Praise for Jessica Hopper and
The First Collection of Criticism by a Living Female Rock Critic

"*The First Collection* is a game-changer, a godsend, and a Holy Grail for those who have been forced to reside on the fringes of the notoriously 'male-dominated sphere' of rock criticism and fandom . . . Hopper's work, influence, and unwavering support for the diversification of voice and perspective within music journalism have altered the landscape of rock criticism for the better. It may be the *First Collection* of criticism written by a female rock critic, but it's definitely not the last." —*The Village Voice*

"A game-changing collection of writing . . . Hopper has created a bible for aspiring writers, not just music critics." —Jessica Goodman, *HuffPost*

"An airtight case for why the professional critic still matters, and why it is a thrill to spend time in the presence of someone whose job it is to care so much and so intelligently." —Kathleen Rooney, *Chicago Tribune*

"In this crucial book, Hopper schools us all in the art of criticism. You will be reminded, as I was, why you care to read and write about (and listen to!) music to begin with. Hopper's relationship with music is a joy to behold." —Tavi Gevinson

Mercedes Zapata

JESSICA HOPPER

The First Collection of Criticism by a Living Female Rock Critic

Jessica Hopper is a Chicago-based music journalist and documentary producer. Formerly an editor at *Rookie*, MTV News, and *Pitchfork*, her writing has appeared in *Rolling Stone*, *The New York Times Magazine*, *Punk Planet*, and *The Village Voice*.

ALSO BY JESSICA HOPPER

Night Moves

The Girls' Guide to Rocking

**The First Collection of Criticism
by a Living Female Rock Critic**

MCD X FSG ORIGINALS
FARRAR, STRAUS AND GIROUX
NEW YORK

THE FIRST
COLLECTION
OF CRITICISM

BY A LIVING
FEMALE
ROCK CRITIC

JESSICA
HOPPER

REVISED AND EXPANDED

MCD × FSG Originals
Farrar, Straus and Giroux
120 Broadway, New York 10271

Library of Congress Cataloging-in-Publication Data
Names: Hopper, Jessica, author.
Title: The first collection of criticism by a living female rock critic / Jessica
    Hopper.
Description: Revised and expanded. | New York : MCD x FSG Originals,
    2021.
Summary: "A revised and expanded edition of celebrated critic Jessica
    Hopper's pioneering music writing" —Provided by publisher.
Identifiers: LCCN 2021002668 | ISBN 9780374538996 (paperback)
Subjects: LCSH: Rock music—2001–2010—History and criticism. | Rock
    music—2011–2020—History and criticism. | LCGFT: Essays.
Classification: LCC ML3534 .H673 2021 | DDC 781.6609—dc23
LC record available at https://lccn.loc.gov/2021002668

Designed by Gretchen Achilles

They sung in code
But their message clear:
Don't shun the world, shed it

—LUNGFISH

CONTENTS

PART III: DEATH/REDEMPTION

PART IV: NOSTALGIA

PART V: CALIFORNIA

PART IX: SHE SAID

FOREWORD

Samantha Irby

I don't know how to write about music. I can buy a ticket and stand crushed against the guardrail in a puddle of spilled beer while singing my heart out with whoever is on the stage, but I don't know how to sit down at my computer and capture the transcendent vibe of a thrilling live show through the keyboard. I can download an album, crank it through a pair of very fancy noise-canceling headphones while lying very still in a dark room, and listen to it all the way through, but it's doubtful I'd come up with anything more eloquent than "Wow, that was a jam" to describe it.

Everyone is a critic, but not everyone should be? No one is better at writing about music, and the artists who make it, than Jessica Hopper. I've been reading her work for forever. I used to cut her articles out of *Punk Planet* and the *Chicago Reader* and stash them in a notebook. I searched tirelessly for the records by the bands she wrote about so I could listen to them while rereading her words.

It's so dope when a woman fights her way into a space that has historically been hostile to her and forces the people already in it to make some room. Jessica kicked down the door of the boys' club and made a space for herself—and then took it over. That's fucking cool. Jessica Hopper is a producer, a critic, a journalist, and a really nice, down-to-earth person. I feel like that's an important distinction to make, that in addition to having a career that spans a couple of decades, and having broken down barriers along the way, she's also somehow not an asshole.

I love Jessica because she's always the coolest person in the room. She's fucking fearless. It's a joy to read her, to follow along with a woman whose passion for music radiates from the page. Jessica's writing is powerful (please know that I am cringing to death on the inside by referring to something as "powerful," but it's true!) and funny and keenly observational and feminist as fuck. She's profiled Robyn! And Cat Power! And Chance! And Björk!!! I'm thrilled that a new audience will be introduced to her with this expanded reissue of her greatest works and, in the process, will have their minds blown and their hearts torn open by her words.

JULY 2020

INTRODUCTION

I Have a Strange Relationship with Music

HIT IT OR QUIT IT #17, SPRING 2002

I have a strange relationship with music. It is strange by virtue of what I need from it. Some days, it is the simple things: distraction, entertainment, the sticky joy garnered only from Timbaland beats. Then, sometimes, usually in the part of the early morning that is still nighttime, most especially lately, I am painfully aware of every single thing that I need from music, embarrassed by what I ask of it. Having developed such a desperate belief in the power of music to salve and heal me, I ask big, over and over again. I have an appetite for deliverance, and am not particularly interested in trying to figure out whether it qualifies me as lucky or pathetic.

The stereo is just past halfway to as-loud-as-it-will-go, the rolling bass of Van Morrison's "T.B. Sheets" (the first song on side two of the album of the same name) is moving throughout the house, its punctuating bump 'n' grind ricocheting off the parquet floor, sound filling every room. This is the fourth night of the last five that I'm doing this same routine—lights out, alone, in a precarious emotional state not worth explaining, dancing—though in a way that is barely dancing—because lying down is out of the question on a night as hot as this, and lying down means motionless, and there's really no being still right now.

Seven of the eight songs on *T.B. Sheets* are about Van Morrison and a girl he loves, who is dying of tuberculosis. I can count on one hand the times that I have made it through the entire album without crying. It's brutal and never fails to deliver in its relentless humanity. Some songs detail the recent past, a golden reminiscence of some then-average day ("Who Drove the Red Sports Car") that now will have to be enough for a lifetime; he's asking her, "Do you remember?" insinuating some intimate exchange, some forgotten little secret. He needs her to remember. "Beside You" is a fierce, rambling pledge—he's pleading for her confidence, in a torrential cadence of nearly unintelligible half sentences that sound like they could be directions someplace, before the decimating crescendo. He sounds drunk, a little off-key, hysterical, now saying everything he ever meant to say to her and didn't, confessing himself, as if this act of deathbed desperation, this unbearable love, this compassion to the point of oneness with her, if she knew it, if she could really understand it, and take it in—it might just save her. All of this is cast out among ominous trilling B3 sustain and repetitive guitar, droning off into bottomless tension.

The title track, "T.B. Sheets," is nine minutes and forty-four seconds of Van rending an exquisite topography of bleak human expanse, an outline of him collapsing under the weight of incontrovertible mortal pall, in a dialect too casual and acrimonious for how well he knows her. He's unable to be of any use—unable to get far away fast enough from his fear, evading the knowledge of exactly what all this means, the finality of it. Details give way to a much deeper reckoning: "I can almost smell / The T.B. sheets," audibly choking for air, and repeating, with frail cogency, "I gotta go," over and over, like a mantra of absolution, he's seeking another set of chances, burdened by survival.

But it's too late, he's in for all he's got.

It's a song of failure. It's realizing that sometimes the best you've got to give isn't much of anything at all.

Dancing in pitch-dark rooms, rooms illuminated exclusively by the tiny light on the turntable, fits very well with my ideas of rock-critic behavior, which is like normal music-fan behavior, but substantially more pitiful and indulgent. It's behavior that comes from an inextricable soul entanglement with music that is insular, boundless, devoted, celebratory, and willfully pathetic. It's my fantasy of what a *real* rock-critic scenario is like: a "special" manual typewriter, ashtrays full of thin roaches, an extensive knowledge of Mott the Hoople lyrics, a ruthless seeking for the life of life in free jazz sides. It may also include: a fetishizing of THE TRUTH (which always turns gory, no matter what records you listen to), detoured attempts to illuminate the exact heaven of Eric B. & Rakim or Rocket from the Tombs with the fluorescent lighting of your 3:00 a.m. genius-stroke prose, and, most of all, an insatiable appetite for rapture that cannot be coaxed by any other means.

It's the exhaustive chronicling of what it is that artists

possess that we mere mortals do not, what it is that they offer up that we are unable or unwilling to say ourselves. Offering connection to the disconnected, their songs make our secrets bearable in their verses and choruses: ornate in their undoing; gambling with their happiness, their personal irredemption, their humility; using failure to build a podium to reach god; their faked orgasms amid in-between-song skits; their solos, clever rhymes, crippled expectations, spiritual drift, still-unmet Oedipal needs, fuckless nights, not-so-gradual disappearance from reality, rodeo blues, unflagging romantic beliefs; being an outlaw for your love; a love supreme; Reaganomics; the summer they'll never forget; the power of funk; hanging at the Nice Nice with the eye patch guy; American apathy; taking hoes to the Cheesecake Factory; getting head in drop-top Benzes; isolation; the benefits of capitalism; screwing Stevie Nicks in the tall green grass; the swirling death dust; the underground; and none of the above.

I want it. I need it. All these records, they give me a language to decipher just how fucked I am. Because there is a void in my guts that can only be filled by songs.

PART I

CHICAGO

CHANCE THE RAPPER IS THE NEXT BIG THING FROM CHICAGO

CHICAGO, JUNE 2013

Chance the Rapper doesn't want to go home. He just came from there, he says. The twenty-year-old rapper is in the passenger seat of my car. We were slated to drive around his South Side neighborhood, Chatham, where he grew up and now lives with his girlfriend. There is a flurry of excuses: It's hot out. It will take too long and he has to be at the studio in an hour. The 'hood where he lives is just where he lives, he says. His story of how he went from half-dropped-out burner kid to Chicago's next big thing, he insists, "happened here." He gestures to indicate that *here* means exactly where we are—this few-block stretch of downtown surrounding the Harold Washington branch of the Chicago Public Library.

Despite his casual air and congenial charm, Chance is very aware of his image, his origin story, and how much it constitutes his appeal. Beneath his earnest demeanor lies an artist who has mapped every inch of his hustle. Chance is a favorite with high school kids, in part because his story could be theirs. He got busted smoking weed while ditching class at Millennium Park and spent

3

his subsequent ten-day suspension recording a mixtape of songs that birthed his rap career. His is a ground-level stardom, someone fans can talk to when they see him on the train or in the street; he is someone they could ostensibly become. The young MC is very clear on the importance of his apocryphal tale and that is the only one he is inclined to tell. And so we will not begin our story of Chance the Rapper in Chatham, we will begin where he says it began: downtown.

We park and step out of the car outside of the Columbia College dorms. There is the waft of marijuana and someone yells, "Whattup, man!" A former classmate from Jones appears and pulls Chance in for a half hug, and explains, "He was the craziest motherfucker in school!" The old friend passes Chance his joint. Chance plugs his upcoming mixtape by title and street date. They exchange numbers after the kid offers his in case Chance needs a hookup for weed.

It is difficult to ascertain whether Chance is famous citywide, but in this six-block proximity of where we walk, he is the Mayor of the Underage. He is greeted constantly, by name, with handshakes, pounds, dap. He gamely poses for pictures, is offered lights for his ever-present cigarettes, and kids prod his memory to see if he remembers the last time they met—at the library, in the parking lot of their school when he was selling tickets to one of his shows, that one time their cousin introduced them.

We head down the street to Jugrnaut, the hip-hop clothing store that has hosted all of Chance's mixtape release parties, drawing hundreds more kids than they can accommodate in the tiny space. Owner Roger Rodriguez brags that they've known him since back when he was "just Chance. Before he was Chance *Thee*." In the store, the half dozen dudes shopping look up but play it like they are not noticing Chance, who refers to the store as "home." He would sometimes spend six hours a day there, writing rhymes or just hanging out. That doesn't really happen anymore. Two middle school–age boys in uniforms pass by and pause to gawk when they catch sight of Chance through the open door. Chance gives them an acknowledging wave. They wave back before running away.

After Jugrnaut, we head into the YOUMedia center on the ground floor of the Harold Washington public library. "The first time I came here was to rap," he explains. Kanye-obsessed Chance was in a duo with a friend ("We were terrible") and had heard that the library had free recording studios. The center also offers free workshops: "Production, software, piano lessons, music theory. I took all of them." He quickly became the star of the popular Wednesday-night open mics. "This place made me what I am today." He swings open the door to the recording studio and pops his head in. Five teenage boys are inside; one is behind the mic, the rest behind the computer. "Y'all recording?" he asks. "I used to be recording in here—I don't mean to hold up your session." Chance acts oblivious but the boys are stunned silent. This is a little like Derrick Rose suddenly sidling up while you're free-throwing in the driveway.

By the time he ducks back out a minute later, nearly a dozen boys have amassed in a semicircle. "All y'all rap?" he asks them. They all giddily introduce themselves by the names they rap under: Dre Valentine, E-Man, Vic-Ivy, Psycho Ten Times. The iPhones come out and there is a group shot. They are all fifteen, sixteen, seventeen— the same age as Chance when he started camping out at YOUMedia—and all of them are from Chicago's South Side, too. A kid who raps as Esh explains, "Everyone knows this is where Chance made *10 Day*." We decide to leave, as it becomes apparent that every kid in the library has realized *Chance is here.*

Within the next half block he is stopped and recognized by a janitor from Jones Prep. He takes a succession of selfies with three girls he knows from YOUMedia, the cousin of his DJ, and, finally, three rappers he knows from street ciphers. I ask one of them, Pres, why Chance's success is so important to Chicago. "Everyone feels like he's on his way up. He's the voice of the youth in the Chi—but he is just part of it. He's the lightbearer."

VIVA LA FILTHY NOISE!

Coughs' *Secret Passage*

CHICAGO READER, OCTOBER 2006

Every time Coughs count off a song, it's like a ticking toward detonation; every show they play is rumored to be their last, threatening both explosion and implosion. These locals' most recent "last show" was last month at the Empty Bottle, during *The Wire*'s Adventures in Modern Music fest, and their fiercely kinetic cacophony was as tight as it's ever been, awing and frightening an already timid crowd. (People who can afford a fifteen-dollar cover are not Coughs' usual demographic.) The audience formed a polite arc a safe distance from the stage, but the band refused them their distance—only four of the six members stayed behind their monitors. Front woman Anya Davidson took to the floor, shuffling around like an expiring windup toy, her eyes shut as she bumped gently but obliviously into people and screamed out a dialogue with a talking pimple ("Life of Acne"). And keyboardist and saxophonist Jill Flanagan barreled into the front row, charging ass-first into the laps of the people sitting on the steps as she blew sick, squalling runs. You could almost see what the crowd was thinking: *These people are wet with sweat and stink and they are trying to touch us.*

Coughs use every instrument as a percussion instrument, not just the trashed, monolithic two-man megakit at the back of the stage—a multicolored heap of snares, cymbals, soup pots, floor toms, metal barrels, and bass drums mounted flat like tabletops. The guitar and bass pile on with more banging and chomping, and even the vocals and saxophone steer clear of melody—the songs could be sketched out with only two or three symbols, one for the thuds and another couple for the breaks and scree between the thuds. There's little that compares to the sound Coughs make, unless you abandon bands as points of reference: it's like a massive conglomeration of screeching worn-out cab brakes, assembly-line machines, and pneumatic nail guns, the whole thing driven by the maniacally rapid heartbeat of a small mammal. The closest aesthetic antecedents are either early Boredoms or a car crash.

On their new album, *Secret Passage* (Load), they play like they're trying to tear apart the songs themselves and maybe take down whoever's listening as well. But the mushroom cloud rising from this destruction has a silver lining—the explosion is more like the Big Bang, and it feels like something huge is happening inside that bubble of blast heat. Coughs' intensity makes them seem bigger and more important than just a band; they stand for the destruction of contemporary pop with all its rote prescriptions and attendant soul death. They're a cleansing fire purging the earth of the swagger of the Rolling Stones, the tired aggro posturing of punk and hardcore, the vapid "I can't live without you"s of R & B. Their music clears a space for the clever-whatever that's coming in their wake. Direct and unmediated, not referencing much of anything, it's at times purposefully ugly, even gloriously so. But the fury doesn't come out of hate; it's purehearted, boldly altruistic. On their Myspace page, the "Sounds Like" box says "genres collapsing." That is in fact what they sound like, and they're doing us a favor: lighting a path out, delivering us to the future via filthy noise.

When I saw Coughs play for the first time this spring, I was filled with prommy sentiment: I leaned and yelled into the side of my best friend's head, "I don't want this night to ever end." But I've also seen the band bring out the worst in an audience, usually when some damaged Reagan babies try to up Coughs' ante with extra insolence. This summer at a Coughs show in some crumbly warehouse, I watched a modelescent girl with long golden tresses and expensively wrong clothes stand amid the surging crowd and carefully hock gobs of spit onto Davidson. The girl's pupils were pinpricks and she had blood on her face, like she'd gone over her handlebars on the way to the show. But she couldn't top the damage Davidson had already done to herself: her too-small dress was shredding and slipping off her as she heaved, screaming, her hands yanking at the nest of her hair.

The way Davidson acts is just not how you ever see women present themselves in bands. Even when the most ferocious and confident women perform, there's almost always an allusion to the expectations they're sidestepping—to come across as "bad girls," they need the rules hovering close at hand. But Davidson doesn't seem aware those rules ever existed—half the time she doesn't even seem aware of the audience. I've never seen a woman so naturally give less of a fuck. You could call it feminist if she seemed more conscious of what she's doing—it's like she was dropped here by aliens and never suffered the patriarchal damage that makes girls bend involuntarily to the watchful eyes of convention. She's our very own Iggy, unzipping her pants to expose the delicate print of some Hanes Her Ways as beer drips from her hair, howling like Patti Smith if she'd come up on bunk acid and small-town metal bands instead of blues and Baudelaire. She's Niki de Saint Phalle, riddling her canvas with bullet holes out of love and rage.

The other members of the band—a motley, *Bad News Bears* assortment—are hardly cookie-cutter personalities themselves. Percussionists Jon Ziemba and Seth Sher play standing up, often shirtless, like they're trying to beat their way out from behind the piled-up barricade of their gear with constant colossal rolls and the martial rattle of a meth-powered high school marching band. Guitarist Vanessa Harris, who often sports a crooked coonskin hat, is the band's melodic glue, though that's not saying much—air-raid-siren squeals and one-note unsolos are her specialty. Bassist Carrie Vinarsky dresses like a hausfrau; last time I saw her she was wearing a turtleneck, high-waisted pleat-front jeans, and an embroidered vest—but her bass tone is so punishingly swampy it'd make the guy from Killdozer jealous.

Coughs began in 2001 as a cross between an experiment and a dare—no one in the band was allowed to play an instrument she already knew how to play. Their earlier recordings rip, but their haphazard spazziness makes them sound like the product of an accident rather than a collective aesthetic decision. From its first atonal bleat, by contrast, *Secret Passage* pounces with a purposeful ferocity. Coughs' wretched, razor-sharp skronking still has a homemade charm, but now it has a keen and assaultive focus, proving that they've figured out how to engage their instruments for maximum damage. Their early insistence on learning as they went has made their playing more idiosyncratic and unsettling as they've developed chops—though "chops" is a relative term, of course, and in this case it just means they can stomp and churn in unison when they want to.

Secret Passage is also a joyous record, positive and uplifting, despite its calamitous clanging and murder screams. Davidson may sing like she's trying to punch a hole through a wall with her voice, but her lyrics are genuine, colored with a strange innocence. You'd never guess, watching her force every ounce of air from her lungs till she's beet red, that she's screaming about mountains, birds, dreams, gardening, freedom, or pining for a lover who arrives on goatback. On "Quinze Trous (15 Holes)," when she barks "Je suis bombe atomique," it's as much a promise as a threat.

SWEET THINGS

VILLAGE VOICE PAZZ & JOP CRITICS POLL, JANUARY 2006

Dear Sufjan,

I enjoyed your new album about my city and state and I am wondering if you are available, one day soon, perhaps when you are less busy being a newly famous Christian troubadour, to drive around Chicago and listen to "Sweet Thing" by Van Morrison over and over, and see who cries first, you or me. I do not know what "losing" would consist of—crying first or not crying. It wouldn't be a date or anything weird like that, just a friendly contest. Then I could show you the cool things around town that you did not sing about on your record. We could drive under the Green Line tracks where a car chase from *The Blues Brothers* took place, visit the Fern Room at the Garfield Park Conservatory; the top-floor atrium of the Harold Washington Library, where the floors are marble and cool and very clean and no one is ever there so you can lay on them and look up into the downtown sky or just read the books you checked out; the Soul Vegetarian vegan soul food restaurant run by the African Hebrew Israelites; the Bahá'i temple in

13

Wilmette, which gets a lot of god in the architecture and is ringed with seven gardens. If you aren't scared of dark, isolated places, there is always the land bridge that runs through the industrial corridor to downtown, where there are tons of baby rabbits and people discard great things; last time I was there I found part of an old fair ride and a sign for a mid-'60s hair salon that had fluttering, sequin letters. We could sneak onto the elevators at the Drake Hotel and look at the lake at night, and if it's fall there will be apples in baskets in the hallways. They are for decoration, but if you are me, they are for stealing and eating.

Maybe you wrote songs about that stuff for your *Illinois* record but they did not fit on the album, or the choruses were weak, or the song about Decatur was more fun to sing because of those half-funny half rhymes ("aviator"?!). If you did not already write those songs, you are going to wish you had.

Yours very truly,
JH
Chicago, Illinois

LIL' SQUIRT

Juiceboxxx Takes His Show on the Road, Right After He Graduates High School

CHICAGO READER, JUNE 2005

Juiceboxxx is a senior at Homestead High School in Mequon, Wisconsin, a suburb of Milwaukee. But his weekends, his post-homework nights, and his summers are taken up with the business of being the Juice, DJing, rapping, producing, and promoting the monthly all-ages Milwaukee dance party Get Wacky, now in its sixth month. While he could be just another precocious teen anxious to make a name for himself, Juiceboxxx has something beyond determination and kid guile, something most scene entrepreneurs twice his age would kill for: talent.

Get Wacky is held in a fifteen-by-forty-foot storefront currently decorated to look like a cave: every surface is painted dark gray; there are stalactites and stalagmites and a bevy of ferns and potted trees. At the March installment, Juiceboxxx—known to his mom as John Chiaverina—seems unaware of just how good he is, furiously finessing the records and mixer with long, wiry arms that he's yet to grow into. A geeked-out missing-tooth smile spans his baby face when a crowd calls his name. He's got impeccable taste and a preternatural ability to sustain a wall-to-wall leg-humping frenzy for the duration of his sweatsational sets. Watching him behind the turntables, I get the feeling I'm seeing something big while it's still kicking around in its amniotic sac.

"I've only DJed out, like, I dunno, under ten times. No, maybe exactly ten," Chiaverina says. "Just at Get Wacky and some parties around Mequon." This is hard to believe. He might be the best DJ to come out of the Midwest since Tommie Sunshine. His familiarity and comfort with a breadth of genres—from German minimal techno to Chicago house to R & B hits from when he was in sixth grade—make Sunshine an easy comparison. When I ask him about his influences, he's at a loss: outside of what he's read in magazines, his primary exposure to other DJs has been at school dances. At eighteen, he's still too young to get into clubs.

"I have been buying records like crazy since I was thirteen," he says. "Maybe two and a half years ago I got some shitty Numarks [turntables] and a mixer. I have not really dedicated myself to DJing, it's just kind of happened." Guided by a ska-loving cousin, Chiaverina began listening to local college station WMSE, hearing for the first time and falling in love with the sounds of multiple undergrounds: house, techno, punk, Midwestern hip-hop, postrave music from the UK. "I started going to Massive Record Source, which was a local record store owned by Dan Doormouse, a local electronic fixture," he says. "And through him and the store I got into drum 'n' bass and started buying hip-hop. It was the tail end of the rave scene, and there was a lot still coming out of the Midwestern underground, acid and house. I was picking up the UK imports I was taping off all these radio shows."

"John has always loved music," says his mom, Ginny. "In middle school he played in bands, so there was a lot of picking up and dropping off. I come from a musical family—my brother and his son are professional country-and-western singers—so I have always encouraged him to follow his passion with it. I don't necessarily see him going far with Juiceboxxx, but I'm no hip-hop aficionado, I'm a middle-aged lady, so hip-hop is not really my thing. Whether he makes a living doing it one day is beside the point. I just like that he's having fun doing it and it keeps him out of trouble."

Chiaverina assembled Juiceboxxx as a rap crew of his junior high friends, jumping on whatever bills they could get at basement shows and local rec centers. It quickly shrank to Chiaverina on the mike and making the beats, and he quickly developed a sizable fan base for a kid in ninth grade. "Initially the songs were kind of novelty songs, you know, about, like, food, or gambling," he says. "About seventy-five or maybe one hundred kids were showing up every time. No, maybe just seventy-five."

He released his debut album, *2K3: The Year of the Juice* (produced by local hip-hop booster Kid Cut Up), in tenth grade, burning copies on his computer and eventually selling "around five hundred" at basement rock and hardcore shows. "I haven't really played any hip-hop shows yet—it's a hard thing to break into," he says. "Hip-hop in Milwaukee, it's as exclusive as anywhere, and it's about proving yourself and I'm not really interested in that. But I want it to be known that I am not ironic or mocking hip-hop. Though it might be goofy, there is no irony. Silly and ironic are way different."

His sincerity may be what's most striking about Chiaverina, given the scene he's associated with. Get Wacky's home base, the cave, is the General Store in Milwaukee, a gallery that's ground-zero for Milwaukee's burgeoning experimental noise-band scene as well as the visual- and performance-art scene anchored by General Store owner Tyson Reeder. At one recent show, Frankie Martin, who makes art as Frankie Forever, performed under the name Airbrains. She wore rainbow-bright pajamas and Pippi Longstocking braids to sing and "rap" in a singsongy squeak from the point of view of "a family of balloons," pausing between numbers to ask the audience with cheerleader-like enthusiasm, "Are you having a good time?" Juiceboxxx followed with a performance so heartfelt that it could have been mistaken for ironic, opening with the anthemic "Do U Want 2 Hear It?" and ripping off his shirt Hulk-style mid-set. "I know that's where Tyson and Frankie are coming from and it's not really the same place I am coming from aesthetically," he says. "I cannot dispute that, but I consider them to be in the same arena. It's just about having fun."

This month Chiaverina graduates from Homestead High, and between then and the start of his freshman year at the University of Wisconsin–Milwaukee, he's got a lot going on. Vicious Pop, a Milwaukee label, is releasing his sophomore album, *R U There God?? Itz Me, Juiceboxxx*. It's not in stores outside of Milwaukee yet, but it can be ordered from www.viciouspoprecords.com. Chiaverina has already sold twenty-two copies at school. His inaugural U.S. tour, an eight-day venture to the East Coast and back, kicks off in Detroit in July; it incorporates performances by Reeder and Martin and work by visiting Japanese painter Akiko Niimura. "We're working within a variety show format," explains Chiaverina. "Tyson warms up the crowd with some performance art and stand-up comedy. Then Frankie performs, and debuts her new dance video, which is kind of a *Dirty Dancing*–style thing she made with some friends. Then there is a sketch—we're still working out the kinks on that. Then I do a normal Juiceboxxx set, then Frankie and I perform a retooled duet version of Kelly Clarkson's 'Since U Been Gone.'"

Then there are more Get Wackys, and a Chicago DJing gig is in the works. Juiceboxxx's rep is spreading outside Wisconsin and even outside the Midwest. "I think what Juiceboxxx is doing is so refreshing—it's so inspired and unironic," says San Diego–based DJ and music writer Anna Klafter, who wrote to me after I raved about Juice on my blog. "I first saw him when he was maybe sixteen. I was the tour DJ for MC Paul Barman, and Juiceboxxx opened for us in Madison. He had dancers—it was hard not to love him, he was so young and in love with music."

At the March installment of Get Wacky, the juxtaposition between art-school aesthetics and Juiceboxxx's gentle geniuneness is nonexistent. The store windows are steamed up, the walls are sweating, the people are dripping. Everyone is grinding, people are taking turns showcasing solo moves on homemade platforms meant for art displays. "There's candy, pop, fresh-baked cookies, or costumes over by the cooler for free, so help yourself," Chiaverina announces through the PA, mixing an old U.K. rave anthem into DMX on the wrong speed over the thick bass bounce of a Baltimore club record. Get Wacky offers reduced cover (four dollars instead of five) for people who dress according to the night's theme. Tonight it's "Olympics/Athletics." Girls are rocking looks last seen in Jazzercise class, guys wear running shorts and papery New Jersey mall-mom tracksuits—except the one who showed up in a regulation hockey goalie getup, but even he's dancing. Chiaverina piles a cappella from some obscure Detroit techno onto a New Order song with the high end turned all the way up for a blastro effect; then it's Tego Calderón and Kylie into M/A/R/R/S into some jackin' Trax twelve-inches first issued the year he was born into the a cappella of Terror Squad's "Lean Back" dropped over "Ms. Jackson." Chiaverina watches the room go rabid. He checks his watch, then cedes the decks to the next DJ to the sound of the crowd yelling, "Juice! Juice! Juice!" He flashes that tooth-missing smile and bounds into the throng.

SAN FRANCISCO, LOS ANGELES, NEW YORK, OSWEGO

An Up-and-Coming British Post-punk Trio Wows the Preteens at a Suburban High School Gym

CHICAGO READER, FEBRUARY 2006

Last Friday evening, two dozen kids between the ages of seven and fifteen milled around nervously in front of the stage in the auditorium at Oswego East High School. They were VIPs, hanging out in a reserved section that had been roped off with actual rope, while 350 other kids filled up the stadium seating. They'd all come to see Black Wire, an up-and-coming post-punk trio from Leeds, England, and for most of them this was their first show. When front man Dan Wilson asked at the beginning of the band's set, "Who here has ever been to a concert before?" six little hands went up.

One of the hands belonged to Gia Muzzalupo, a ten-year-old VIP who came with her three best friends. "I saw Rascal Flatts this summer," she said later. "I'm here because my friend's mom runs the label that put out Black Wire. I've never heard them before, but I know it'll 21 be good 'cause it's rock 'n' roll. I'm really excited—I love rock 'n' roll. I'm in a band too. We're called Hot Goth Chicks. We're a mix of rap, hip-hop, and rock 'n' roll. I'm the lead singer."

This was Black Wire's first U.S. tour, a short jaunt with stops in San Francisco, Los Angeles, New York, and Oswego, the home base of the band's U.S. manager, Bjorn Forsell. Along with an old friend, Meredith Wittich, Forsell started Giant Pecker Records, which released the band's self-titled debut CD stateside. "I just thought it would be cool to expose the kids to a band that's well on its way to breaking," Forsell said. "Most of them had never seen a concert, and those who had, it was at Rosemont Horizon. Meredith and I both have kids, and it's not like we can take them to shows at the Empty Bottle." Forsell, thirty-six, who has previously worked as a studio engineer and as a guitar tech for the Cardigans and the Hives, discovered Black Wire through their debut seven-inch and signed on to work with the band after seeing them a few times in England. Wittich, thirty-four, who has no previous experience in the music business, left her job as a science teacher at Oswego High six months ago to work on the label full-time.

Black Wire formed in 2003, and their first single, "Attack Attack Attack," was named an *NME* single of the week in April 2004. Their second, "Hard to Love, Easy to Lay," cracked the U.K. Top 75 singles chart the first week of its release the following December, and they've spent the last year touring in support of their first full-length, opening for bands like the Kaiser Chiefs and the

Arctic Monkeys. Playing a high school was a first for them. "We've never played an all-ages show before," said Wilson, twenty-three. "Generally, we just play to drunk old people. It was cool to play to people who weren't jaded, people who were just happy to be out of the house with something to do."

Oswego East's auditorium, which features an elaborate professional lighting rig and an unbelievably loud sound system, is frequently rented for public events, according to the school's theater manager, Todd Mielcarz. "We mostly just get recitals in here," he said. "This kind of show, a punk band, that's a pretty big deal for us in a presenting season. Our main concern is safety. We're keeping the VIP roped off so people don't rush the stage. I don't think they will." But physical safety wasn't the only concern. Though Forsell had submitted copies of Black Wire's album, along with T-shirts and posters, to the school's administrators for approval several months earlier, it wasn't until the day before the concert that objections were raised. Several parents took issue with the title "Hard to Love, Easy to Lay" and also with the explicitness of Forsell's label name. In order for the concert to go off as planned, "Giant Pecker" had to be blacked out from all posters and promotional materials, no merchandise could be sold, and the band had not only to agree not to play "Hard to Love" but to not say the word "lay" at all.

The audience, a total of 420 people including guests and chaperones, ran the gamut from JV basketball cheerleaders (still in uniform) who had never heard the band to serious fans like fifteen-year-old Charise Walters, who normally does sound for the theater but tonight was working as a runner for the band's soundman. "I got into the band about a year ago," she said. "I heard about them from family in England, actually. It's really cool that they are actually playing my high school." Other kids took fashion cues from pictures they'd seen of people at concerts. One boy wore a dark green wool suit he'd borrowed from his dad, which was five or six sizes too big for him. Another had on a shirt that simply read "reggae" under his letter jacket. There were fur coats and Zeppelin T-shirts and sunglasses worn indoors. Gia Muzzalupo and her friends had spent all week planning their outfits over the phone. "We have to dress attractive," she said. "What if we want to marry someone in the band?"

Once the house music—live Warren Zevon—was cut and the lights went down, the VIP rope was moot. Black Wire entered to high-pitched screaming, the kids rushed the stage, and the screaming continued throughout a well-honed, Clash-inspired half-hour set. The kids screamed when the band danced. They screamed for guitar solos. A group of girls from Waubonsie Valley High School screamed "I love you!" every time Wilson neared the lip of the stage. They screamed when he kicked a water bottle and when he chewed the banana-flavored gum that had been thrown onstage. They screamed when he announced before the band's second song, "This one's about London." They imitated his moves: pogoing, rock-steady ska dancing, throwing arms to the beat. Wilson, clearly amused, had to catch himself in the middle of his standard

in-between-song banter, stopping after he began to thank
the kids for "coming out tonight."

As their set progressed, the band never once said the
word "lay," although "fuck" was uttered twice: once ac-
cidentally by Wilson, and once quite intentionally by
an eager young man who grabbed the mike and cussed
a female teacher. Then for their final song, in spite of
their promise, they launched into "Hard to Love." Wilson began pulling audience members up onto the stage,
who in turn pulled up their friends, and by the song's
second chorus, almost the entire audience was bouncing
around up there, jostling for spots next to band members
and screaming into the microphones. Eventually Wilson
was squeezed off, and as his band finished the song, he
watched the kids.

POGOING ACROSS BORDERS

CHICAGO READER, JUNE 15, 2006

From the parking lot of the Black Hole, an arcade in a strip mall in Chicago's Little Village, it seemed like an ordinary Saturday night. Guys cruised by in cars, kids zoomed past on bikes, couples walked in the street. The only sign that anything unusual was taking place was the three teen boys and a girl, covered in zits and Amebix patches, hitting up people for spare change, trying to scrounge together enough money to pay the arcade's ten-dollar cover charge. The girl was trying to sell a filthy, wadded-up dreadlock the size of a fist, displayed on a napkin on which she'd scrawled "$500 O.B.O." These may have been the first white punk kids with the balls to panhandle on Twenty-Sixth Street.

More than four hundred kids and adults were gathered inside the arcade for the second night of Southkore, the first Latinx punk festival ever held in America. Put on two weekends ago, it featured twenty bands playing punk and hardcore in Spanish, including a surprise Friday-night reunion of the influential South Side band Los Crudos. Some audience members had come from

just down the block, others from as far away as Nicara-
gua. The walls were covered in cartoon Day-Glo murals,
and next to the stage a bank of TVs showed a scene from
Santa Sangre with a guy having his penis burned off.
When music wasn't playing, the room was filled with the
din of arcade games and conversations in Spanish.

Southkore is a South Side collective that books shows
and runs its own record label and distribution network.
Benny Hernandez, one of the founders and a festival organizer, says it started in 1999 after the breakup of Los
Crudos, whose popularity among traditional hardcore
fans had temporarily opened doors for other Spanish-
speaking groups. "After Crudos broke up, none of us
were getting opportunities to play on the North Side,"
he says. "So we had to make things happen for ourselves,
here." The collective was anchored by bands like Eske,
Sin Orden, I Attack, and Tras de Nada, and though the
idea of hosting an international fest had been discussed
for years, the ball didn't get rolling until 2005. "We didn't
have the money to put it together, and we had to save
to make it happen," Hernandez says. "There were some
Spanish rock promoters who offered to help us put it
together, but that would have meant corporate sponsor-
ship and radio stations advertising it, and we're a DIY
operation."

Drawing on contacts he'd made through Southkore's
distribution channels, Hernandez began reaching out to
bands all over the United States and Puerto Rico, and
word spread. "When we contacted Juventud Crasa, who're
from Puerto Rico, they wrote back and suggested we

contact La Armada Roja, who're actually the first punk band ever from the Dominican Republic." Even after the lineup was confirmed, he kept hearing from bands all over the world, and he says he already has commitments for next year's festival. "We approached a bunch of different kinds of bands, but most of the ones that could do it were all hardcore," he says. "Next year is more about showcasing Latino DIY bands of all kinds.

"One of the most important things to come out of the festival is the networking," says Hernandez. "Now that all these bands have met each other, made connections, made friends, they can book tours nationally and play with each other." Hernandez says Latinx punks have never truly been accepted in the white-dominated scene, where solidarity and connections are often taken for granted. "White punks are okay with Latinos as tokens, but the minute you want to be counted, forget it. I think we made a lot of them uncomfortable by doing this, and I think that's wonderful. It's important for them to get the opportunity to go to a festival where not a single song is in their language. It gives them a chance to understand, one that they may not get otherwise."

Within the Latinx community, being punk has often carried a cultural stigma. Martin Sorrendeguy, singer for Los Crudos and Limp Wrist, and whose documentary on the Latino punk scene, *Beyond the Screams*, played as part of a Saturday-afternoon Southkore film screening at Metzli Gallery, says when he was growing up, punk was viewed "very much as a white thing. If you were into punk you were seen as trying to assimilate—you were trying to be white." Hernandez, the thirty-year-old son of Mexican immigrants, says the scene is viewed as a threat to cultural traditions. "Having a band like Condenada play," he says, referring to the local all-female quartet, "seeing all those Latinas up front, singing along, it really means something when you have grown up in a traditional, patriarchal Mexican home."

But one of Saturday night's headliners, the Puerto Rican band Tropiezo, playfully showed it was possible to use Latinx punk to bridge the gaps between the different cultures it straddles. Before their set, the band played a ten-minute mash-up over the PA that incorporated salsa and cumbia hits with sound bites from Martin Luther King, Jr.'s "I Have a Dream" speech, Univision shows, and a sample of a soccer announcer yelling "Gooooaaaallll!" Several couples, clad in black and well-tattooed, broke out in effortless and precise salsa moves, only to join everyone else pogoing and throwing elbows in the pit when the band started. Midway through the set, Tropiezo's singer, who, like his bandmates, was wearing a campesino hat, tore off his shirt to reveal a classic Bad Brains T-shirt with a lightning bolt striking the dome of the U.S. Capitol.

"The bands that played the festival, their angst is real," says Hernandez. "In some of the bands, half the people are unemployed, they're dealing with friends being shot, some of them are living in poverty. Some have members who're here illegally and we had to think about whether to even announce them, because just three weeks ago there were immigration raids up and down Tweny-Sixth

Street. Even the bands that aren't overtly political, every single one of them is being touched by immigration and what's happening politically. And in the face of that—for all of us to come together, to have all these bands sing in Spanish, for us to celebrate our culture together—it's true protest music."

THE "STOMACH-CHURNING" SEXUAL ASSAULT ACCUSATIONS AGAINST R. KELLY

A Conversation with Jim DeRogatis

THE VILLAGE VOICE, DECEMBER 2013

It has been nearly fifteen years since music journalist Jim DeRogatis caught the story that has since defined his career, one that he wishes didn't exist: R. Kelly's sexual predation on teenage girls. DeRogatis, at that time the pop-music critic at the *Chicago Sun-Times*, was anonymously delivered the first of two videos he would receive depicting the pop star engaging in sexual acts with underage girls. Now the host of the syndicated public radio show *Sound Opinions* and a professor at Columbia College, De-Rogatis, along with his former *Sun-Times* colleague Abdon Pallasch, didn't just break the story, they did the only significant reporting on the accusations against Kelly, interviewing hundreds of people over the years, including dozens of young women whose lives DeRogatis says were ruined by the singer.

This past summer, leading up to Kelly's headlining performance at the Pitchfork Music Festival, DeRogatis posted a series of discussions about Kelly's career, the charges made against him, and sexual assault. He published a live review of the singer's festival set that was an indictment of Pitchfork and its audience for essentially endorsing a man he calls "a monster." In the two weeks since Kelly released his latest studio album, *Black Panties*, the conversation about him and why he has gotten a pass from music publications (not to mention feminist sites such as *Jezebel*) has been rekindled, in part because of the explicit nature of the album and also because of online arguments around the Pitchfork performance.

I was one of those people who challenged DeRogatis and was even flip about his judgment—something I quickly came to regret. DeRogatis and I have tangled—even feuded on air—over the years; yet, amid the Twitter barbs, he approached me offline and told me about how one of Kelly's victims called him in the middle of the night after his Pitchfork Festival review came out, to thank him for caring when no one else did. He told me of mothers crying on his shoulder, seeing the scars of a suicide attempt on a girl's wrists, the fear in their eyes. He detailed an aftermath that the public has never had to bear witness to.

DeRogatis offered to give me access to every file and transcript he has collected in reporting this story—as he has to other reporters and journalists, none of whom has ever looked into the matter, thus relegating it to one man's personal crusade.

I thought that last fact merited a public conversation about why.

In this interview (which has been condensed significantly), DeRogatis speaks frankly and explicitly about the many disturbing charges against Kelly and says, ultimately, "The saddest fact I've learned is nobody matters less to our society than young Black women. Nobody."

JESSICA HOPPER: Refresh our memories. How did this start for you?

JIM DEROGATIS: Being a beat reporter, music critic at a Chicago daily, the *Sun-Times*, R. Kelly was a huge story for me, this guy who rose from not graduating from Kenwood Academy, singing at backyard barbecues and on the L, to suddenly selling millions of records. I interviewed him a number of times. Then *TP-2.com* came out. I'd written a review that said the jarring thing about Kelly is that one moment he wants to be riding you and then next minute he's on his knees, crying and praying to his dead mother in heaven for forgiveness for his unnamed sins. It's a little weird at times. It's just an observation.

The next day at the *Sun-Times*, we got this anonymous fax—we didn't know where it came from. It said: R. Kelly's been under investigation for two years by the sex-crimes unit of the Chicago police. And I threw it on the corner of my desk. I thought, "Player-hater." Now, from the beginning, there were rumors that Kelly likes them young. And there'd been this Aaliyah thing—*Vibe* printed, without much commentary and no reporting, the marriage certificate. Kelly or someone had falsified her age as eighteen. There was that. So all this is floating in the air. This fax arrives and I think, "Oh, this is somebody playing with this." But there was something that nagged at me as a reporter. There were specific names, specific dates, and those great, long Polish cop names. And you're not going to make that crap up. So I went to the city desk and I asked, "What do we do with this?" They said, Abdon Pallasch is the courts reporter, why don't you two look into it and see if there's anything there? And it turns out there had been lawsuits that had been filed that had never been reported.

When you cover the courts in Chicago or any city, you go twice a day and you go through the bin of cases that have been filed and every once in a while Michael Jordan's been sued or someone went bankrupt and it's this sexy story and you pull it out. These suits had been filed at 4:00 p.m. on Christmas Eve. Ain't no reporter working at 4:00 p.m. on Christmas Eve, and they flew under the radar. So we had these lawsuits that were explosive and we didn't understand why nobody had reported them.

JH: Explosive in what regard?

JD: They were stomach-churning. The one young woman, who had been fourteen or fifteen when R. Kelly began a relationship with her, detailed in great length, in her affidavits, a sexual relationship that began at Kenwood Academy: He would go back in the early years of his success and go to Lena McLin's gospel choir class. She's a legend in Chicago, gospel royalty. He would go to her sophomore class and hook up with girls afterward and have sex with them. Sometimes buy them a pair of sneakers. Sometimes just letting them hang out in his presence in the recording studio. She detailed the sexual relationship that she was scarred by. It lasted about one and a half to two years, and then he dumped her and she slit her wrists, tried to kill herself. Other girls were involved. She recruited other girls. He picked up other girls and made them all have sex together. A level of specificity that was pretty disgusting.

Her lawsuit was hundreds of pages long, and Kelly countersued. The countersuit was, like, ten pages long: "None of this is true!" We began our reporting. We knocked on a lot of doors. The lawsuits, the two that we had found initially, had been settled. Kelly had paid the women and their families money and the settlements were sealed by the court. But of course, the initial lawsuits remain part of the public record.

JH: So her affidavit, this testimony—it's all public record?

JD: To this day, any reporter who cares can go to Cook County and pull these records, so it drives me crazy, even with some of the eloquent reconsiderations we've seen of Kelly in recent days, that they keep saying "rumors" and "allegations." Well, "allegations" is fair, okay. You're protected as a reporter, any lawsuit that has been filed as fact. The contents of the lawsuit are protected. So these were not rumors. These were allegations made in court.

JH: Do you think part of how it's been handled and why it's been underreported is that music writers may not know how to deal with it in a journalistic sense?

JD: Let's start with the most mundane part. A lot of people who are critics are fans and don't come with any academic background, with any journalistic background, research background. Now, nobody knows everything, and far be it from me to say you've got to be a journalist or you have to have studied critical theory in the academy. Part of what we do is journalistic. Get the names right, get the dates right, get the facts right.

Sometimes, on a very rare number of stories, there's a deeper level of reporting required.

There's another reason: people are squeamish. I think a lot of people don't know how to do it, don't care to do it, and it's way too much work. It's just kind of disgusting to have to write about this and bum everyone out when you just want to review a record.

JH: You and I got into it over Twitter around *Pitchfork*, in part over the fact that you were saying, "If you are enjoying R. Kelly, you're effectively cosigning what this man has done." At the time, I was being defensive, saying people can like what they like.

JD: To be clear, I think, *Pitchfork* was cosigning it. I think each and every one of us, as individual listeners and consumers of culture, has to come up with our own answer. I don't think there's a right or wrong answer. The thing that's interesting to me is that *Pitchfork* is a journalistic and critical organ. They do journalism and they do criticism.

And then when they are making money to present an act—that's a cosign, that's an endorsement. That's not just writing about and covering it. They very much wanted R. Kelly as their cornerstone artist for the festival. I think it's fair game to say: "Why, *Pitchfork*?"

JH: I had purposely not listened to his music since the initial charges came out and I saw these ninth- and tenth-grade girls interviewed on TV, talking about how he was in the parking lot of their school every day and everyone knew how come. That is what it took for me.

JD: Part of our reporting was sitting with those girls, sitting with their families, seeing their scars on their wrists, hearing the emotion.

JH: Some of our young critical peers, they're twenty-four and all they know of Kelly's past is a vague idea of scandal; they were introduced to him as kids via *Space Jam*. A lot of your reporting on this is not online, it is not googleable. Collective memory is that he "just" peed in a girl's mouth.

JD: To be fair, I teach twenty-year-olds at Columbia. Ignorance is nothing to be ashamed of. Nobody knows everything. A lot of art, great art, is made by despicable people. James Brown beat his wife. People are always, "Why aren't you upset about Led Zeppelin?"

I got the Bonham three rings [tattooed] on my foot. Led Zeppelin did disgusting things. I read *Hammer of the Gods*, I'm disgusted by the group sex with the shark. [Note: it was actually a red snapper! Still gross.] I have a couple of responses to that: I didn't cover Led Zeppelin. If I was on the plane, like Cameron Crowe was, I would have written about those things if I saw them.

The art very rarely talks about these things. There are not pro-rape Led Zeppelin songs. There are not pro-wife-beating James Brown songs. I think in the history of rock 'n' roll, rock music, or pop culture people misbehaving and behaving badly sexually with young women, rare is the amount of evidence compiled against anyone apart from R. Kelly. Dozens of girls—not one, not two, *dozens*—with harrowing lawsuits. The videotapes—and not just one videotape, numerous videotapes. And not Tommy Lee/Pam Anderson, Kardashian fun video. You watch the video for which he was indicted and there is the disembodied look of the rape victim. He orders her to call him Daddy. He urinates in her mouth and instructs her at great length on how to position herself to receive his "gift." It's a rape that you're watching. So we're not talking about rock star misbehavior, which men or women can do. We're talking about predatory behavior. Their lives were ruined. Read the lawsuits!

JH: And there was a young woman who was pressured into an abortion?

JD: That he paid for. There was a young woman that he picked up on the evening of her prom. The relationship lasted a year and a half or two years. Impregnated her, paid for her abortion, had his goons drive her. None of which she wanted. She sued him. The saddest fact I've learned is, nobody matters less to our society than young Black women. Nobody. They have any complaint about the way they are treated, they are "bitches, hoes, and gold-diggers," plain and simple. Kelly never misbehaved with a single white girl who sued him, or that we know of. Mark Anthony Neal, the African American scholar, makes this point: one white girl in Winnetka and the story would have been different.

No, it was young Black girls and all of them settled. They settled because they felt they could get no justice whatsoever. They didn't have a chance.

JH: And they learned that after putting these suits forth and having them get nowhere? Do you think they didn't get traction because of the representation they had, or Kelly's power? Were certain elements in concert with that?

JD: I think it was a lot of things, including the fact that Kelly was fully capable of intimidating people. These girls feared for their lives. They feared for the safety of their families. And these people talked to me not because I'm super-reporter—we rang a lot of doorbells on the South and West Sides, and people were eager to talk about this guy, because they wanted him to stop!

JH: Going back a little bit to our original question, you get this tape dropped in the mail . . .

JD: Well, the tape came a year after we ran the first story. We ran this story and the world shrugged. Associated Press picks it up: "*Chicago Sun-Times* has reported a pattern of sexual predation of young women by Robert Kelly," and everybody says, "Ah, well, okay." Then one day I get this call that says: "Go to your mailbox. There's this manila envelope with a videotape in it."

We had gotten one videotape already after the first story, and we gave it to the police. When I say "we," I mean a roomful of editors sitting around asking, "What is the right thing to do here? This would seem to be evidence of a felony, we should give it to police." There was one tape, but the police could not determine the girl's age. The forensic experts they had looking at it said judging by the soles of her feet, they could tell she was thirteen or fourteen at the time this tape was made, but we can't identify who the woman is. Videotape No. 1.

There were tapes on the street. And I had heard of another videotape with a girl who was part of an ongoing relationship. This is the girl who was in the tape that was in the lawsuit.

JH: And some forty people testified that it was her?

JD: Yeah. Coaches, best friend's parents, pastor, half the family, grandmother, aunt—but the mother and father never testified, the girl never testified. When we wrote our story about the tape, the girl and mother and father took a six-month vacation to the South of France. We'd been to the house several times. We'd rung the doorbell. This was an aluminum-siding, lower-middle-class house on the South Side, with a station wagon which is thirteen years old—you know what I mean? And now they're in the South of France. And one time the dad got a credit as a bass player on an R. Kelly album. He didn't play bass.

The situations are incredibly complicated, and sometimes there is an element of "We're gonna exploit this situation for our favor." That doesn't mean that it's legal or it's right or that girl wasn't harmed. It tore that family apart.

JH: How many people do you think you've interviewed? How many people came forward?

JD: I think in the end there were two dozen women with various levels of details. Obviously the women who were part of the hundreds of pages of lawsuits—hell of a lot of details. There were girls who just told one simple story, and there were a lot of girls who told stories that lasted hours which still make me sick to my stomach. It never was one girl on one tape. Or one girl and Aaliyah.

JH: The other thing, the thing that people seem to not know: she was fresh out of eighth grade in this tape.

JD: Fourteen or fifteen. That puts a perspective on it. She's not sophisticated enough to know what her kinks are.

JH: Let's talk about what it is, aside from not just having reportorial chops, that might hold somebody back. I feel that a lot of younger journalists came up through blogs, not journalism school. They are fearful to write about it because they don't know what they can say, what language they can use, if they can be sued for even acknowledging charges.

JD: You may not know how to report, but you should know how to read. The *Sun-Times* was never sued for the hundreds of thousands of words that it wrote about R. Kelly. You cannot be sued for repeating anything that is in a lawsuit. You cannot be sued for repeating anything that was said during the six- or seven-week trial. It's in his record, and then there's Kelly's own words. Then read [Kelly's biography] *Soulacoaster*. It was not a pleasant experience for me to read *Soulacoaster*! But read it, and read what he says in his own book! Do your goddamn homework!

JH: What are the other factors?

JD: Here's the most sinister. This deeply troubles me: there's a very—I don't know what the percentage is—some percentage of fans are liking Kelly's music because they know. And that's really troublesome to me. There is some sort of—and this is tied up to complicated questions of racism and sexism—there is some sort of vicarious thrill to seeing this guy play this character in these songs and knowing that it's not just a character.

JH: Songs like "Sexasaurus" make it novel. The ironic, jokey *Trapped in the Closet* series airs on the Independent Film Channel and features Will Oldham—that has these other hallmarks of "art" that read to a white, hipster, indie-rock audience.

JD: It puts it in the realm of camp or kitsch. If you have an emotional reaction to a work of art and you use all your skills as a critic to back it up with evidence and context, that's all we can ask of anybody. We're all viewing art differently. The joy is in the conversation. *Pitchfork* is the premier critical organ in the United States for smart discussion of music, books, and artists, but it doesn't have this discussion. The site reviews his records but doesn't have the conversation about "What does it say for us to like his music?"

I think, again, everybody has to individually answer. I can still listen to Led Zeppelin and take joy in Led Zeppelin or James Brown. I condemn the things they did. I'm not reminded constantly in the art, because the art is not about it. But if you're listening to "I want to marry you, pussy" and not realizing that he said that to Aaliyah, who was fourteen, and making an album he named *Age Ain't Nothing but a Number*— I had Aaliyah's mother cry on my shoulder and say her daughter's life was ruined, Aaliyah's life was never the same after that. That's not an experience you've had. I'm not expecting you to feel the same way I do. But you can look at this body of evidence. "You" meaning everybody who cares.

JH: You told me about the night after your critical review of R. Kelly's performance at Pitchfork ran, one of these women called you at 2:00 a.m.

JD: This happens a lot. If you are a good reporter, you are accessible to people and you cannot turn a story off. And that sucks! The number of times since I began this R. Kelly story that I was called in the middle of the night, was talking to someone on Christmas Eve or on New Year's Day or Thanksgiving . . . Yeah, I got a call from one of the women after the Pitchfork festival review. "I know we haven't spoken in a long time," and said thank you for still caring and thank you for writing this story, because nobody gives a shit.

It was a horrible day and a horrible couple of weeks when he was acquitted. The women I heard from who I'd interviewed, women I'd never interviewed who said, "I didn't come forward, I never spoke to you before, I wish I had now that son of a bitch got off." Jesus Christ. Rape-victim advocates—I don't believe in god—they do god's work. These young women who volunteer to be in the emergency room and sit with a woman throughout the horrible process, I don't do that. I'm not saying I'm even in the same universe. But somebody calls you up and says I want to talk about this, or thank you about writing this, or "I can't sleep because I'm haunted, can you hear what I want to tell you?" We do that as a human being. I would like to forget about this story. I'm not saying I'm super-reporter. I'm saying this was a huge story. Where was everybody else?

JH: There is a disregard for your ongoing concern about

this. "Let this go, Jim. Get over it, Jim. He was acquitted." You have never dropped this, and your peers are pissed because it puts the rest of us over a barrel. I can speak to this, too. It's often uncool to be the person who gives a shit.

JD: "You're jealous of R. Kelly, you're trying to make your name off his career."

JH: Because you would love nothing more than to have to report and carry these stories of sexual assault.

JD: It is on record. In the dozens. So stop hedging your words, and when you tell me what a brilliant ode to pussy *Black Panties* is, then realize that the next sentence should say: "This, from a man who has committed numerous rapes." The guy was a monster! Just say it! We do have a justice system and he was acquitted. Okay, fine. And these other women took the civil lawsuit route. He was tried on very narrow grounds. He was tried on a twenty-nine-minute, thirty-six-second videotape. He was tried on trading child pornography. He was not tried for rape. He was acquitted of making child pornography. He's never been tried in court for rape, but look at the statistics. The numbers of rapes that happened, the numbers of rapes that were reported, the numbers of rapes that make it to court, and then the conviction rate.

I mean, it comes down to something minuscule. He's never had his day in court as a rapist. It's fifteen years in the past now, but this record exists. You have to make a choice, as a listener, if music matters to you as more than mere entertainment. And you and I have spent our entire lives with that conviction. This is not just entertainment, this is our lifeblood. This matters.

PART II
REAL/FAKE

WE CAN'T STOP

Our Year with Miley

VILLAGE VOICE PAZZ & JOP CRITICS POLL, JANUARY 2014

Is there a scribe among us—save for *Wire* writers and those who eagerly reviewed that Larry Coryell reissue— who didn't pull down at least forty dollars for Miley musings in 2013? Perhaps a shock-and-awe news item, a post-VMAs reaction, a pondering of that preponderance of her tongue? If not, I hate to break it to you, but you got ripped off. It was her year, whether we liked it or— well, yeah.

We wrote about Miley perhaps not so much because she fascinated but galled us with her every move. And to be sure, it was the moves: the videos, performances, mas- turbatory fingers, nudity, twerking, tongues, the way she used Black women's bodies, and her own, as props. Her actual new album, *Bangerz*, was a tertiary concern at best.

It was a long year for pop aggrievement. With the ex- ception of Bruno Mars's five-week run at the top of the year, the number one spot on *Billboard* in 2013 was oc- cupied exclusively by white artists. While Baauer, Mack- lemore, Robin Thicke, and Lorde hits got their share of controversy and think-piece lather, nothing disquieted the critical corps as thoroughly as Miley. "Wrecking Ball" reigned for a mere three weeks, but then spent the last half of the year as a lightning rod of censure and outrage. We cut off her head and she just kept writhing, unchastened.

Writing about Miley was—and is—simple. Critics often treat young women as billboards. Because they are impossible to define and easy to vilify, they can dependably carry water for any idea we attach to them. Miley is enrapturing, repulsive, hysterical, ignorant, white, young, ultra-rich, ultra-famous, sexy, scary, skeezy, feminist, an artist, not feminist, privileged, talented, sad, visceral, powerful, plastic, real, too real, and friends with Terry Richardson. What can't we say about her? Apparently nothing. Bad girls are infinite. Miley holds America's attention in a way that fully clothed Lorde may never.

Yet Miley's sins were real, and she made egregious missteps as she attempted to telegraph her own artistic primacy by appropriating hip-hop culture and tangling herself in Black cultural idioms. She claimed she didn't see or consider race—of *course* she doesn't have to consider race; she's a very rich and very successful white woman. To ask her to see the scope of her privilege, to understand what it means to mean-mug and then push in her grill, to really comprehend how a swipe of her tongue across Amazon Ashley's ass might play, what it could mean to anyone but herself, is seemingly futile. Miley's irreverence, and her defensive assertion that we were all prudes with a problem, illustrated how wide the chasm between her actions and her awareness was. Her ignorance was willful and emblematic, which made her continual triumph enraging.

Then there was the other matter: the paucity of imagination with which Miley served herself up in 2013. She was permanently lensed in a hetero-pornographic gaze that forced viewers to either imagine what it is to fuck her, or imagine ourselves *as* her, begging for consumption with knowing doe-eyes. By the time the video for "Adore You" dropped in December, Miley's uncomplicated invitation began to feel ruthless in its continual deployment. Her cheap power was fatiguing.

If there was any discernible depth behind her image, *Bangerz* could have been a masterful Top 40 long con, a work of weapons-grade performance art reminiscent of, say, Valie Export's actionist peep show *Action Pants: Genital Panic*. Miley engaged her audience's baseness and biases, forcing them to confront how much they want to see—and are turned on by—a rich, white teenage girl daring us to want her, watching us as we watched her. By year's end, she'd utterly failed to shock anyone who was still paying attention. Which, if we're being honest, was everyone.

In the same week that her second single, "Adore You," dropped, Miley offered up a revision of herself in an interview with *The New York Times*. Taken at face value, it would seem we've misunderstood her all along: she's a Mandela-mourning, big-tent feminist living in hope for America's post-racial future. She doesn't want to be a bad example to the youth, but she's got a rebel nature. She respected the brand Disney built for her enough to curtail it till she was legal. In fact, that's the only part of Miley's narrative that actually makes sense. To believe in her new, grown-up image requires an awareness of her *Hannah Montana* past; it is the most effective way to understand how bad Miley is *now*. Disney made millions branding Miley as a clean-fun-loving, purity-ring-clasping everygirl. Disney forced her to formally apologize for taking bikini selfies after the then-teenage singer's phone was hacked and her pics were disseminated. It is only natural that the adulteration of Miley's emblematically pure image would be sensational, that it would have the power to horrify.

Miley's *Bangerz*-era story is a transformation fantasy built on proximity to what she once was. How quickly she traveled from super-sweet to super-freak is meant to suggest she was an authentic bad girl all along, hiding underneath that darling Disney guise. Her drifting orientation from the Mouse mothership is meant to tell her audiences as much about who she is now as when she cried real tears for Richardson's camera on the set of "Wrecking Ball," then followed them up with real fellatio on a sledgehammer. This is her ceremony to show, whether we want her or not, she belongs to us now.

GAGA TAKES A TRIP

NASHVILLE SCENE, APRIL 2011

There's this photo. In it, Lady Gaga is framed tight, center of the picture, shot from far away by staked-out paparazzi perhaps hiding out behind a row of chairs or a plastic ficus. There are blurred objects around the edges; distant glass security cordons make frames within the frame. The dark, lumpy figure of a TSA agent looms to the left, hands near the star, extended rigidly, officially. Lady Gaga does not acknowledge the camera: she is not looking at it, yet there is no part of her presentation that does not anticipate the camera's gaze, and subsequently, ours as well.

Lady Gaga is taking a trip and has arrived at Los Angeles International Airport in full pop regalia. She is not like the other blond pop singers, Madonna or Jessica Simpson, who deplane in comfort sweats, their makeup-free faces looking strangely unfamiliar, a ponytail sticking out from their ball cap. Gaga does not dress like she is headed home from a yoga workshop even when flying across the continent. Gaga teases out the fan fantasy of the pop star by never dropping the act. Like a superhero, she never appears out of uniform. She never snaps us back to reality; we stay with her in the weird, glamorous world that her presence has made real.

In this, she is conceding the duality of pop stardom: this is all surface and finessed-to-please presentation, an impossible manufacture. She one-ups all those who decry her work and platinum pop as not "real" music—because it's all "fake"—by making it *the most fabulous fake that ever faking faked*. To be sure, Gaga's "fake" is at least as real as the "real" of any self-conscious Brooklyn beardo about to be discovered by *Pitchfork*.

Here, amid her TSA-administered security screening, Gaga is looking spectacular—as in, *like a spectacle*, which is how we want her to be—and she is not disappointing. She is wearing perilously tall (ten-inch) Alexander McQueen snakeskin platform heels, which the designer is said to have modeled after an armadillo. They arch from the ankle, a smooth half-moon that is blunted where it meets the floor, like a toucan's bill if it pointed down instead of out. The snakeskin leather gleams; they are unlike any shoes I have ever seen. Their protrusion is strange but there is something familiar about them, hoof-like. From the waist down, Gaga is wearing only nude underwear and fishnet pantyhose. Looped through her shiny black belt is a pair of metal handcuffs. Her flowing white wig cascades down to her stomach, she wears round, Lennon-style sunglasses, and there is a phone in her hand. Most of her outfit is accessories; she's also wearing a bra and one sleeve of a golden jacket; the other half is tucked into her waistband. It's a curious slip of modesty to cover one's ass while appearing nearly naked in public.

With this picture, we see Gaga become White Swan to out-of-control Britney Spears's Black Swan. This outfit is similar to the one worn by a distressed Spears in summer of 2008, in one of the bleaker paparazzi shots taken during those years. A pale, blemished Spears is shown exiting a black SUV, clad in ripped black fishnets, black cowboy boots, a black jacket, her miniskirt hiked up to her waist, revealing her blood-stained underwear. She wears oversized black sunglasses, her hair is dyed black, her weave a ratted mess, and there is a phone in her hand. She is heading into L.A. boutique Kitson for a private shopping spree at 2:00 a.m.

Though Gaga's work is nearly as platinum-perfect as Britney's, Gaga's work is rife with irony and self-possession; she satisfies with a cultivated and purposeful strangeness. As she plays with the idea of pop's real fake, she winks at us from atop her skyscraper heels. Nearly nude in LAX, she obliges her audience's most debased wish: to see celebrities naked, to ogle them, completely. She acknowledges the ironies, she ruptures the fantasies of pop, yet she abides by them as she rips them apart. In doing so, Lady Gaga shows that she understands the only real rule of popular entertainment: give the people what they want.

DECONSTRUCTING LANA DEL REY

SPIN, JANUARY 2012

1. The Origin Story: A Star Is Made

The myth, as it presently stands: Lana Del Rey is a vanity project bankrolled by the singer's dad and honed, over several years, by a series of lawyers and managers who've shaped her image and plotted her career path. She is a canvas of a girl, and a willing one at that. The truth, as it is presently understood: Her legal name is Lizzy Grant, "Lana Del Rey" is her stage name. She is twenty-five and grew up in Lake Placid, in upstate New York. She spent her time as a teen wandering in the woods and writing, feeling like a secret weirdo and having her first real connection to music through Biggie's "Juicy." She says that back then she was something akin to trouble, which got her shipped off to Kent, a private prep school in Connecticut. Her remembrance of her cherry-schnapps-swilling party-girl era can be heard on her song "This Is What Makes Us Girls."

At eighteen, she moved to New York City to attend Fordham University, where she studied metaphysics, looking for proof of God, and began writing songs. She stopped drinking and got sober. She played shows, performing versions of songs that now make up her major-label debut, *Born to Die*. Just before her senior year, she landed a deal with the small independent label 5 Points, through a songwriting competition. The label, which specialized in electronic and worldbeat artists, gave her an advance, which she used to move into a New Jersey trailer park shortly after graduating from Fordham.

David Nichtern, who runs 5 Points, solicited producer David Kahne (who has worked with everyone from Paul McCartney to Sublime), who agreed to helm the Lizzy Grant record. "It was a bit of a coup because he is a big name, and we are a tiny record label," says Nichtern. In the studio, Kahne saw in Del Rey a singer who was motivated and self-directed, always looking for ways to move her work forward. "What she's doing goes against the grain of chart pop," says Kahne. "The country is fraying at the edges. She wanted to look at that edge, at destruction and loss, and talk about it." According to Kahne, Del Rey was "solitary" and often spent her nights riding the subway alone out to Coney Island, exploring.

The songs from these sessions were split into two releases, the *Kill Kill* EP and her debut full-length album, *Lana Del Ray A.K.A. Lizzy Grant*. According to Nichtern, after the release of the EP, the singer said she wanted to change the name she recorded under. "First it was 'Del R-A-Y,' and then she settled on 'R-E-Y.' This story that it was anyone but her making the decision is complete fiction," says Nichtern. "If she is 'made up'—well, she is the one who made herself up. She has very strong ideas about what she does. The idea someone could manage her into a particular shape—it's impossible."

Shortly before the *Lizzy Grant* album was to be released, Nichtern says Del Rey decided she was unhappy and wanted to add tracks, among other changes. "It became difficult to go forward," he explains. Del Rey decided to shelve the record, and 5 Points obliged, striking a deal for her to buy back her masters. Nichtern is adamant that, counter to rumor, the deal's dissolution was all aboveboard and there were never any hard feelings. "She is a great artist," he says, "a real artist. I have always thought so and still do."

"It was very unusual," says Interscope's executive VP of A&R Larry Jackson of his first serious meeting with Lana Del Rey. "We sat for an hour and talked, without her playing any of her music. Just conversation, honing in on the philosophy of what she was doing, what she saw for herself. It was a totally unorthodox meeting, and I thought, 'I've got to do this.'" When asked if anyone else was involved, if there is someone orchestrating Lana from behind the curtain, Jackson is emphatic. "The only Svengali in this thing is Lana."

"I've never understood this controversy about whether she is real or fake," says rapper-producer Princess Superstar. "All artists have a persona." A year prior to the Interscope deal, the two women spent a few months honing Del Rey's songs, with the rapper serving as mentor. "She's not put together by some company. These are her songs, her melodies, her singing—she's always had this '60s aesthetic."

Interscope don Jimmy Iovine gave Jackson his bless-
ing to sign Del Rey on the basis of seeing an unfinished
version of Del Rey's video for her song "Video Games"
on YouTube. Del Rey signed a worldwide, joint deal with
Interscope and Polydor in March 2011, which means she
was a major-label recording artist a full six months before any blog was speculating whether the former choir-
girl was an indie ingenue or a purely plasticine creation.

2. The Look: Baddest of the Good Girls

A pretty singer with a cool voice is one thing, but Lana
Del Rey fascinates because of the tension in her persona.
She's the good girl who wants it all: the boy, his heart, and
nothing short of pop stardom. In short, Lana Del Rey is
Amy Winehouse with the safety on. While Winehouse's
complicated image was that of an unrepentant bad girl, Del
Rey plays it differently: her image is one of a bad girl who
knows better, a bad girl held back by her conscience. Her
ballads are about self-control (and sometimes the lack of
it) and being hopelessly dedicated to bird-dogging dudes
("You're no good for me / But, baby, I want you" goes Del
Rey's "Diet Mountain Dew"). The Lana of "Blue Jeans"
and "Video Games" is enchanted by the darkness and
thrilled by the prospect of losing herself in this bad boy,
dissolving or finding form in disappearing into his needs.
The Lana of these songs is alive in that vicarious freedom,
further evidence that there's still some teenage intensity
lingering around her Chantilly edges. "I've had to pray a
lot because I've been in trouble a lot," she told *GQ* last year.

"I remember that she had really specific feelings about what she wanted to portray about girls," recalls Kahne. "We were talking about Marilyn and Natalie Wood, these iconic actresses of the '50s, and she said, 'They were good girls.' She liked that image."

"In her, I see the struggle between the good girl and the bad girl," says Larry Jackson. That duality was part of what made him want to sign her. After a dinner meeting in Los Angeles last spring, he saw her kick a cab that cut her off as she was walking away. "She cursed out the cab. I saw her do it, but she didn't see me. She epitomizes the loose-cannon star."*

In a YouTube video from 2008, back when she was still firmly Lizzy Grant, Del Rey gives a writer from *Index* magazine a tour of her New Jersey trailer park. Gracious and proud, she smiles easily. It's a year after Winehouse's "Rehab" hit ubiquity, and Del Rey is done up in a Jersey approximation of the British singer: She's wearing a silk bomber, her white blond flip teased up into a bouffant and tied up with a bandana, batting long false lashes. She looks miscast, like a too-young housewife or a teen bride trying to look grown. Her baby face and coquettish giggle give her away. The sound on the video is awful and

---

* Admittedly, much of this story is accorded to men's recollection and rests on their perception of LDR's artistry, based on what parts are visible to them, and all of them have varying stakes in the public reception of her work. This was supposed to be a profile-interview with her, and when her publicist repeatedly pushed back the interview, I started working on a write-around. I was seven months pregnant and this buck-a-word feature was my maternity leave. My interview with Lana never materialized.

the questions tepid, but Del Rey answers the two most important ones clearly and directly to the camera: this is where she wrote her record; and she moved to Jersey for the state's surplus of metal boys. She wants no confusion about what matters to her.

"She has many different qualities that women in our culture aren't allowed to be, all at once, so people are trying to find the inauthentic one," says Tavi Gevinson, the founding editor of teen-girl mag *Rookie*, of the heated online debates and gossip that surround Del Rey's rise. "She's girly, but not infantilized. I relate to her aesthetic the way I think other girls relate to Taylor Swift lyrics— her femininity isn't too sexy or too pure, and that's something I can get behind."

How Del Rey defines herself in the classic-pop cosmos has changed as her music and image have evolved over the past year: "Gangsta Nancy Sinatra" gave way to "Lolita lost in the 'hood." More recently, she catchphrased her *Born to Die* as "Bruce Springsteen in Miami," effectively trading up on that South Jersey striving. *Born to Die* features familiar Springsteen tropes—no-future kids tangled in sin and forever making promises they can't possibly keep; Del Rey's songs are like answer-back dispatches direct from "Candy's Room," but the door's slammed shut and the stereo's up. She's telling the missing side of the story, Candy's side, revealing a new, true character, a young woman living behind that scrim of male desire: *Born to Die* is an album about a good girl who wants it just as bad as *he* does.

3. The Backlash: It's About the Music, LOL

The issue with Lana Del Rey is not whether she is, as alleged by the music press, a corporate test-tube babe, but rather why some are unwilling to believe that she is animated by her own passion and ambition. The big question here is not "Is she real?" but, rather, why it seems impossible to believe that she could be.

On its surface, the online Lana Del Rey Authenticity Debate™ swings between two depressing possibilities: (1) that she's been Frankensteined together by conspiratorial old white guys in order to exploit the now substantial "indie" market, or (2) that she is a moderately talented singer who is getting over by pushing our buttons with nostalgia and good looks. This is the distracting crux, a pointless debate that casts a long shadow over *Born to Die*. For cynical critics and anonymous commenters alike, the reality of Lana Del Rey seems to be an unsolvable equation: the prospect of an attractive woman artist who sings plainly about her desire because she has it, with an earnest and ambitious vision, who crafts her own songs and videos, who understands what it takes to be a viable pop product and is capable of guiding herself to those perilous heights—all of this is somehow impossible to believe. Yet Lana Del Rey is doing it all, before our very eyes.

Being sexy and serious about your art needn't be mutually exclusive, even when your art involves being a pop package. Defending herself to *Pitchfork* last fall, Del Rey said, "I'm not trying to create an image or a persona. I'm just singing because that's what I know how to do." If her ambitions were to "just" sing, she'd still be making the rounds at Brooklyn open mics, but here she's attempting to refocus our attention on her music. Which, for a short time, was the only reason we cared about her. Perhaps if she'd faked us out with a record on a modest indie label like Merge first, shown some hesitation toward major labels or the mainstream, her ambition would've been palatable instead of outrageous.

The central, mistaken assumption being made about Del Rey is that she is a valence for DIY/indie culture, which she's never been. She played daytime, industry showcases at overlit venues in Midtown Manhattan for years, and was taking meetings at majors in 2010. These are the steps of someone who wants to be a pop star, not signed by Matador. Bloggers and tastemaking websites believed they noticed her first when, in fact, they were two years behind a pack of lawyers and A&R scouts who were eager to sign an artist who was the total package.

While a few blogs got on the Del Rey wagon early, the successive waves of attention in late spring of 2011 were prompted by press releases. No one can rightly claim to have discovered her; even the coolest blogs were being jumped into LDR awareness by publicists or a "grassroots" marketing firm, their earliest LDR posts repeating her origin story just as it was fed to them. Many of these same blogs are now indignant, fronting like they were duped into caring about her or lending her credibility, though they certainly weren't so discerning before. They were just eager to claim "first," as is the law of the jungle.

In the weeks surrounding the release of Del Rey's

Born to Die, every interview and TV performance be-came a new proving ground. Video interviews showed Del Rey as both self-aware and funny, as when a VH1 interviewer condescendingly comforted her for not being on this year's Coachella lineup. She deadpanned, "Aw, thanks," before cracking herself up. Her much-maligned *Saturday Night Live* performance sounded just as awk-ward as every other band that performs on the show. Still, her unevenness was taken as resounding proof that she was "Born 2 Fail" by no less an authority than, uh, NBC news anchor Brian Williams.

In other interviews, Del Rey has talked about study-ing cosmology and a six-year stint doing homeless out-reach, suggesting that she's more engaged in the real world than her ardent critics. Though she aims high, she's still hardly acting like a star, telling MTV, "I consider being able to pursue music a luxury, but it's not the most important thing in my life. It's just something that's really nice that ended up working for me for right now." Still, she doesn't bother hiding her ambition; she's even cited the self-actualization classic *Think and Grow Rich* as her recommended reading.

Surprisingly, it's still easier for people to believe the ancient model of a major-label star system, the familiar fable of a girl of moderate talent being polished up and posed to appeal, rather than accept that a young woman could plot her course by her own force of will. Mean-while, sexist critiques of Del Rey's appearance, songs, and videos get spun and offered up as knowing analysis of a deceptive product. Her songs are assailed as "trying too hard" to be sexy, as if listeners have slept through the past three decades of liberated pop-star sexuality as written by Madonna/Janet/Britney/Rihanna and are now shocked by Del Rey's own approximation. She's by-the-book, and yet she's seen as breaking the rules. Would anyone even be this intrigued by a young woman artist being subtle or modest in her ambitions? As an audience, we make a big stink about wanting the truth, but we're only really interested in the old myths.

ST. VINCENT, *STRANGE MERCY*

THE VILLAGE VOICE, NOVEMBER 2011

Annie Clark is too perfect a rock star, but she will do. She has china-doll features; she is put-together and glamorous; her manner is refined. She's beautiful, and you can tell she is used to being looked at and watched, as if she was famous long before now.

Looking at her when she's offstage, you imagine she should be doing something else, not staying up late with a guitar slung round her back and commanding a band into loud swells of her own design. It seems like the wrong job for her hands. She seems more coquettish than rock 'n' roll as she's curled up on the couch backstage in her emerald crepe dress before her show.

When Annie Clark gets onstage as St. Vincent, her image is mere collateral. What fixes your gaze to her is the confidence, the ease, and the naturalness she exudes. You cannot imagine she was meant for anything else but stomping around the stage, coaxing new noise from her guitar, her eyes surveying the sold-out crowd. She solos; they scream.

"I'm not qualified to do anything else," she says,

sounding a little concerned—as if she had been browsing Craigslist ads for admin positions while casting about for a post-Berklee-dropout plan B. "I didn't think I needed it. Which sounds insane when I say it aloud."

It's not. It's only reasonable. Clark's third record, *Strange Mercy*, is her best and most pop album. The signs of her success are ample. For one thing, *Mercy* sold twenty thousand copies in its first week of release. Still, she plays modest, or at least presents as the anti-diva—"It would be interesting to know exactly how many people have heard my songs," she says. Her guess: "Like, one hundred thousand?" Perhaps that would be the case if everyone who'd bought a copy of her last few albums had kept them entirely for themselves, she'd never toured, file sharing didn't exist, and her songs weren't presently all over radio and the blogosphere.

With *Strange Mercy*, Clark moves closer to her audience, lowers the transom a bit. On her previous two albums, *Marry Me* (2007) and *Actor* (2009), it was hard to tell what, if anything, was personal. Her debut seems to be made up of vignettes and stories. She cited "Pirate Jenny" and Nick Cave as her inspirations for its theatricality. It seemed the work of someone eager to impress—to show off, even. *Actor*, purportedly a tribute to Clark's favorite films, resulted in Clark rhapsodizing over Woody Allen's work as much as explaining her own. She says of her progress as a songwriter since: "I care less about impressing. Well . . . maybe. It's no longer about trying to impress people with my wit."

Audiences want confessional bits from rock icons,

and expect them from female singer-songwriters. Clark doesn't give them up easily, but *Strange Mercy* is being called "candid." The singer is still cagey, though there is discernibly more of her on here. Was it intentional?

"Was I trying to be candid? Hmm." She munches an apple and considers what to say. "I want to give you answers, but I am also aware this is to be printed in a magazine, so I'm at a bit of an impasse. But I don't want to give you a rote answer, though that rote answer is quite true. There are songs here that are very, actually, candid. But I won't say which those are."

Although she hemmed over making her art more personal, the candor came naturally, which she characterizes as scary. She didn't have as much time or ability to dress up or intellectualize what was coming out of her, so some songs remained as visceral as they were when initially written. "Two thousand ten was a rough year. Tough stuff. Rough time. When life was actually hard, I had less time to wring my hands about music. It got to be what it should be, a great thing—a replenishing thing." She adds, apologetically, "Not to use a spa word."

Much has been made of the album closer, "Chloe in the Afternoon," which is somewhere between "Afternoon Delight" and Anaïs Nin lyrically; it depicts soft sadism with a girl in a hotel room. Is Clark put off by how this one song has resulted in people calling *Strange Mercy* "sexual"? "It's not like I should have called the record *Get Down to Fuckin'*," she laughs. "I think people focus on something like that because it's titillating." Given that female performers often have their work sexualized, regardless of whether their work is sexual or not, was she hesitant to make a song so blatantly erotic? "I was more reluctant to write a song about that power/sex/domination trifecta, that murky water where it all swims around together," she says. "That felt more complicated than it being about something sexual."

If there is a theme to be found on *Strange Mercy*, it involves dissolving an identity, or another person's idea of that identity. Clark's modesty is belied by her awareness of and use of her own image as a beautiful woman, as a gossamer shredder of skill and confidence, as a woman in charge of her career, as a popular singer of pop songs. She knows what she is working with. She understands the machinations of fame, of why her audience likes (and loves) her; she is careful but solicitous enough with the press that pokes at her. "I have one answer for you if the tape recorder is on, and another if it's off," she says when asked about her awareness of her own image. "That's my answer there."

Still, Clark says she feels like a fraud much of the time. "It's complicated to exist in the world—everyone feels that, whether or not you have a modest amount of notoriety," she says. "I was reading this Miranda July piece in *The New Yorker*, and it ends with a line about how feeling like an adult also means feeling like a fraud. I think if anyone has any kind of self-awareness, they've felt like a fraud—with other people or in relationships. I feel that way. And maybe it's more powerful to put that out there. To just own that, than to keep being, like, 'Watch me sing and dance, I've got all the bases covered, don't worry.'"

The singer's measured control seems to keep her from

truly letting it all (or, even, some of it) hang out. She credits her politeness to her mother, whom she describes as a saint, and to her cultural inheritance as a Texan. She says she learned the value of professionalism from her aunt and uncle, the folk duo Tuck & Patti, whom she toured with as a teen. "It's not the '80s or the '90s anymore; it's not a gravy train," she says of the music business. "If you want to have a career for a long time, you need to act right. I know it's counterintuitive to the whole rock 'n' roll thing, but I have never acted like I was a person who was so unimpeachably great that I could afford to be an asshole to people, nor would I want to be. I take it seriously."

To be a rock star involves more than just charisma, or good songs, or talent (talent usually least of all). One must be a capable player and have an appealing image—and, perhaps, most of all, a clear confidence that one deserves to be in front of an audience. In that regard, Annie Clark is a natural-born rock star; she just happens to be working below the arena level. She doesn't disagree. "There are plenty of things I am not confident about, but *this* I can do."

KACEY MUSGRAVES, *PAGEANT MATERIAL*

PITCHFORK, JUNE 2015

From its opening notes, Kacey Musgraves's *Pageant Material* sounds like a sigh of relief. Musgraves's voice is largely unadorned, her sound analog and organic; she is backed by a small band, sweetened by pedal steel and strings. The songs are not overworked; the choruses do not explode, they merely unfurl. Her near-perfect major-label debut, 2013's *Same Trailer Different Park*, positioned her as something akin to the country Kendrick Lamar; like she could save country music from itself. Musgraves stands in stark relief to some of her CMA-hoisting peers, and her ascendance as a corrective at a time when bro-country's red cup runneth over with EDM's structural dynamics, NRA talking points, and "rapping." She's rightfully hailed as a new model, the inverse of what dominates Nashville's Top 40. Musgraves is a perpetually stoned real girl, fixating on fine '70s countrypolitan flourishes and focusing on self-acceptance.

Musgraves grew up rural and working class in East Texas and firmly orients herself as someone not that far removed from a small-town fate. Country, historically, espouses nothin'-fancy humility, but in 2015, these qualities are often illustrated by naming things—cheap beer, old trucks—that signify one's down-homeness. Mainstream country is currently a few years deep into a circa-2004 hip-hop rut, where recitation of the familiar nouns of late-stage capitalism replace narrative altogether; moral certitude and purchasing power are a constant broadcast in every song. The lone examples of this sort of signaling on *Pageant Material* are a citation of Willie Nelson (who duets on his own lovely "Are You Sure"), the invocation of a room shared with Gram Parsons's ghost on "Dime Store Cowgirl," and the title-track entendre of "the only Crown is in my glass." When Musgraves sings "Just 'cause it don't cost a lot / Don't mean it's cheap" on "Dime Store Cowgirl," it's as much a personal thesis as it is a repudiation of capitalist culture values.

Musgraves's "not"-ness is the pivot point of her artistic identity. Her songs exude a relaxed resonance because they have a lot less to prove. They feel personal, and you can locate Musgraves the artist in them ("And if I end up goin' down in flames / Well, at least I know I did it my own way"). Mainstream country often posits an Us vs. Them divide meant to performatively alienate those who cannot identify or ally themselves with the lifestyle or values represented; for Musgraves, openness and acceptance are the paradigm. One of the remarkable things about Musgraves is not how much she has deviated from country norms but the way that she expands them.

The most obvious one, and the one that the press and the public have latched on to, is the feminist-at-her-liberty narratives with songs (most of which are cowritten by her producers, Luke Laird and Shane McAnally, who were also behind the boards on *Same Trailer*). While this is worth noting and celebrating, in Musgraves's case it's overstated simplification, one that pits her as a straw-(wo)man against the easy villainy of bro country, instead of within a canon that spans from Kitty Wells's "It Wasn't God Who Made Honky Tonk Angels" to Loretta Lynn's "Fist City" through Miranda Lambert's "Kerosene." With *Pageant Material* there is less good-for-the-gander agenda than anticipated. Musgraves is confident and self-contained, the Big Machine–subtweeting "Good 'Ol Boys Club" and its chaser, "Cup of Tea," showing that she's not measuring herself against anyone's standards but her own, a credo she reiterates on most every song on the album. Under the microscope, it's more than confidence, it's more than self-help, self-love maxims; it's a disregard of the system. It's Musgraves shrugging off the mantle of Southern Girlhood ("I'd rather lose for what I am / Than win for what I ain't" she sings on the title track).

Unlike some of her peers, Musgraves doesn't use her not-ness to position herself as a bad girl; in her world that dichotomy doesn't exist. Being a country music bad girl would be giving traditional ideals too much credit. While Musgraves may occasionally traffic in cliché, she doesn't abide by stereotypes. Instead she spends much of the record refusing the obligation to a good reputation ("Biscuits," "Late to the Party," or boasting "I'm always higher than my hair" on "Pageant Material"). She celebrates an authentic self-expression above all; Musgraves's tendentious *realness* is what lends the album its quiet politics.

Unpacking her on-record presentation of persona is fun and engaging work, but it's Musgraves's songcraft that provides the *whoa* moments. She has the ability to shift a phrase—like "family is family" or "you can take me out of the country, but you can't take the country out of me"—out of rote and into poignancy, or hell, even into something deep. She can pin ten of these plainspoken lines back-to-back, without ever straining the song or its narrative or appearing to do any hard work at all. Her ability to pair song to sentiment is fairly flawless.

Pageant Material is a bit smoother than *Same Trailer*, and musically there is less to grab on to. The album's maudlin center, the triptych of "Somebody to Love," "Miserable," and "Die Fun," gives it some gravitas. Her voice on these world-weary bits, especially "Miserable," give the album some of the heft it could use a little more of. It's an easy listen that clocks its fourteen tracks swiftly and can feel a little lightweight on repeated listens.

The binary of "good" country vs. "bad" is one we'd be wise to retire, and is the wrong narrative to frame a songwriter of Musgraves's caliber. She remixes all that we might call corny and shopworn in other, less deft hands. She's making gold records in service to small-town DGAF burner girls who managed to half get their shit together.

Which is a strange universe for a burgeoning pop star to be working in, nestling in with the ex-Swiftie fuck-up fringe, young folks imagining lives beyond the dead ends and expectations set before them. While much of women's work in mainstream pop is hung up on pleasure (still important!) and what freedom disposable income nets them (ditto), Musgraves is musing in a more quotidian space of struggle and acceptance. It's a strange and forgiving album, less toothsome than the ones that preceded it, but Musgraves's resistance makes this album important, even when it's imperfect.

LOUDER THAN LOVE

My Teen Grunge Poserdom

FOR EXPERIENCE MUSIC PROJECT CONFERENCE, SPRING 2005

There was a time, not too terribly long ago, when I was not cool. In 1990, I was fourteen, almost fifteen, and had just entered the ninth grade at the largest high school in Minneapolis. I orbited somewhere between loner dork and amorphous weirdo. My wardrobe consisted of a lot of black clothes, a lot of orange clothes, and my mother's business apparel from the eighties; I wore cowboy boots and long, unbelted tunics that made me look like I was in a cult. I spent a lot of time alone, sewing hats and reading news magazines to keep up on international politics. The music I knew about was from the radio. I had a few tapes I liked: the B-52's *Cosmic Thing*, Deee-Lite, the first Tracy Chapman album. I mostly listened to the tapes on the weekend, when I was delivering my newspaper route, though sometimes I would lie in bed at night and listen to the Tracy Chapman tape over and over and cry a little.

Six weeks after I started high school, I was sitting on the bleachers during freshman gym, which I was already failing for refusing to dress for class, along with all the other weirdos, who were also refusing gym on principle.

Andrew Semans, also of the ninth grade, came and sat next to me and asked, "Are you a punk or a hippie? I can't tell." I told him I liked the Clash, and he started drilling me about a million bands I had never heard. The next day he handed me a cassette tape, a mix made from a very specific subsection of his big brother's record collection. Butthole Surfers, Babes in Toyland, Boredoms, BALL, Big Black, Bongwater on side one; Pussy Galore, Voidoids, Stooges on the flip. By week's end I was a convert and punk-identified.

As punk rock began to ravage and motivate my life, so did my adolescent hormones. I began to pine for the attention of punk boys, of whom I knew three. One was Andrew S.; we could barely stand each other but were bonded by conversations about Sonic Youth. His friend Ted wore a Jane's Addiction T-shirt and was on JV bowling; he thought *All Shook Down* was the best Replacements record—making him a no-go. Then there was Andrew B., who was in the tenth grade, who wasn't so much punk as he was proactively grunge.

He became my crush by virtue of the fact that he knew my name and he knew who Hüsker Dü was, and at the time that was more than I had going with anyone else. His look was proto-grunge: he wore his hair long and parted in the middle, all of his jeans were ripped, he wore a faded Mudhoney *Superfuzz Bigmuff* T-shirt and a flannel. He played drums in a cover band of sorts with his college-age brother; they were called Korova Milkbar and their only gigs took place in their basement. Their repertoire read like a best-of Sub Pop Records sampler: Tad's "Loser,"

Nirvana's "Lovebuzz" and "Floyd the Barber," a Sound-garden song, a Screaming Trees song, and they usually closed their set with a Mudhoney medley that included an infinite version of "In 'n' Out of Grace" that would alternate between the chorus and long drum solos. Because I "loved" Andrew and wanted him to love me back, and though I was approximately four feet tall, had a mouth full of braces, and looked as much like a fourteen-year-old boy as I did a fourteen-year-old girl, I took the only route available—I became a grunge devotee.

The process was simple: I made the rounds to every record store in the Twin Cities, spending my hard-earned babysitting and paper-delivery savings on anything with a Sub Pop logo on it, every release in multiple formats—Mudhoney, Nirvana, Fluid, Tad, Dwarves, Soundgarden, L7, and Dickless. I saved up one hundred dollars for the out-of-print *Sub Pop 100* compilation. I mail-ordered five Mudhoney, one Soundgarden, and two Fluid shirts and then made my own Nirvana shirt with a Sharpie.

I parted my hair in the middle, ripped holes in the knees of my jeans, scrawled the names of every band I liked on my Chuck Taylor high-tops in pen. I am not sure why I thought dressing *exactly* like Andrew B. might lure him to me, but I wanted to show him we were kindred spirits in the world, toughing out our teenage times with Tad's *8-Way Santa* in our Walkmans.

Alas, the pose did not end there. I did things like casually wander past his classes as they got out, holding nothing but a Mudhoney tape in my hand, as if it were required material for ninth grade. I took the same

Russian class as him so that I would have the chance to tell him such things as I was considering getting a tattoo of Mudhoney bassist Matt Lukin, "once I got the money together." My project for film class was a documentary on his band, and it was twenty minutes of carefully edited footage of band practices in his parents' basement. (I got a C–.) I went to see Fluid twice that year, despite hating them, in hopes of seeing him at the show. When I saw him that following Monday, after lingering outside his AP English class again, I said, "I figured I would have seen you at the show last night." He told me he was *no longer into Fluid*. I was crushed. I had spent dozens of hours listening to their records, which I found to be unbearable, fantasizing and prepping for conversations about Fluid minutiae that we would one day have.

All soul soon left my pose. My obsession with detail slipped. I was coming to the agonizing conclusion that all of this, my teen-girl masking, was in vain. I'd dedicated several months and several hundred dollars to trying to cultivate a connection that was never going to be. Still, I wasn't quite ready to give up.

At the end of the school year, I managed to get invited to a party where all three of the school's grunge cover bands were playing. I would soon have the chance to see my crush-object one last time before the span of summer. I went to the party wearing a Soundgarden *Louder Than Love* T-shirt, which I had purchased for the occasion. I slouched up against a wall, peacocking my ennui, sipping a Miller Lite and pretending to be way into that, too. I was standing next to Andrew's best friend, Mike, who was setting up a bass rig. I ventured to ask him what awesome record we were listening to. He gawked at me, appalled. "Uh? *Louder Than Love*?" I scrambled, mortified, and insisted I was "too wasted" to recognize Soundgarden, the most distinctive band of the grunge genre.

I then had the torturous experience of watching Mike walk over to Andrew and relay this anecdote. Andrew looked toward me and snickered. I left the party, walked home, and cried myself to sleep.

Less than a month later, I picked up a compilation album called *Kill Rock Stars*. My purchase was initially fueled by the inclusion of Nirvana and Melvins tracks, both potential conversation topics with Andrew, but something entirely different happened when I heard a band on side B, Bikini Kill. Kathleen Hanna's rebel yell freed me from my teen grunge misery; I had found music that meant everything to *me*. The band's *Bikini Kill* fanzine and the cassette demo meant I no longer had a reason to be obsessing over music that *meant nothing*. I was liberated from my days spent walking past some boy's locker, loudly humming Nirvana songs. Bikini Kill songs taught me something that neither Mudhoney nor Andrew B. ever could—that my teen-girl soul mattered. That who I was mattered, what I thought and felt mattered, even when they were invisible to everyone else.

PART III

DEATH/
REDEMPTION

THE PASSION OF DAVID BAZAN

CHICAGO READER, JULY 2009

"People used to compare him to Jesus," says a backstage manager as David Bazan walks offstage, guitar in hand. "But not so much anymore."

It's Thursday, July 2, and Bazan has just finished his set at Cornerstone, the annual Christian music festival held on a farm near Bushnell, Illinois. He hasn't betrayed his crowd the way Dylan did when he went electric—this is something very different. The kids filling the fifteen-hundred-capacity tent know their Jesus from their Judas. There was a time when Bazan's fans believed he was speaking, or rather singing, the Word. Not so much anymore.

As front man for Pedro the Lion, the band he led from 1995 till 2005, Bazan was Christian indie rock's first big crossover star, predating Sufjan by nearly a decade and paving the way for the music's success outside the praise circuit. But as he straddled the secular and spiritual worlds, Bazan began to struggle with his faith. Unable to banish from his mind the possibility that the God he'd loved and prayed to his whole life didn't exist, he started drinking heavily. In 2005, the last time he played Cornerstone, he was booted off the grounds for being shit-faced, a milk jug full of vodka in his hand. (The festival is officially dry.)

I worked as Bazan's publicist from 2000 till 2004. When I ran into him in April—we were on a panel together at the Calvin College Festival of Faith & Music in Grand Rapids—I hadn't seen him or talked to him in five and a half years. The first thing he said to me was, "I'm not sure if you know this, but my relationship with Christ has changed pretty dramatically in the last few years."

He went on to explain that since 2004, he's been flitting between atheist, skeptic, and agnostic, and that lately he's hovering around agnostic—he can't flat-out deny the presence of God in the world, but Bazan doesn't exactly believe in him, either.

Pedro the Lion won a lot of secular fans in part because Bazan's lyrics—incisive examinations of faith, set to fuzzed-out guitar hooks—have a through-a-glass-darkly quality, acknowledging the imperfection of human understanding rather than insisting on an absolute truth. As the post-9/11 culture wars began to heat up, Pedro the Lion albums took a turn toward the parabolic: an outraged Bazan churned out artful songs about what befalls the righteous and the folly of those who believe God is on their side.

Bazan's relationship with the divine was once pretty uncomplicated, though. Raised outside Seattle in the Pentecostal church where his father was the music director, he hewed closely to Christian orthodoxy, attended Bible college, and married at twenty-three. Now thirty-three, he didn't do a lot of thinking about politics until the 1999

WTO protests. "Growing up, Christianity didn't feel oppressive for the most part, because it was filtered through my parents. They were and are so sincere, and I saw in them a really pure expression of unconditional love and service," he says. "Once I stepped away, I could see the oppression of it."

Bazan's *Curse Your Branches*, due September 1 on Barsuk, is a visceral accounting of what happened after that. It's a harrowing breakup record—except he's dumping God, Jesus, and the evangelical life. It's his first full-length solo album and also his most autobiographical effort: its drunken narratives, spasms of spiritual dissonance, and family tensions are all scenes from the recent past.

Bazan says he tried to Band-Aid his loss of faith and the painful end of Pedro the Lion with about eighteen months of "intense" drinking. "If I didn't have responsibilities, if I wasn't watching [my daughter] Ellanor, I had a deep drive to get blacked out," he says. But as he made peace with where he found himself, the compulsion to get obliterated began to wane. On *Curse Your Branches*, Bazan sometimes directs the blame and indignation at himself, other times at Jesus and the faith. He's mourning what he's lost, and he knows there's no going back.

"All fallen leaves should curse their branches / For not letting them decide where they should fall / And not letting them refuse to fall at all," he sings on the title track, with more than a touch of fuck-you in his voice. On "When We Fell," backed by a galloping beat and Wilson-boys harmonies, he calls faith a curse put on him by God: "If my mother cries when I tell her what I discovered /

Then I hope she remembers she told me to follow my heart / And if you bully her like you've done me with fear of damnation / Then I hope she can see you for what you are."

The album closer, "In Stitches," may be the best song Bazan's ever written. It's the most emotionally bare piece on the album, and works as a synopsis of the story:

> *This brown liquor wets my tongue*
> *My fingers find the stitches*
> *Firmly back and forth they run*
> *I need no other memory*
> *Of the bits of me I left*
> *When all this lethal drinking*
> *Is hopefully to forget*
> *About you*

He follows it with an even more devastating verse, confessing that his efforts to erase God have failed:

> *I might as well admit it*
> *Like I've even got a choice*
> *The crew have killed the captain*
> *But they still can hear his voice*
> *A shadow on the water*
> *A whisper in the wind*
> *On long walks with my daughter*
> *Who is lately full of questions*
> *About you*
> *About you*

The second "about you" comes in late, in a strong fal-
setto, and those two words carry his entire burden—the
anger, desire, confusion, and grief.

Since the jug-of-vodka incident, Bazan has kept a
pretty low profile, doing a couple of modest solo tours
and releasing an EP of raw-sounding songs on Barsuk.
Pedro the Lion was a reliable paycheck—most of its albums
sold in the neighborhood of fifty thousand copies, and
the group toured regularly, drawing four hundred to six
hundred people a night. His most recent tour couldn't
have been more different: Bazan doesn't have a road
band put together yet for his solo stuff, but he couldn't
afford to wait for *Curse Your Branches* to come out. So
he found another way to keep in touch with his most
devoted fans, booking sixty solo shows in houses and
other noncommercial spaces. He played intimate acoustic sets to maybe forty people each night, at twenty dollars a ticket, and took questions between songs—some of
them, unsurprisingly, about the tough spiritual questions
his new material raises.

Despite his candid answers to those questions, he was
invited back to Cornerstone for the first time this year.

"I know David has a long history of being a seeker
and trying to navigate through his faith. Cornerstone is
open to that," says John Herrin, the festival's director.
"We welcome plenty of musicians who may not identify
themselves as Christians but are artists with an ongoing
connection to faith . . . We're glad to have him back. We
don't give up on people; we don't give up on the kids
here who are seeking, trying to figure out what they

don't believe and what they do. This festival was built on patience."

At Cornerstone, where I catch up with him behind the fair-food midway, Bazan laughs when I suggest that he's there trying to save the Christians. "I am. I am really invested, because I came up in it and I love a lot of evangelical Christians—I care what happens with the movement," he says. "The last thirty years of it have been hijacked; the boomer evangelicals, they were seduced in the most embarrassing and scandalous way into a social, political, and economical posture that is the antithesis of Jesus's teaching."

With *Curse Your Branches* and in his recent shows, he's inverting the usual call to witness: "You might be the only Christian they ever meet." He's the doubter's witness, and he might be the only agnostic these Christian kids ever really listen to.

When I talk to some of those kids in the merch tent the day after Bazan's set, many of them seem to be trying to spin the new songs, straining to categorize them as Christian so they can justify continuing to listen to them. One fan says it's good that Bazan is singing about the perils of sin, "particularly sexual sin." Another interprets the songs as a witness of addiction, the testimony of the stumbling man.

Cultural critic and progressive Christian author David Dark, who since 2003 has become one of Bazan's closest friends, claims that Bazan's skepticism and anger are in line with biblical tradition. "I doubt this is what your average Cornerstone attendee means, but when David is addressing his idea of his God, the one that he fears exists but refuses to believe in, when he is telling God, 'If this is the situation with us and you, then fuck you—the people who love you, I hope they see you for who you are,' when he's doing that, he is at his most biblical. If we are referring to the deep strains of complaint and prayers and tirades against conceptions of God in the Bible—yes, then in that way he's in your Christian tradition. But I disagree that he's an advocate *for* the biblical."

When I tell Bazan that there are kids at Cornerstone resisting the clear message of his songs, he's surprised. "That someone could listen to what I was saying and think that I was saying it apologetically—like, in a way that characterizes [doubt] as the wrong posture—bums me out, but that's pretty high-concept given how I'm presenting this stuff. So I have to hand it to someone who can keep on spinning what is so clearly something else." He pauses for a long moment, then adds, "I don't want to be that misunderstood."

During the two days I follow Bazan and his fans around the Cornerstone campus, though, it becomes clear that he isn't really misunderstood at all. Everyone knows what he's singing about—his listeners are taking great pains to sidestep the obvious. "Well, his songs have always been controversial," one says, but when asked to pinpoint the source of the controversy suggests it's because he swears—nothing about not believing in hell or not taking the Bible as God's word. Bazan's agnosticism is the elephant in the merch tent.

Fans rhapsodize about Bazan's work: they love his

honesty, they love how they can relate to him, how he's not proselytizing, how he's speaking truth—though they don't delve into what exactly that truth might be. Brice Evans, a twenty-four-year-old from Harrisburg, Illinois, who came to Cornerstone specifically to see Bazan's set, dances artfully around it. "He's showing a side of Christianity that no other band shows," Evans says. "He's trying to get a message across that's more than that."

It's hard to say if anybody is conscious of the irony: the "side of Christianity" Bazan sings about is actually disenfranchisement from it.

"I think with *Curse Your Branches* David expands the space of the talk-about-able," says Dark. "It's not confessional in the sense that he's down on himself and trying to confess something to God in hopes of being forgiven. I think that's what crowds are trying to make of him, but they're going to have a tougher time when they get the record."

Bazan is known for his dialogues with fans, and during his set he's affable, taking questions from the crowd. Tonight's audience, openly anxious and awed, keeps it light at first: "Would you rather be a werewolf or a vampire?" Then he opens with the new album's lead track, "Hard to Be," a sobering song with an especially hard-hitting second verse:

Wait just a minute
You expect me to believe
That all this misbehaving
Grew from one enchanted tree?

And helpless to fight it
We should all be satisfied
With this magical explanation
For why the living die
And why it's hard to be
Hard to be, hard to be
A decent human being?

By the time he finishes those lines I can see half a dozen people crying; a woman near me is trembling and sobbing. Others have their heads in their hands. Many look stunned, yet no one leaves. When the song ends, the applause is thunderous.

After Bazan plays a cover of Leonard Cohen's "Hallelujah," reinstating the sacrilegious verses left out of the best-known versions, someone shouts, "How's your soul?" Bazan looks up from tuning his guitar and says, "My soul? Oh, it's fine." This elicits an "Amen, brother!" from the back of the tent.

Following Bazan's set, a throng of fans—kids, young women with babies on their hips, a handful of youth pastors—queues up around the side of the stage to talk to him. Some kids want hugs and ask geeked-out questions, but just as many attempt to feel him out in a sly way. "I really wished you had played 'Lullaby,'" says one kid, naming a very early Pedro the Lion song that's probably the most worshipful in Bazan's catalog. A few gently bait him, referring to scripture the way gang members throw signs, eager for a response that will reveal where Bazan is really at.

During discussions like this, Bazan doesn't usually get into the subtle barometric fluctuations in his relationship with Jesus, but that still leaves room for plenty of post-show theological talk. "This process feels necessary and natural for these people," he says. "They're in a precarious situation—maybe I am, too. To maintain their particular posture, they have to figure out: Do they need to get distance from me, or is it just safe enough to listen to? I empathize as people are trying to gauge, 'Is this guy an atheist? Because I heard he was.'"

Bazan has chosen sides, but old ideas linger. "Some time ago, we were discussing [the Pedro the Lion song] 'Foregone Conclusions,'" Dark says. "I told him I was impressed with the lines 'You were too busy steering conversation toward the Lord / To hear the voice of the Spirit / Begging you to shut the fuck up / You thought it must be the devil / Trying to make you go astray / Besides it could not have been the Lord / Because you don't believe He talks that way.' I thought, what a liberating word for people who've been shoved around by all manner of brainwash. But also, Dave's doing something even more subtle, as many interpret the unforgivable sin to be blasphemy against the Holy Spirit—confusing the voice of God for the voice of the devil—so there's a whole 'nother level of theological devastation going on in the song.

"When I brought it up, he laughed and told me he still worries about going to hell for that one. He knows that it's horribly funny that he feels that way, but he won't lie by saying he's entirely over it. He's both one hundred percent sincere and one hundred percent ironically detached. He's haunted even as he pushes forward, saying what he feels even though he half fears doing so will be cosmically costly for him."

After a long few years in the wilderness, Bazan seems happy—though he's still parsing out his beliefs, he's relieved to be out and open about where he's *not* at. "It's more comfortable for me to be agnostic," he says. "There's less internal tension by far—that's even with me duking it out with my perception of who God is on a pretty regular basis, and having a lot of uncertainty on that level. For now, just being is enough. Whether things happen naturally, completely outside an author, or whether the dynamics of earth and people are that way because God created them. If you look around and pay attention and observe, there is enough right here to know how to act, to know how to live, to be at peace with one another.

"Because I grew up believing in hell and reckoning, there is a voice in me that says, 'That might not cut it with the man upstairs,' but I think that that has to be enough. For me it is enough."

FLIRTING WITH RELIGION

Rickie Lee Jones

CHICAGO READER, MARCH 2007

Contemporary praise pop may posit Jesus as a personal savior, but much of the language it uses is a sort of Christian jargon that hardly speaks to the uninitiated. Worship is formal, salvation is personal, God is in his distant heaven, and the sinners are still here on earth. The salvation songs on Rickie Lee Jones's new *The Sermon on Exposition Boulevard* (New West), on the other hand, have all the hallmarks of love songs: the lust and the longing, the desperation and solitude, the new love raising its defiant head, the wounded heart healed. Yet these love songs are about something far less tangible than romance: they're songs of faith. On *The Sermon on Exposition Boulevard* it's as if Jones has divorced the secular world and her rebound boyfriend is Jesus Christ.

Jones improvised the bulk of the lyrics for the album's thirteen songs while the tape was rolling in the studio. She riffed on *The Words*, a book published by her friend Lee Cantelon that removes the words of Jesus from their biblical context and arranges them by topic—a kind of CliffsNotes to the New Testament. The record starts easy enough, with the sleepy jangle of "Nobody Knows My Name," over which Jones—her voice still the sinewy, reedy cry muscled into insistent girl-soul that made "Chuck E's in Love" a hit back in '79—sings of a God present in both the elemental and man-made, an everywhere-at-once spirit, moving freely, unknown and unrecognized. It's a lament of faith in a faithless world, but it also establishes a theme that recurs throughout *Sermon*: that Jesus and belief in Jesus have been co-opted and codified by the religious Right, who set rigid parameters for who can worship and how. They narrowly define what a relationship with God can look like: Jesus is in the church, a white man on the cross, on the side of the good and the righteous. Jones returns to us the gnostic Jesus, the table-flipping, temple-cleansing people's savior of Matthew 21:12, who's down with everyone and everything, not just the pious uttering heavy hosannas between the pews.

Most of *Sermon* is in first person, but the songs aren't personal testaments of belief per se. On the second track, "Gethsemane," she voices Jesus's internal monologue, a prayerful pleading with his father as he awaits his fate in the Garden of Gethsemane. The first few times I heard it, I thought it was baby-please-take-me-back, post-breakup desperation: "You wake up one morning and you're someone else / You're on your own," Jones sings, and later, "All I want is your hand." Christ's willing obedience to God's plan is the very model of Christian faith, but Jones cleaves it and renders Jesus casually; these songs are far from typical hymns.

Yet the most remarkable thing about the record isn't Jones's recasting of Jesus as more human than holy, but rather the way she transmits her own faith. It's a soft sell, relying on the beauty and aliveness of her message rather than traditional witness. Underneath the metaphors and the transmuted bits of the Gospel of Luke that pass for a chorus lies the true light of the record, Jones's own eureka moment, like a tiny jewel laid carefully in each song. You get the sense that therein lies her hope for the world, a hope not of universal conversion but of peace for all. It'd sound insufferably New Agey and annoying if Rickie weren't something akin to West Coast, California-cooled Patti, who fell hard for jazz instead of rock 'n' roll and preferred her own diary-poems to Rimbaud's. Both ecstatic and world-weary, she sings of the "soft-shoed devil" in "Circle in the Sand," as though they're well acquainted, like the devil might be a local bad boy she knows from back in her wild-girl days.

Last Saturday night, when Jones came through Chicago, those days seemed behind her. She blew in from the blizzard and walked up the theater aisle directly onto the stage, her scarf and coat still on, a to-go coffee cup in her hand. She pulled out the piano bench, dropped her outside clothes in a pile on the floor, pushed up her shirt-sleeves, and sat down to get to work. She was wearing lace-up shoes, a sweatshirt, no makeup, and cargo pants with a bunch of stuff in the pockets—she looked like this was just a stop she had to make on her way to Petco for some litter. But then, in the quick silence between the end of a song and the start of the applause, someone yelled

"Rickie!" She looked up from beneath her long, blond tangled hair and flashed a huge, knowing smile, and in that moment she was our star.

For the first few songs of the set it was just Jones at the piano. She gave some forgotten cuts the once-over, seeming purposeful and confident and comfortable with her dominion over the music and the crowd. After "The Last Chance Texaco," she was joined by her six-piece backing band, most of whom appear on *Sermon*—and which included Cantelon himself, doing backup incantations. They ambled through almost the entire album, their fuzzed-out churning recalling the Velvet Underground rather than the sometimes adult-contemporary sound of *Sermon*'s studio recording. Jones strapped on an electric guitar and occasionally did double duty as a shaman: her voice shrank and expanded, at one extreme tiny enough to be mistaken for a child's, at the other clarion and full. She let loose whispers, holy howls, and even a swampy Waits-ian growl on "Tried to Be a Man."

The songs meandered and circled back on themselves, picking up and shedding new instrumental layers as they went and almost never doing the same thing twice—sometimes they threatened to get away from the band entirely. But Jones was the real show. She nearly yelled the words to "It Hurts," giving voice to the loneliness of the A.D. world—"It hurts / To be here / When you're gone." The song could be a love letter from Mary Magdalene to an absent Jesus or a prayer from a disappointed disciple: "My only precious thing I had / Has been broken." But as electric guitar arced and receded, as furious strumming and choral aahs welled up around Jones, as she squeezed her eyes shut and bent in half, pulling the mic down with her, as her agony turned to ecstasy and her accusing wail turned triumphant, it became clear what we were hearing—a redemption song.

SUPERCHUNK, *I HATE MUSIC*

SPIN, AUGUST 2013

Death is everywhere on *I Hate Music*, Superchunk's tenth studio album. It is sidling up right beside us, doing air-guitar windmills on its scythe, from album opener "Overflows" (where "dead" is the third word front man Mac McCaughan sings) all the way to bittersweet-ever-after closer "What Can We Do." This is a record of grief, bristling with the anguish of what it means to survive, to have to reevaluate your life after someone else's death: "Now everything is different / And everything's the same."

As if that wasn't quite heavy enough, McCaughan also dredges up a rhetorical question from that emotional swampland of punk-after-thirty-five: What does music mean in the face of mortality? "I hate music—what is it worth?" goes the opening salvo to "Me & You & Jackie Mittoo." "Can't bring anyone back to this earth." It's a line that pulls you up short—after decades of insisting this song or that album "saved your life," you're suddenly confronted with the fact that *it actually won't*. It can't.

It's a line that leaves you embarrassed in your vulnerability; to have ever asserted otherwise seems like a denial of life's terms. When you are past that youthful period when your whole identity is tied up in a faith affirmed by music, when the mortal aspects of life start to catch up with you—*how do you orient yourself*? The small god who lives in a perfect beat or solo, in the raw, chest-beating howl of some puerile punk . . . Is that the same god you curse out and bargain with when you are trying to keep the people you love alive? On this album, McCaughan reckons with the belief system that has informed so much of his life. Yet the idea that music is everything is rather naive on this side of forty, and saying music is nothing is equally hopeless, and too cynical; it disorients the past. What to cling to?

I Hate Music is crushing in its poignancy, its ruthless weighing of what this whole mess adds up to (or doesn't). "Put up your feet on the dash," McCaughan cheers; he's doing the math on life's beauty-to-agony ratio, reasoning with memories from before his friend's death and after. *I Hate Music* acknowledges music's power to impart meaning, to be a blessed distraction. It can distract us from our mourning, too, though that's all it can do; grief and music both have the power to distort reality as much as they cut through the bullshit of it all. Title aside, *I Hate Music* eventually (thankfully) comes down on the "everything" side of the argument.

All this is a heavier orbit than the usual "Teenage angst has paid off well / Now I'm bored and old" sentiment of post-punk forty-somethings singing of their disenfranchisement from the scene they helped build. Chalk it up to the liberation of middle age or the certainty of an audience that has held fast (and aged with them), but the band clearly feels no compulsion to keep it light; they trust their music to hold up under all the weight of such examinations and trust their listeners to be able to handle it as well.

All the frustration and anger at play on *I Hate Music* energizes songs like "Staying Home," wherein the Hüsker Dü echoes that have trailed McCaughan since 1991's "Cast Iron" have never been louder (the last thing you expect ten albums in is Superchunk breaknecking like it's *Land Speed Record* or bust). Ironically, it's an anthem about *not* going out—the ultimate geezer cop-out—set to hardcore, the very sound of youthful vigor. Out of step, indeed. Other songs sit in awe of death, alive in the fresh hell of it, McCaughan's eager-teen squeak of a voice still stretching toward those high notes. His voice is full of love and restless sadness, which tells as much of a story as the lyrics do, atop heartbreaking lines like "Oh, what I'd do / To waste an afternoon with you."

It's a perfect place for Superchunk to wind up, given this is a band that initially wooed us twenty-five years ago with "Slack Motherfucker," indie rock's quintessential bratty-kid anthem. Now, just as confidently, they have given us songs that map adult life, even if these anthems are more a mortality blues. But with *I Hate Music*, Superchunk proves that it wasn't naive to believe in what music could do.

WHY MICHAEL JACKSON'S PAST MIGHT BE GARY, INDIANA'S FUTURE

THE VILLAGE VOICE, JULY 2009

The first thing I noticed was that Michael Jackson was gone. Downtown Gary, Indiana's main drag hosted a wide-scale mural project in 2002, presenting fantastic possible futures for the city's boarded-up buildings painted directly onto the boards. A larger-than-life MJ adorned the old record store, symbolically turning his back on Gary, three digits of his bejeweled-glove hand blotted out with graffiti, as if he were giving his birthplace the finger. It was an odd touch of realism amid the inaccurately scaled office scenes of ferns and giant computers; Michael had been painted with care and detail. Now much of downtown has been boarded up again, and he has once more disappeared.

I'd been driving from downstate Illinois all day while radio news reports of his death became more and more detailed as time passed. Shortly after arriving home, a friend texted what I was already thinking: "We should go to Gary." Hitting one of Chicago's impromptu MJ-tribute nights didn't seem right. *Thriller* had taught me what it meant to have music be your whole life, to be a devoted fan; *Thriller* was the first album that was all mine, not my parents'. A vigil seemed more appropriate than a dance party. Gary is where it began, and it was only thirty-three miles from my house. In every lane, the tollbooths on I-90 West pumped *Off the Wall*.

The Jackson family home is about a mile off an unlit freeway exit. You pass the bank, the only one in town. When I did a travel piece on Gary a few years ago for the *Chicago Reader*, people were quick to tell me about how things were looking up: after several years without one, they had a bank again. Its gleaming exterior stands in sharp contrast to a downtown filled with stately, half-burned buildings with saplings growing from rooftops and terraces. A fire took much of the area in a single night in 1997: what survived still stands. Boarded-up stores are emblazoned with loping midcentury fonts and signs for chains that haven't existed for decades. It's like Pompeii of the Midwest, a postapocalyptic-looking cityscape created by plant closings, white flight, decades of divestment, and arson.

The Jacksons left Gary in 1968, right before the Steel City began its economic freefall: between 1960 and 2000, the city's population was nearly halved. Their house shows no mark of its former occupants' success, save for the renamed streets; it sits at the corner of Jackson Street and Jackson Family Boulevard. It's difficult to imagine how a family of eleven lived in the tiny two-bedroom bungalow.

When we roll up to 2300 Jackson, it's almost 11:00 p.m., seven hours since the news hit. Slow-cruising cars blare different eras of MJ as two thick cops perched on ATVs shine their headlights on the crowd milling in the yard. This is not so much a gathering as a lookie-loo, a chance to observe the coterie of stuffed animals and notebook-paper tributes that had amassed. A Gary Fire Department shirt on a hanger clings to the front window's security bars with a note taped to it: "Goodbye Michael J5 forever." There's not a lot of talking up by the actual shrine and its safety candles: everyone just snaps pictures with their cell phones and slaps at mosquitoes. Some people are crying.

Back at the edge of the yard, locals trade stories, theories, and firsthand reminiscences: Michael's appearance at a Gary high school in 2003, older siblings who went to high school with Tito, guesses of what will become of the house. Everyone weighs in on where he'll be buried: everyone hopes for Gary, thinks it should be Gary—maybe even right here in the backyard. I imagine the modest, fenced-in lot overtaken by a mausoleum, ringed with teddy bears and white gloves.

The next day, Mayor Rudy Clay talks of turning the tiny house, which would take four minutes (max) to thoroughly examine, into a Graceland. Grim as it is, Jackson's death could mean new life for Gary. A stretch of downtown is set to be razed in the next year; no doubt an MJ shrine would be its star attraction. Interviewing residents a few years back, the idea that Michael could return and somehow save their city was a collectively held notion. Some held his abandonment against him and considered such a return his duty as a native son, while others were sympathetic, asking why would the King of Pop ever want to come back to Gary? Few had guessed that this is how it might happen.

The mosquitoes are getting to us, and we've taken all the pictures we want of the memorial heap of mini-mart roses and stuffed animals. Across the street, a man affixes a flashlight to a lawnmower, fires it up, and starts cutting the grass. We get back in the car. On our way out, we stop and take pictures of the long-abandoned Palace Theater's marquee. Since Donald Trump had the place spruced up for the 2002 Miss USA pageant, it has read JACKSON FIVE TONITE—another fantasy future for the Magic City, come and gone.

BETWEEN THE VIADUCT OF YOUR DREAMS

On Van Morrison

TINYLUCKYGENIUS, JULY 2008

When the chasm of human experience feels unbridgeable, and the past is keeping you like the stocks, and there is no absolution to be had, no forgiveness to salve you, and the world feels too much in its infinite newness, and it's midnight and people are screaming, when all you see is difference and a long string of your own unqualified failures, there is Van singing, "Lay me down . . . to be born again." There is so much wanting in "Astral Weeks," but it's not desperation, it's all vessel; it's faith enough to cover anyone listening. He waits until 4:55 to slip the big one, "I'm nothin' but a stranger in this world"—after he's sung all this future-hope, he's just fucking untangled joy over pipping flutes—here, he flashes his wretch-like-me makings and dovetails his abyss with deliverance: there is something beyond this. He sounds like he's about to giggle, he's so delighted, he's so *sure*. It's fine, fixed sureness, an easy sureness when he repeats it this last time, in this final, ecclesiastic glee coda. He has all the reasons not to believe, but he does. The Buddhists say hope is a trap, it's a setup for suffering, but the hope in this song is free, it drags nothing with it, it is only onward, onward in love and frailty.

PART IV
NOSTALGIA

WHEN THE BOSS WENT MORAL

Bruce Springsteen's Lost Album

THE AMERICAN PROSPECT, NOVEMBER 2010

What is pop music for if not escape? It lifts us out of our everyday to stoke and coalesce our fantasies about an alternate life, far away from where we've landed. In 1977, Bruce Springsteen began recording the album that would become the landmark *Darkness on the Edge of Town*. Informed by Elvis, Orbison, and Brill Building songwriters, he was penning from this tradition: grand, lovelorn tunes of cars and girls and memories. Springsteen was eager to prove himself more than a one-hit wonder off the popularity of *Born to Run*, and was feeling the schism between where his new success had placed him and the blue-collar caste from which he'd risen. This is very much the place from which pop offers refuge, and it's what drove and shaped *Darkness*. Springsteen wanted to speak from that unresolvable place, to confine the listener in that discomfort.

The tracks that didn't fit that vision made up *The Promise*, a lost album of sorts. The twenty-two tracks are immaculate, a glut of fine work from The Boss at the dawn of his prime. Some of the tracks here reappear in slightly different forms on *Darkness* and later albums ("Candy's Boy," "Racing in the Street ('78)"; the opening refrain of "Spanish Eyes" would later appear in "I'm on Fire"). It's easy to sense that some of these could have become hits for Springsteen and wonder why they're absent from *Darkness*. As an album, *Darkness* is lean and ready, marks of the influence of Springsteen's recent conversion to both punk rock and Hank Williams; many of these tracks are ballads and polished anthems with large debts to the formalist sensibilities of Spector, Leiber and Stoller, King and Goffin. More than their sound, what kept these cuts off *Darkness* is that the story that Springsteen wanted to tell was a moral one.

Darkness was an attempt to ask big questions about life and liberty in America, what it meant to be a white working-class man, the (de)meaning of work in a capitalist system, and, as Springsteen explained later, how to deal with sin in a good life. He spent five months in the studio with the E Street Band working out the hungry ghosts of his Catholic boyhood, until he found a way to contain them in *Darkness*'s anxious blaze. He refused the gleaming pop tracks and lovelorn balladry that make up *The Promise*; he turned "Because the Night" over to Patti Smith because he *knew* it was a hit, a song that would define him, and he wasn't interested in that.

Whether Springsteen was seeking to become rock's beleaguered blue-collar conscience or he just wanted to be more than a standard-issue rock star is debatable, but it's safe to assume that one doesn't spend years laboring over the allegorical language with which to illuminate the spiritual longing of the American underclass if one isn't fully convinced of one's own powers. Whether Springsteen was interested in being rock's great moralist is beside the point; *Darkness* is what earned him the job.

Listening to *The Promise*, it's easy to understand that if any of these tracks would have made it onto *Darkness* it would have changed the record's entire character. These are songs about kisses ("Fire," "The Little Things"), fourteen of them are about his feelings for a girl. All this lovin' and radio-listenin' and engine-buildin' on *The Promise* doesn't emotionally align with a *Darkness* track like "Adam Raised a Cain," a song about shouldering the legacy you inherit from your parents, or the album's reconciliation of rage and powerlessness in "The Promised Land." Even as desperate as "Because the Night" is— Springsteen sounds so plaintive and vulnerable—it would have worked against the macho confidence he exudes on "Candy's Room." "The Promise" chronicles disenfranchisement from the American Dream *and* could have fit, but its bathos would have undercut the hope that is *Darkness*'s covenant with the listener.

While *The Promise* comes as a standalone double disc, it's perhaps better to take it in its other form, sandwiched within the context of the *Darkness on the Edge of Town* box set: a reproduction of Springsteen's notebook from the sessions, three CDs (*The Promise* and *Darkness*), and three DVDs, including a making-of-*Darkness* DVD that is culled from archival footage from rehearsals and sessions and a phenomenal vintage concert performance. Seeing the scope of Springsteen's bright-eyed intent and his commitment—to *Darkness*'s message, to his music, to his talent and his fans—and his belief in the power of music to communicate something so complex, makes the man seem heroic. By aiming to make such moral music, he made a new mimetic mold, one that successfully fulfilled the boomers' altruistic belief in rock's duty to *meaning*. *Darkness*-era Springsteen is everything you'd want your rock stars to be: the longing loverman, the prove-it-all-night rock star, and the regular guy staking his guts to the stage, the craftsman capable of putting all your too-familiar restlessness into a song you'd wanna hear a thousand times.

The album's emotional truth mirrors its political one. The Carter-era malaise into which *Darkness* was born is palpable. It was made in a time where no one could buy the lie anymore; a long, bad war had made that impossible. The album's metaphor of lost innocence and consequence is best illuminated on "Racing in the Street," a tale of good people adrift in their betrayal, wanting to wash the sin off their hands. *Darkness* is the album that established Springsteen as one of the great communicators of a certain sort of American dilemma; it is the work of someone born to a country founded on moral covenant, always striving to be that exemplar city on the hill but forever falling shy of its mark.

FLEETWOOD MAC, *RUMOURS* BOX SET

PITCHFORK, FEBRUARY 2013

Upon its release in 1977, *Rumours* became the fastest-selling LP of all time, eight hundred thousand copies per week at its peak; that success made Fleetwood Mac a cultural phenomenon. The million-dollar record that took a year and untold grams of cocaine to complete became a totem of 1970s excess, a yardstick by which to measure just how '70s the '70s were. Yet for all its legendary indulgences, it's an album of a certain innocence, a true product of its time. In 1976, the crisis of AIDS could not be predicted, Reagan had just left the governor's manse, cocaine was touted as a nonaddictive recreational drug, it was the twilight of the free love era, and there would be no going back. *Rumours* seized that moment and wrapped it in heavy harmonies. It set a template for pop—a gleaming surface with something dark, desperate, and complicated resonating underneath.

Setting aside the album's weighty history, listening to *Rumours* is easy pleasure. Its omnipresence means even if you've never owned a copy of it, it's possible to be familiar with nearly every song. When you make an album

115

this big, your craft is, by default, accessibility. Yet these songs weren't generic pablum; they were personal songs of love and loss.

Two years prior to recording *Rumours* Fleetwood Mac was approximately nowhere. In order to reestablish the group's flagging stateside reputation, in early 1974 Fleetwood Mac's drummer and band patriarch, Mick Fleetwood, keyboardist/singer Christine McVie, and her then-husband, bassist John McVie, moved from England to Los Angeles. The quartet was then helmed by their fifth and least-dazzling guitarist, the American Bob Welch. Not long after the band's British faction had relocated, Welch quit the band. Around the same time, Mick Fleetwood was introduced to the work of local duo Buckingham Nicks, who'd just been dropped by Polydor after their debut failed to chart. The drummer was enchanted by Lindsey Buckingham's guitar work and Stevie Nicks's complete package, and when Welch quit, he offered them a spot in the band outright.

The group, essentially a new band under an old name, quickly cut 1975's self-titled *Fleetwood Mac*, an assemblage of Christine McVie's songs and tracks Buckingham and Nicks had intended for their second album, including the eventual smash "Rhiannon." It was a huge seller in its own right and they were now a priority act, and given considerable resources by their label, Reprise. But by the time Fleetwood Mac made it to Record Plant in Sausalito to record *Rumours*, the band's personal bonds were frayed, and there was serious resentment and constant drama between members. Nicks had just broken up with Buckingham after six years of domestic and creative partnership. Fleetwood's wife was divorcing him, and the McVies were separated and no longer speaking.

While *Fleetwood Mac* was a bit of a mash-up of existing work, Lindsey Buckingham effectively commandeered the band for *Rumours*, giving their sound a radio-ready revamp. He redirected John McVie and Fleetwood's playing, pushing them to abandon blues-rock's past and pursue pop's promise. Fleetwood Mac wanted hits and gave the wheel to Buckingham, a deft craftsman with a vision for what the album had to become.

He opens the record with the libidinous "Second Hand News," inspired by the redemption Buckingham was finding in new partners, post-Stevie. It was the album's first single and is perhaps the most giddy ode to rebound chicks ever recorded. Buckingham's "bow-bow-bow-doot-doo-diddley-doot" is a bit hammy, but it works along with the percussion track (Buckingham drummed on the seat of an office chair after Fleetwood was unable to properly replicate the beat of the Bee Gees' "Jive Talkin'"). Like "Second Hand News," Buckingham's "Go Your Own Way" is an upbeat fuck-you. He croons "shackin' up is all you wanna do," accusing an ex-lover of getting around on a song where his ex-lover harmonizes on the hook. Save for "Never Going Back Again," a vintage Buckingham Nicks composition brought in to replace Stevie's too-long-for-the-album side "Silver Springs," Buckingham's songs are turnabout-as-fair-play with lithe guitar glissando on top.

"Second Hand News" is followed by a twist-of-the-knife Stevie showpiece, "Dreams," a gauzy ballad about what she'd had and what she'd lost with Buckingham. She wrote the song in a few minutes on one of the days where she wasn't needed for tracking. Nicks recorded it onto a cassette, and returned to the studio with it in hand and demanded the band listen to it. It was a simple ballad that would be finessed into the album's jewel; the quiet vamp, and exquisite sketch of loneliness, laced with Leslie-speaker vibrato and spooky warmth. "Dreams" would become Fleetwood Mac's only number one hit.

Though Fleetwood Mac was always the sum of its parts, Nicks was a singular artist both in terms of the band and in rock history. She helped establish a feminine vernacular that was in league with the so-called cock rock of the '70s but didn't present as a diametric vulnerability; it was not innocent. While Janis Joplin and Grace Slick had been rock's most iconic heroines at the tail end of the '60s, they were very much trying to keep up with boys in their world; to be rock 'n' roll was to align yourself with the macho aesthetic of more. Femininity was considered antithetical to rock itself. Nicks was creating a new space. Fleetwood Mac was still very much an anomaly, unique in being a rock band fronted by two women who were writing their own material, with Nicks presenting as the girliest bad girl rock 'n' roll had seen since Ronnie Spector. She took the stage bearing a tambourine festooned with lengths of lavender ribbon; people said she was a witch.

Like her macho rock 'n' roll peers, Nicks sang songs about the intractable power of a woman (her first hit,

"Rhiannon"), and used women as a metaphor ("Gold Dust Woman"), but her angle of approach was wholly different. At the time of *Rumours*'s release, she maintained that the latter song was about groupies who would scowl at her and Christine but light up when the guys appeared. She later confessed that it was about cocaine getting the best of her. In 1976, coke was the fuel of the scene; to admit you were growing weary would have been gauche. Nicks's expressive, husky voice made it sound like she'd lived her lyrics, that she'd experienced the pathos and independence she sang of, that she'd been played. The way her image, voice, and lyrics resolved with one another made Nicks easy to identify with; real and mysterious, she possessed a natural glamour worth aspiring to.

You might almost miss Christine McVie for all of Nicks's superstar mystique. McVie had been in the band for years, but never at the fore until they regrouped in America. Her song "Over My Head" was the single off *Fleetwood Mac*, and the commercial breakthrough and first Top 20 hit. *Rumours*'s two biggest singles, "You Make Loving Fun" and "Don't Stop," were written by her, and both were Top 10, career-defining hits for the band. McVie's "Songbird" starts as a plaintive devotional ode and until the elegiac tell of "And I wish you all the love in the world / But most of all I wish it from myself," it doesn't reveal itself fully; this is about a love clarified in letting go. The directness, pep, and sweetness of McVie's songwriting obfuscates the emotional complexity of her work on *Rumours*: she didn't hate her husband, she adored him. She wished it could work between them, but after years of being in the band together, she knew better. "Oh Daddy," a song she wrote about Mick Fleetwood's pending divorce, is melancholic but ultimately maintains its dignity. McVie, with typical British reserve, confessed she preferred to leave the bleakness and poesy to her dear friend Stevie.

As much feminine energy as *Rumours* wields, the album's magic is in its balance: male and female, British blues versus American rock 'n' roll, lightness and dark, love and disgust, sorrow and elation, ballads and anthems, McVie's sweetness against Nicks's gritty introspection. They were a democratic band where each player raised the stakes of the whole. The addition of Buckingham and Nicks, as well as McVie's new prominence, kicked John McVie's bass playing loose from its blues mooring and forced him toward greater simplicity and dimension. Mick Fleetwood's playing itself is just godhead, with effortless little fills, light but thunderous, and his placement impeccable throughout. The ominous, insistent kick on the first half of "The Chain," for example, colors the song as much as the quiver of disgust in Buckingham's voice when he spits "never."

In the liner notes to this new, deluxe *Rumours* 4xCD/DVD/LP box set, Buckingham describes the album-making process as "organic," but the listener's experience of *Rumours* is anything but; it's so flawless it feels far from nature. *Rumours* is Olympic-level studio craft. It was made better by its myopia, its songs informed by circumstances: the wounded pride of a recently dumped Buckingham made him all the more exacting and competitive;

"Rhiannon" went to number eleven on *Billboard* half-way through the recording of *Rumours*, which emboldened Nicks to fight for the inclusion of her own songs on the new album; Christine McVie attempting to salve her heart with "Songbird," and John's with "Don't Stop." That *Fleetwood Mac* would spend thirty weeks on the charts and become the biggest record their label, Warner Bros., had released to date *while* the band was making *Rumours* meant the group was granted a long tether for writing in the studio and then perfecting that album until it was immaculate.

Given the standalone nature of *Rumours*, it's difficult to argue that any other part of the box set is necessary. The live recordings of the *Rumours* tour are fine, lively even (perhaps owing to Fleetwood's rationing of a Heineken cap of coke to each band member to power performances). Only a handful of tracks on the two discs of the sessions outtakes lend any greater understanding of the process behind it. "Dreams (Take 2)," which features only Nicks's voice, some burbling organ chords, and rough rhythm guitar, underlines her fundamental talent as well as Buckingham's ability to transform it; it makes the case for how much they needed each other. Another is "Second Hand News (Early Take)," which features Buckingham mumbling lyrics so as not to incense Nicks. By the time you make it to disc four, the alternate mixes and takes (More phaser! Less Dobro! Take twenty-two!) only underscore the fact that *Rumours* did not hatch fully formed. One does not need three variously funky articulations of Christine's burning "Keep Me There" to comprehend this.

Nevertheless, it is difficult not to buy into the mythology of *Rumours* both as an album and a cultural artifact: a flawless record pulled from the wreckage of real lives. As one of classic rock's foundational albums, it holds up better than any other commercial smash of that ilk (*Hotel California*, certainly). It's now used as a nostalgic benchmark—they don't make groups like Fleetwood Mac anymore; there is no rock band so palatable that it could have the best-selling album in the United States for thirty-one weeks. Things work differently now. Examined from that angle, *Rumours* was not exactly a game changer, it was merely perfect.

SHOUTING OUT LOUD

The Raincoats

THE PORTLAND MERCURY, OCTOBER 2009

These days, the Raincoats' legacy is most often defined by *who* remembered them. In 1992, Kurt Cobain recalled in his *Incesticide* liner notes that the British post-punk girl-band's debut album had served him as a lifesaving device, a reprieve from his depression and boredom, something cool he wished to be in on. The plaintive mash notes of punk's living Jesus revivified the Raincoats amid the dude-driven grunge boom. Underground, there was riot grrrl salvation and Fugazi, sure, but up top, *cool* was Pearl Jam (not yet sanctified, or anything more than macho qua rebellious) and the best-selling album of the year was Whitney's last stand, the *Bodyguard* soundtrack.

In 1994, when DGC reissued the trio of records that constituted the Raincoats' discography, the rock-star boy's stamp of approval was necessary to accept the genius girl's work. Cobain was *the* acceptable boy bridge to girl culture; he was part of popping the escape hatch to a better world, his endorsement served as a kind of atonement for the crush of corpo-grunge that Nirvana's success seeded. Then, as now, as ever, the Raincoats were needed; there was *still* no other band quite like them.

This week, Kill Rock Stars has reissued the Raincoats' self-titled 1979 debut album on vinyl and the timing couldn't be more perfect. Amid an epic mire of aesthetics-first indie bands, and the post-ironic post-punk era that hath wrought an inscrutable wave of bands utterly resistant to meaning (swastikas as album "decoration"/neon hippie bullshit, et al.), *The Raincoats* serves as a reminder that discernable earnestness isn't proprietary folk or emo, and asserting meaning doesn't mean the work isn't open to dynamic interpretation. People keep tending to the Raincoats' legacy, with good reason. They were special, yet everygirls, and they made music that was, and still is, personal, expressive, artful, and full of joy.

Cobain's notes imagined the band perhaps making him a cup of tea, which would be very polite and grandmotherly coming from such a trenchant band. Maybe it's because on the opening track, "Fairytale in the Supermarket," Ana da Silva sings about cups of tea marking time, right after she shouts out in a derailing, defiant yelp, "No one teaches you how to live!" She sounds like she figured it out anyhow. Listening to the debut, it's easy to see why the Raincoats of Cobain's imagining were gentle and doting; in the wake of British punk's formative, nihilist, no-future thrashing, the Raincoats had that PMA. They are sunny without being pop, and while they were as rudimentarily skilled as their string-bashing punk peers, there was a sense of cohesion, another vision of the world offered in this album. They were out-punking punk, defying its leather/spitting/anarchy trope with lively possibility, art-school playfulness, and absurdity, down to the pink drawing of a children's choir right on the cover. They liberated the ultimate girl instrument—the violin—from its school orchestra realm.

Yet for all of this, *The Raincoats* is often referred to as a harsh, clanging album, their genius usually framed as accidental: girls in the wilderness of their own stuttering hands, their invention chalked up to not knowing the rules. The implication is that the Raincoats couldn't have been serious or intentional for as excited and rough and fun as they sound. Punk was full of amateurs, as was post-punk (which was more their scene), but girls were always the outsiders, the exception. But as Brilliant Amateurs, they fared a bit better than their compatriots/peers, the Slits, whose amateurness got compared to wild animals by the punk press.

The Raincoats is not harsh or shrill. It's filled with space, grace, and living. "I am the music inside," they sing together on "No Side to Fall In." Their disregard is audible; they were absolutely following their own cues. They sha-la-la'd about their own minds and thinking ("The Void")—they made a record about being young women knee-deep in the formative adventure of their young lives. There's not even a love song until deep into side two, "You're a Million," and it's vague at that.

The Raincoats understood the meaning of covering the Kinks' "Lola" and keeping in all the *she/her* gender pronouns. Just the year before, the Pretenders had made their debut with a totally straight (in every way) take on another Kinks song, "Stop Your Sobbing." These girls' "Lola" was hardly an homage to the Kinks, and more about exploding all that rock 'n' roll boy seriousness they represented.

The special quality of *The Raincoats* is willful and girly: it flaunted its gentleness, its otherness, its disdain for the shoulds of rock virtuosity. They were not naive. *The Raincoats were reactive.* In BBC concert footage from 1980, Ana da Silva sings about the sad dating life of a girl with bad skin, and how the world judges and devalues women, while she clunks two woodblocks together like she's fighting rhythm, resisting the linear path, letting the song disintegrate. The song does not rock so much as it trembles. There is a singsong to their singing, something (or someone) is chirping, there is thudding or skronking in lieu of a solo, and none of it obscures the importance of the words, what the band has to say.

The Raincoats are the sound of learning and having fun and making it up as you go along; may they be revivified, rediscovered, and reissued infinitely.

CHALK CIRCLE, *REFLECTION*

CHICAGO READER, APRIL 2011

What a different world punk rock could've been. "We wanted Henry to be our drummer, but he wants to sing," teenaged Sharon Cheslow wrote in her diary on May 13, 1980. Cheslow and her pal Cheryl Celso were forming what would become Chalk Circle, the first—and for several years, incredibly, the only—all-girl punk band in Washington, D.C. Their friend Henry? He was about to discover Black Flag, a band he'd soon go on to front as Henry Rollins, becoming the apogee of macho in American hardcore. It's hard not to wonder if history would've taken a different shape, not just for Chalk Circle but for girls in punk, had Rollins done even a few rehearsals behind the kit with that fledgling D.C. band. Maybe Chalk Circle would've played more than four shows before breaking up in early 1983. For sure their first record wouldn't have taken twenty-eight more years to see the light of day.

Reflection compiles Chalk Circle's complete recordings, which are either unreleased or beyond rare: a single that Dischord declined to release, some songs that appeared on local tape compilations, a demo. In many ways Chalk Circle were like the other bands they came up with—a bunch of high school misfits hanging around Georgetown, watching Bad Brains practice, going to their friends' hardcore shows at night. The difference was they were girls, and in that scene girls playing punk could expect a reception somewhere between awkward and awful. During a D.C. punk panel at SXSW last month, Minor Threat's Lyle Preslar remembered that his bandmate Brian Baker was fond of saying, "Punk rock was invented so that ugly women would have something to do on Saturday night."

Given that dismissive atmosphere and the fact that these women played post-punk, not hardcore—which the likes of Minor Threat, the Untouchables, and Government Issue were codifying as the D.C. sound—it's not terribly surprising that Chalk Circle ended up absent from histories of the scene. A local zine review of their first show described it as "bimbo nite at dc space." While there were pictures of them in the photo book *Banned in DC*, the crucial scene history that Cheslow coedited, playing one of their few shows, dancing front and center at an early Bad Brains gig, there were no records to dig up. Given the often ephemeral nature of punk bands, it was easy to assume they'd broken up before anybody could document what Chalk Circle had done.

The genuinely surprising thing about *Reflection* is just how good Chalk Circle were. There's no reason they couldn't have been a band that truly mattered. They were brave, artful, and strange, with Cheslow and front woman Mary Green (who replaced Celso in 1981) trading vocals and shouting in unison over sputtering, angular unriffing and swampy bass. (The band was a brief and formative entry point for roughly a half dozen women musicians to make their way into the scene.) The lyrics—which address identity politics, feminist ideas, and friendship between women—are sharp, poetic, and earnest, and despite the seriousness of the songs you can tell the band's having fun. The twelve tracks on the comp are split between seven made in 1982 with de facto Dischord house producer Don Zientara and five recorded live. Listening to "The Slap," "Subversive Pleasure," and the anti-love love song "Easy Escapes," it's hard not to feel like punk rock got robbed of something cool and feminine in its early years.

Rehashing and documenting the birth of punk and hardcore has become a burgeoning little industry in the past half decade or so, with coffee-table books, oral histories of long-dead scenes, and a constant stream of documentaries that invariably feature Rollins[*] and Keith Morris and all the other major white dudes sharing the

[*] Henry Rollins has, as of this writing, published forty-four books of memoir, poetry, tour journals, and columns. Rollins's post–Black Flag career seems to be a project of mutual reinscription within punk music culture, a perpetual and mistaken affirmation that *his history is our history.* This has made him a durable icon, and the primary authoritative voice of punk history. I do not begrudge his career per se, but am careful to note that Rollins's work has failed to widen the path for anyone else, such as the women, queer, trans, Black, and Latinx folks who pioneered and defined punk. The omnipresence of Rollins's perspective has created the gravitational pull of punk's popular history and continually reified punk space as white, heteronormative, and masculine; punk becomes whatever Rollins did, wherever he was, and whatever he remembers it to be.

same old nostalgic version of how it went down. Every one of those accounts is missing its women. Just outside of these heroes' tales hover the ghosts of bands and folks who existed on punk's margins, of feminist arty goth-punk trios and queer work that went undocumented. And, still, not one of those boring documentaries tells the story of how Cheslow, after the demise of Chalk Circle, talked long and seriously with her good friend Ian MacKaye about the way hardcore had become so macho and exclusive that there was no safe place for women within it. This burst MacKaye's bubble, fueling D.C. punk's major transformation of the 1980s, the Revolution Summer of 1985—which in turn gave us Fugazi and emo (in its visceral, pre-commercial form). *Reflection* is a small but mighty blow to the version of punk history written by the winners. May there be many more.

YOU'RE RELIVING ALL OVER ME

Dinosaur Jr. Reunites

CHICAGO READER, APRIL 2005

It was about an hour after dusk in the early summer of 1991, and I was sitting on a log in the half woods near my parents' house with a guy I'd met a few weeks earlier in the front row at a Dinosaur Jr. show. I had the names of my favorite bands scrawled in pen on the toe caps of my Converse high-tops ("Fugazi" on the left, "Dinosaur" on the right), and I studied them intently, trying to keep my teenage awkwardness under control. Two dorks alone in the dark, we avoided the obvious question by engaging in deep conversation: *Was Dinosaur Jr. better with or without Lou Barlow?*

I'd hung out with this guy a few times, and every night was the same: as he rattled off Dinosaur Jr. minutiae, I'd nod attentively, hoping that'd charm him. He was one of two boys who would actually talk to me. I was sixteen, but I still had braces and could easily pass for twelve. I also knew more about Dinosaur Jr., and all his other favorite bands, than he did, but I kept that to myself. If I intimidated him, he wouldn't want to sit on area logs with me anymore. I decided to act docile and tried not to show my teeth when I laughed.

Maybe it was particular to the time and place—Minneapolis in the early '90s—but from what my girlfriends told me, lots of boys thought going to the woods with a girl and regaling her with an hour and a half of Dinosaur Jr. trivia was a perfectly acceptable courtship ritual. If you liked him (or Dinosaur Jr.) enough, you could pretend it was a date. I withstood many hours of Dinologue during those awful teen years, and my memories of the band's early albums—with their noisy, shimmery solos and shots of warm feedback—are inextricably tied to memories of some dude that never liked me back. Actually, there was a series of dudes; they only seem to blend into one because they all shared the same bell-shaped, grunge-bob hairstyle, unflagging devotion to J Mascis, and polite disinterest in me.

Dinosaur Jr.'s first three full-lengths, *Dinosaur* (Homestead, 1985), *You're Living All Over Me* (SST, 1987), and *Bug* (SST, 1988), have only been out of print for five years or so and have never been too hard to find on eBay or in used bins. Nonetheless, on March 22, Merge Records reissued all of them. They're the only albums with the band's original lineup: guitarist and front man Mascis, one-named drummer Murph, and bassist Barlow, who quit (or was fired) in 1989. Barlow subsequently dedicated himself to the tape-hiss horn o' plenty Sebadoh, which he'd started as a side project a couple years before, and Mascis and Murph soldiered on with a rotating cast of bassists. In

1990, Dinosaur signed with Sire, and the following year they issued the flawless *Green Mind*.

The band was rumored to have become a Mascis dictatorship, an impression confirmed in the reissues' liner notes, and by the mid-'90s Murph was gone, too. Until Sire dropped Dinosaur in 1997, Mascis and a lineup of scabs rewarded a devoted fan base with diminishing returns. Then Mascis became the Fog, a studio project that only turned into a proper band to tour. He receded into the distance, dwindling to a speck on the horizon; if you'd been able to make him out, you'd still have seen his long hair, his guitar, and his flannel, but he'd lost his spot on the main stage to other dudes, dudes with turntables, who were to become our newest heroes.

In the late 1980s, though, Dinosaur were magnets for the devotion of teenage weirdos, combining the huge, thralling Marshall-stack overdrive that made Neil Young famous with the jacked-up amphetamine-pulse of hardcore. Like their SST labelmates Hüsker Dü, they connected punk's mosh-pit machismo to its brooding, emotional side. Often the pummel of the rhythm section would pause, as though Murph and Barlow were trying to fake us out, and then Mascis's guitar would rumble to life, wonderfully too loud, every note gloriously destroyed by the city of effects pedals at his feet. Unlike early punk rockers, Dinosaur weren't lashing out at the bloated, coked-up corpse of the '70s. They were just trying, as Mike Watt suggests in the new liner notes to *You're Living All Over Me*, to be an East Coast version of acid-damaged country punks the Meat Puppets.

Save for Mascis's drawling whine, there isn't much country in Dinosaur's music, but it's plenty damaged.

Dinosaur structured their tunes like miniature, wank-free, classic-rock epics. "No Bones," the second cut on *Bug*, begins as an instrumental dirge with the bass playing distorted chords against a skipping, waltzy beat, segues into a verse in which Mascis sounds like the loneliest, most congested kid in all of Massachusetts, and from there jumps to a chorus overlaid with a track of strummy acoustic guitar. On the strength of songs like this, Mascis became not just a fanboy icon but an icon's icon—Sonic Youth's "Teen Age Riot," from the 1988 album *Daydream Nation*, is reputedly about his dominion over the guitar and the kids.

In their lyrics, Dinosaur doesn't even toy with the nihilistic sloganeering of many of their progenitors and peers. Mascis's singing is endearingly amateurish, his voice gentle, his diction thick, his lyrics vague. He never adopts an obvious pose or persona, but his words don't reveal much about who he is; maybe he's being honest, but he's not being particularly forthcoming. In short lines capped with simple rhymes, he often sketches a blurry metaphor about what stands between him and her; listening to this stuff is like reading a teenager's frustrated, lovelorn poetry, written for an audience of one. Even when Mascis is singing in his most somnambulant monotone, his voice cracks whenever he hits the word "girl." Barlow barely ever takes the mic, but his one star turn on *Bug* is a doozy. On "Don't," he howls with the consuming rage of ten thousand virginal high school seniors: "Why? / Why don't you like me?" Those are the only lyrics, and he repeats them forty-four times—it's emo distilled to its essence.

In Dinosaur's songs, the topic is often romance, but it's hard to tell whether the girl said yes or no or if she never got asked a question in the first place. That fumbling dorkiness is a big part of the charm. It's easy to imagine that the band spent puberty the same way a lot of their fans probably did: perched on the edge of their bed playing along with metal records on a shitty Ibanez, growing out their hair, smoking weed, and getting ignored by their crush. Dinosaur have bastardized everything from folky pop to feral thrash to turgid classic rock, imbuing it with qualities sacred to the indie-rock fanboy: a nerd's aesthetic, virtuosity, and emotionally fraught lyrics. Their albums nodded to the most righteous parts of your record collection, and the songs were open-ended enough that they could easily be about you and your ennui. In the late 1980s, Dinosaur helped create a template that Nirvana would take worldwide when "Teen Spirit" went nuclear a few years later.

Considering how much indie rock has changed since 1986, do these three Dinosaur reissues belong anywhere now? *Bug* is a great record but feels irrelevant in the harsh light of the current post-post-post-punk world, with its skinny ties and drum machines and leg warmers and hedonism. The twenty-year-old snapshots included in the reissues' beefed-up liner notes reveal three greasy-looking dudes who wouldn't have made it past the door at a loft party in Brooklyn in 2005.

These three lost-looking dorkboys made totally monstrous records, though: sprawling, adolescent, and sharp.

Dinosaur's early albums were casually elaborate and masterfully sloppy. Unfortunately, the timing of the band's long-rumored reunion—for their first gig together since 1989, Mascis, Murph, and Barlow are playing *The Late Late Show* on CBS on April 15 (followed by European and U.S. tours)—makes the reissues seem opportunistic. Given the epic bad blood between Mascis and Barlow, their reconciliation seems too convenient to look like anything but a cash-in. Why couldn't they stick to pursuing their increasingly marginal solo careers, leaving us to savor our memories of the great shit they did together back in the day?

At least one beautiful thing might come of this. If Dinosaur's midlife-crisis reunion repels enough of the kids who might've fallen in love with these reissues, it could save a generation of teen punk girls from hours of distortion-pedal discourse on awkward dates in the woods.

BIG STAR, *NOTHING CAN HURT ME*

PITCHFORK, JULY 2013

Big Star weren't perfect. The word gets thrown around a lot, especially in regard to their debut, *#1 Record*, as if perfection were their triumph. Yet they were a band marked by their *lack* of triumph; theirs was a losers' history upgraded by the passage of time and the success of the artists they influenced. Big Star were roiling and volatile, a freak collision between a couple of college kids and an idle teen idol; they were a band who, in every regard but artistic, failed their way through a career that barely qualified as such. How Big Star attempted to bridge that wide chasm between what they wanted to be and what they actually were is what made them great.

Nothing Can Hurt Me is the soundtrack for the new Big Star documentary of the same name. It contains unheard, alternate mixes from their 1972 debut *#1 Record*, rough mixes from the eventual *Sister Lovers*, and other special mixes created for the movie, all bracketed by studio banter. They don't shine like the original album versions, but still, "When My Baby's Beside Me" is just as compelling even if this mix has more pish in the cymbals.

You would have to be at least a six-out-of-ten on the Big Star nerd scale to hear specific differences without cueing up a Big Star album to check.

During the time of these recordings, Alex Chilton was only a few years past "The Letter," the 1967 hit single that made the singer a teenage star with the Box Tops. The single had sold 4 million copies and nabbed them a Grammy nomination alongside the Beatles. Over the next few years, young Chilton saw enough of success to know he didn't want it on its terms; he dropped from the limelight, bailed on his life in Memphis with his teenage bride and newborn son, hung heavy with the Beach Boys in L.A. before he expatriated to the Village at nineteen to fashion himself into a folkie. Embarrassed by the Box Tops, he was aiming to do something earnest. Two years later, he returned to Memphis with a couple of songs and essentially stumbled into Chris Bell's laborious studio project with bassist Andy Hummel and drummer Jody Stephens. With the addition of Chilton, they became Big Star.

If nothing else, *Nothing Can Hurt Me* functions as a will-do-in-a-pinch Big Star best-of. You get a thumbnail of their genesis, but without the movie to provide context, it's jarring to go from Chilton's ode to the purity of teenage love, "Thirteen," with its fragile harmonies and "tickets for the dance," to a markedly less lucid Chilton droning, "Nothing can hurt me . . . I can't feel a thing" five songs later. On "Thirteen," and the songs that precede it, they sounded like what they were: American kids who grew up on the Beatles. Once you get to the brittle distance of "Kanga Roo" and its peals of feedback, there is a sad, reedy quality to Chilton's voice. It's clearly the same repentant boy of "Give Me Another Chance," but on "Kanga Roo" his wavering, narcotized tone makes it seem like he's melting; on "Another Chance," with his promise that "I'm gonna be alright now," he sounds anything but.

Chris Bell, as the saying goes, was just not made for his times. Born into affluence, he was private and volatile; during Big Star's era he secluded himself in the back house behind his parents' home, where he immersed himself in making art and music, taking drugs in an attempt to salve his depression and blunt his sexuality. In the American South in the early '70s, even amid the fringes of rock culture, being queer was hardly spoken of. Bell's friends speak of his queerness euphemistically as "experimentation." Many of the doc's tear-jerking moments are for Bell, the life he had, and the one out of reach.

You can hear Bell's Beatlesmania in his voice here on "My Life Is Right," in his crisp Oxford English *o*'s of the "lonely road" he sings of. There's a quiver in his voice on "Feel," a squeaky stretch as he forces his high notes. Along with the surly bravado he summons on "Don't Lie to Me," he attempts to summon surly bravado as he yelps, "I told my dad / And now I'm telling you / Don't push me 'round," and you hear his proximity to boyhood. For all their finesse, for all of these gorgeously arranged songs and year of Bell-helmed sessions at Ardent, they were still amateurs getting it right, a coupla kids in a good-time band.

What the sad documentary and its accompanying soundtrack of barely alternate mixes reinforce is that there is no justice in pop music; the ones that "deserve" to make it so rarely do, dreams die on the vine. Big Star's fame and acclaim, during their initial three-album run, were directly inverse to their talent. Rock 'n' roll is cruel like that; it's all winners' histories and idiot luck. Music might have been a different place if *#1 Record* had been just that and bumped Jethro Tull's *Thick as a Brick* off the charts in June of 1972, but, then again, maybe not. There are plenty of bands that mapped inspired paths to greatness, but Big Star's story, as told in this film and heard on these songs, is a potent reminder of just how beautiful failure can be.

SONIC YOUTH,
DAYDREAM NATION DELUXE

CHICAGO READER, JUNE 2007

Sonic Youth's *Daydream Nation* is my favorite album, and
has been since the first time I heard it. Or, actually, the
second. The first time I didn't realize the batteries in my
Walkman were dying, and after a few minutes of slurred
behemoth clang, I passed the tape back to my friend Andrew, complaining that it was too weird and slow. It was
1989 or '90 and I was in ninth grade, and Andrew had
introduced me to punk rock just the week before with
a mixtape that included the likes of Chrome and the
Butthole Surfers, so it seemed perfectly reasonable to me
that a band might sound like a lawn mower underwater.

After a little enlightenment and a battery change, I
tried again. Andrew had told me to listen for the fifty-
nine-second noise break in "Silver Rocket." I timed it by
the sweep hand on the clock in the guidance counselor's
office. I'd come to Sonic Youth pretty much straight from
Tracy Chapman and Deee-Lite, and the idea of "noise" as
music was mind-breaking. That was it—I was sold.

Earlier this week, for the third time in nineteen years,
Daydream Nation was reissued, and the new version is a

"deluxe" double-disc set with a whole disc of bonus tracks. Sonic Youth are admittedly an archivist band and the album is undeniably a classic, but what's going to sell this reissue isn't the remastering job or even the stuff from the vaults. The real drivers here are the nostalgia of aging punks and indie rockers and the borrowed memories of kids born too late and hungry for a connection to that bygone era. It's not hard to turn those feelings into money, but to trigger them you need a fresh product.

Accordingly, the past nine months alone have seen the release of a documentary about the glory days of American hardcore and deluxe reissues and reunion shows from indie rock icons Sebadoh, Chavez, and Young Marble Giants. The original lineup of Dinosaur Jr. is on the road behind a new record, the reunited Slint is touring again—this time re-creating the 1991 album *Spiderland*—and both the Meat Puppets and Afghan Whigs have gotten back together in one form or another.

This cultural recycling keeps us stuck in the past, where we're forever twenty-one, favorite bands are kept like secrets, and scenes are protected from co-optation by their sheer inaccessibility. The internet has all but obliterated the potential for a band or a scene to be private, and it fuels yearning for the time when you last felt that special connection. The same technology that's steamrolling what feels important and particular to us also makes it easier to escape into nostalgia. It provides new and improved reproductions of our memories and makes them easy to share in perpetuity throughout the world.

This gets extra weird when it comes to punk rock.

Punk is nihilistic music made by angry kids, and its nature is to die, to be extinguished, to destroy itself. But once the angry kids grow up, the rules change. When you grow up, you learn that the losers don't write history, so old punks engage in historical revisionism, recasting themselves as brave visionaries in order to be remembered by the mainstream.

Sonic Youth might be America's oldest living noise-punk band, approaching their thirtieth year, so you could argue that they really are winners, with the prerogative to tell their own story. Having outlasted New York no wave, SST punk, "pigfuck" noise, and Nirvana-era alternative rock, they now stand alone, totemic and anomalous. Perhaps for lack of a real-world career model in the indie world (the ultra-DIY Minutemen approach stopped being viable circa 1995), they're taking cues from classic rockers. Beginning with the 2003 reissue of *Dirty*, they've been upgrading and boxing up their classics, buffing their wares to a showroom shine. The band may see this as a way to make rarities available to fans who aren't eBay sickos, but it reminds me of the way a piano salesman softens up a retiree by playing golden oldies. Once you tap into those feelings, you can sell people all kinds of things they don't need.

Most of the time it's not even a tough sell. There are apparently hordes of folks anxious to fan the flames of nostalgia with their federal notes. On their current tour, Sonic Youth are playing *Daydream Nation* in its entirety, and the day they headline the Pitchfork festival is the only one that's already totally sold out. (On the same bill are long-defunct and newly reunited Slint, playing 1991's *Spiderland*, and GZA, performing 1995's classic *Liquid Swords*.) The crowd at the Dinosaur Jr. show I saw a couple of weeks ago, also sold out, was thick with middle-aged men, some wearing ragged relic T-shirts, others in tucked-in button-down shirts, pleated slacks, active sandals that signaled their maturity and affluence.

It's easier to take comfort in the things that were meaningful to you in the past than to risk feeling alienated by the new, but you can sink into absurdity doing it. One of the two sets of liner notes to this edition of *Daydream Nation* is another dull procedural courtesy of the band's BFF, Byron Coley, and both his and the band's remarks exude a wistfulness that's alarmingly intense given that "back in the day" is only 1988. Sonic Youth waxing elegiac about a long-ago Lower East Side, amid the crack epidemic and burning mattresses, as the golden era before gentrification drove sandwich prices above five bucks is just shy of offensive.

Given that Sonic Youth have never really fallen out of favor with critics or the public and are still actively evolving on their new albums, it seems a bit self-serving for them to be so eagerly fanning the embers of their past triumphs. Is it only because they've never stopped oozing good taste and credibility that fans don't dare point out that they're working the underground the way washed-up bands of the '70s work the state-fair circuit? And to what end? They're already so thoroughly canonized that they're guaranteed an audience long after they stop playing.

What's to be gained by the remastering of this masterpiece? If you've loved *Daydream Nation* all along it's hard to hear much of a difference on the disc that contains the studio album. The second disc is mostly unreleased live versions of the songs, plus a few covers recorded around the same time. With Thurston and Lee launching plumes of detuned guitar, Kim groaning tough and flipping patriarchal paradigms, and Steve Shelley pounding as if to remind us that his hardcore days are only just behind him, it's a great addition to the band's catalog. It doesn't, however, give a listener any new insight, doesn't add any meaning to the original artifact. *Daydream Nation* was— and is—a brilliant record and a cultural touchstone. But buying the whole new *Daydream Nation* nostalgia package, and the late-'80s/early-'90s nostalgia-fest in general, feels pathetic—as if the only way to sandbag against encroaching obsolescence is with our wallets.

NEVERMIND ALREADY: NIRVANA'S TWENTIETH-ANNIVERSARY BOX SET

CHICAGO READER, SEPTEMBER 2011

Kurt Cobain, the anointed grunge Buddha, is as big now as he's ever been, which is to say nearly ubiquitous. When *Nevermind* hit number one, less than four months after its release, it was selling roughly 1.2 million copies a month. No one sells like that anymore, and no one ever will again, but Nirvana is still popular, and Cobain even more so. Within the past five years, he's knocked Elvis out of the number one spot on *Forbes*'s list of top-earning dead celebrities. You can own him as a figurine or on a lunch box, or you can buy pre-ratty, Cobain-edition Converse and cultivate your own aura of junkie manqué.

It's hard to believe that twenty years have gone by since *Nevermind* came along and changed everything; it's hard to imagine an album doing that now. Nirvana's supersize ghost lingers in our hearts, and every few years the corpo-coffers get to clangin' hungrily for every last penny in the pockets of anyone who's ever had a head-shop Cobain poster pinned to their bedroom wall.

Nirvana retrospectives and reissues to date include the live *From the Muddy Banks of the Wishkah* (1996), a no-nonsense best-of simply called *Nirvana* (2002), the weighty rarities set *With the Lights Out* (2004), a best-of culled from that set called *Sliver: The Best of the Box* (2005), *Live at Reading* (2009), and vinyl reissues over the past two years of *Bleach*, *Nevermind*, *In Utero*, and *Unplugged*. Now, with '90s grunge nostalgia at high tide, Universal is releasing one of the most bone-dry offerings yet. The "super deluxe" four-CD/one-DVD twentieth anniversary version of *Nevermind*, which comes out on Tuesday, is built around two different mixes of the album—as if anyone listening on earbuds on a city bus is going to be able to tell them apart, or cares to A/B them. Does anyone imagine that kids deafened by two decades of increasingly shitty mastering and overcompression will even be able to hear the difference between the familiar Andy Wallace radio polish (most of disc one) and the initial Butch Vig mix (all of disc three), which still has some punk blood coursing through its bass rumble?

The Vig mix made the rounds as a bootleg not long after *Nevermind* hit big, as did the April 1990, pre-Grohl demos recorded at Smart Studios (part of disc two), both of which reveal nothing except that Chad Channing was the inferior drummer. There are eight boom-box tracks from the band's rehearsal space (most of the rest of disc two), but their novelty is short-lived. Who wants to listen to any band's scuzzed-up cassette tape demos? Every track that wasn't on the original release of *Nevermind*—the BBC sessions, the B-sides—has already been well circulated as a bootleg or seen proper release in a better form. And what's on disc four and the accompanying DVD? The reliable filler of live recordings. Zzzzz and good night.

Nevermind is a great record, but lord, what a boring thing to offer fans. There's not even any fresh meat for the obsessives who go for this sort of thing. Yet this bottom-of-the-barrel commemoration also carries wonderful news: there's nothing left to scrape up. The lost tracks, alternate versions, outtakes, live sets, piss takes, and demos have all been packaged and turned out. Nirvana's former labels have had seventeen years to weave those scraps into dollars—and they're clearly diluting what few bits are left in order to make it last. Universal is stacking up the editions of *Nevermind* for a last hurrah, with not just the "super deluxe" set but also a two-disc "deluxe" version and a straight-up single-CD remastered reissue of the album. Oh, and you can buy the DVD by itself, too. This is the beginning of the end—though if you squint, you can see the "'Heart-Shaped Box' in an Actual Box Shaped Like a Heart Twenty-Fifth Anniversary Box Set" and "*Nevermind* in Mono" galloping this way on the horizon.

It's funny, this latest *Nevermind* coming down the pike two weeks after *Winterland*, a five-CD/eight-LP box of live Jimi Hendrix recordings from 1968. Hendrix is, of course, the most repackaged and reissued artist we've got—a model for the dying major labels. Hardly a holiday shopping season has passed in recent memory when he wasn't revivified in some slick, immodest box. Nirvana, as this pitiful set makes clear, doesn't have such an infinitely expandable catalog. Yet Cobain is not our

Jimi—he's our Jim Morrison. Nirvana, punk bona fides be damned, has become an analogue to the Doors for today's misunderstood, stoned teenagers: a died-young druggie poet-totem.

Cobain's sudden exit at the height of his talent ensures we will always wish for more. These endless reissues count on that. These boxes and anniversary editions prey upon the universal, inchoate wish to relive the singular moment of "Smells Like Teen Spirit." That feeling of being possessed by its pure abandon, its stuttering pound, the implacable tension between verse and chorus, the feral grain of Cobain's voice. There is no one among us who cannot pinpoint where we were and what we were doing, what we felt hearing it for the first time. That wish is there in anyone who ever heard Nirvana and loved them. But you never get as high as the first time.

This is clearly understood by every company that owns a piece (labels, publishing houses), everyone with a claim to stake (Love, Grohl, Novoselic), and everybody with some marketable crumb to pimp out (Michael Azerrad, for instance, has made plenty of hay with his Cobain interview tapes). And Cobain, whose heart once beat heavy with Olympia-bred punk dogma, isn't here to refuse any of it. *He's dead—so fuck him.* In life, he was a commodity; in death, even more so. As Everett True wrote in 2007's *Nirvana: The Biography*, the intervention staged shortly before Cobain's suicide focused as much on cajoling him into headlining Lollapalooza as it did getting him into rehab. Now he's no longer an impediment to anyone's potential revenue stream.

It's easy to speculate about what Cobain and Nirvana would have become had he lived. The band's next album could've been a *Chinese Democracy*–like fiasco, especially embarrassing in light of Cobain's original genius-flash. He could've gone Corgan and released music with steadily diminishing returns for a decade plus. He could've joined the Foo Fighters. He could've taken the Reznor path, "retiring" after a steady, respectable career. (Who knew then that Eddie Vedder would turn out to be the real punk among Cobain's grunge-era "peers"?) Revisiting *Nevermind* is like flexing a phantom limb made up of Nirvana records that never were. That's all it means now, all that's left—fantasy. The tomb is empty; let the dead buy the dead.

PART V
CALIFORNIA

KENDRICK LAMAR

Not Your Average, Everyday Rap Savior

SPIN, OCTOBER 2012

On the cover of Kendrick Lamar's major-label debut, *Good Kid, m.A.A.d City*, is a Polaroid dating from 1991. Lamar identifies himself in it as "baby Kendrick," though he was almost five when it was taken. He sits nestled in the lap of his uncle, who is throwing a gang sign with the same hand that's wrapped around his young nephew. On the table sits a forty-ounce and a baby bottle; baby Kendrick is wide-eyed, staring directly into the camera. "We got photo books full of pictures like that," he says. "I was in that atmosphere every day until my teenage years."

He picked the photo "for the innocence in that kid's eyes; not knowing that a baby bottle and a forty-ouncer . . ." He trails off. "It's still so vivid to me. This picture shows how far I really come."

The twenty-five-year-old Compton-born MC is curled up in a corner of the couch at the back of his tour bus, wearing the pajamas he slept in, hoodie drawn and sleeves yanked over his hands. With the air-conditioning on full-blast, the bus feels like a meat locker. Hundreds of fans are queued up across the street, outside the venue, hours

153

before doors open. It is Lamar's first headlining tour and tonight's show in Chicago is sold out.

Lamar may be from Compton, but his roots are here in Chicago. Tonight's *entire* two-hundred-person guest list is made up of family, including Lamar's grandpa, one of several relatives Lamar says he helps support. "I ain't even made my first big purchase yet," he says. "I live in Los Angeles and I don't even have a car. My ends go to take care of my family." He used his Aftermath signing bonus to move his parents out of the Compton neighborhood where they raised him.

Lamar's parents met on Chicago's South Side; his mom was one of thirteen kids, his dad one of seven. In 1984, while still teenagers, they moved to Compton in order to start a family away from the gang war that was tearing up Chicago's South and West Side neighborhoods, where Kendrick's dad was affiliated with the Gangster Disciples. "Compton was just as rough, but they didn't know that," explains Lamar. His parents had him three years later, and his three siblings started coming seven years after that. Lamar's mother also moved much of her family out to Compton as well, effectively transferring their Chicago life to California. In Kendrick's earliest memories, his parents are twenty-five, the same age he is now. He shakes his head in disbelief.

"I always play back these house parties in my memory," he says. "Takin' off my shirt and wilin' out with my cousins, getting in trouble for riding our Big Wheels inside the house. They'd be playin' oldies and gangsta rap.

Just drinkin' and smokin' and laughter. A young crowd enjoying themselves. They were living the lifestyle."

Growing up, his mom worked in fast food, and his dad did, too, sometimes. "My pops did whatever he could to get money. He was in the streets. You know the story." There were stints of being on welfare. "I remember always walking to the government building with Mom. We got our food stamps fast because we lived across the street," laughs Lamar. "I didn't know it was hard times because they always had my Christmas present under the tree and for my birthday."

It wasn't until middle school that he realized that there was a different kind of normal for kids who weren't growing up in his Compton neighborhood. There were kids from the San Fernando Valley, a racially mixed suburban enclave north of Hollywood, who were bussed thirty miles to Compton to attend Kendrick's school. "I went over to some of their houses . . . and it was a whole 'nother world. Family pictures of them in suits and church clothes up everywhere. Family-oriented. Eatin' together at the table. We ate around the TV. Eatin' without your elbows on the table? I'm lookin' around like, '*What is goin' on?!*' I came home and asked my mama, 'Why we don't eat 'round the table?' I think that's when I started to see the lifestyle around us." He pauses and continues. "You always think that everybody live like you do, because you locked in the neighborhood, you don't see no way else."

Lamar says that *Good Kid* is for the kids in those neighborhoods. It's a self-portrait in which others might see themselves. Both of his parents had gang culture in their families, and it was a fundamental part of Lamar's childhood as well. "Being around it, it just seemed like what you gonna do, what you gonna be," he says.

As a teenager, Lamar started drinking and partying, emulating and embracing things he'd grown up around, until his father sat him down at age sixteen. "My father said, 'I don't want you to be like me.' I said, 'What you mean you don't want me to be like you?' I couldn't really grasp the concept." An only child until he was seven, Lamar was, and is, very close to both his parents. His dad took him to the swap meet every weekend for as long as he could remember (a detail that reappears in the song "Westside, Right on Time"), and to see Dr. Dre and Tupac shoot the "California Love" video around the corner from their house (which set off Lamar's dreams of being a rapper). "He said, 'Things I have done, mistakes I've made, I never want you to make those mistakes. You can wind up out on the corner.' He knew by the company I keep what I was gettin' into. Out of respect, I really just gathered myself together."

Lamar began to see life around him with new clarity. "I saw the same things over and over. A lot of my homeboys goin' to jail. Not, like, in and out. *Sentences*. And dyin'; it was a constant. It was a gift from God to be able to recognize that."

Though Lamar has recorded several songs refuting that he's ever been in a gang (most notably, "Average Joe," off *Overly Dedicated*), he says he's not offended that people may not believe him. "Here's the thing about gangbanging. I was born in that area, where you have to be affiliated. The difference was I didn't turn seventeen and say, 'I wanna be a gang member.' Gangs is my family, I grew up with them, I hung with them. So I been around it, but I can't sit here and claim a gang. That's my family more than anything." He smirks, then grows animated. "People saying I am 'gang-affiliated.' Yeah, I almost wanna say that I am because I wanna change the idea. I don't wanna separate myself. I don't wanna be in the hills. I wanna be in the center. I want them to know they can still touch me."

"He's always been humble like that," says Ab-Soul, who has been tight with Lamar since they met eight years ago, and is a member, with Lamar, of the Black Hippy collective. "He hasn't changed. He has a glow about him. He carries it with him; he's just a deep guy." Ab-Soul recalls being humbled by the first time he heard a mixtape recorded under the name "K.Dot." "I was *certain* I was the best MC in my area," he says, laughing. "Or at least my age bracket. But to hear someone rapping at that level at our age, it was incredible."

Lamar began writing rhymes at thirteen, but it wasn't until he saw 50 Cent's early mixtape success that he realized he could be recording and releasing his rhymes on his own. His first mixtape made its way to Top Dawg Entertainment; the story of his audition has since come to signify his dedication. The sixteen-year-old MC stepped into the booth and freestyled for two straight hours, while label founder Anthony "Top Dawg" Tiffith pretended to ignore him, to see what Lamar had to prove. The label had signed Jay Rock two weeks prior and the two MCs began recording at the label's studio house in nearby Carson. Lamar, then barely seventeen, was a constant presence after school. In 2009, as the Top Dawg roster had expanded to include Ab-Soul and Schoolboy Q, the foursome formed Black Hippy, "the conglomeration so cool it could freeze L.A.," rhymes Lamar on the group's quintessential "Zip That Chop That."

Jay Rock was similarly stunned the first time he went into the studio with Lamar, shortly after they'd both been signed. "I was working on lyrics, writing, writing, writing on paper. And Kendrick goes in the booth with nothing. I asked him where's his paper? He'd written it all—the whole song—in his head in about five minutes. That's when I knew he was crazy. And a genius." Jay Rock cribs the trademark line about Dick Clark to describe Kendrick's maturity level at seventeen years old: "He was like the world's oldest teenager."

The first time Ab-Soul was in the studio with Lamar, he saw that he was working on a totally different level. "[Kendrick] was recording full songs with hooks and bridges and melodies and things to keep a crowd. He was not just interested in being the best rapper, he was making songs that the world could sing."

■ ■ ■

Lamar's family hails from Chicago's Seventy-Sixth Street and Stoney Island, two miles from the Parkway Garden Homes' O Block, a significant site of gang violence and the housing project where tendentious teen-rap flashpoint Chief Keef grew up. The two artists are now Interscope labelmates, and the subjects of two of the most sizable bidding wars in recent major-label memory. Keef reportedly pulled down 3 million, Lamar confirms his deal at 1.7 million. Lamar, who has never met Keef in person, grows emphatic when discussion turns to the media's moralizing about the misanthropy and violence in Keef's songs.

"You can't change where you from," he says. "You can't take a person out of their zone and expect them to be somebody else now that they in the record industry. It's gonna take years. Years of traveling. Years of meeting people. Years of seeing the world." It becomes unclear whether, in talking about Keef, Lamar is actually talking about his own experience. He values Keef's success on the same terms as his own. Lamar says that by doing music, they represent two dudes who are *not* in the streets. "Maybe he'll inspire the next generation to want to do music. Convert that energy to a positive instead of a pistol."

With *Good Kid*, Lamar is also trying to shift how South Central Los Angeles has been portrayed historically on record. "He's telling his truth—the typical story of a kid growing up in Compton," explains Top Dawg's president, Terrence "Punch" Henderson. Like everyone around Lamar, Henderson is respectfully mum on what is and isn't on the still-unreleased* *Good Kid*, but he is clear

---

* The album was embargoed by the label, and I had to write the profile without ever having heard the album. The story was published two weeks before the album would be released.

about how it's a departure. "It's not what you know from N.W.A. It's not about gangs he's representing. It's a classic. The only thing separating him from the greats is time."

That potential is what drew the attention of hip-hop legend Dr. Dre, who signed Lamar to Aftermath after being turned on to a K.Dot mixtape by Eminem's manager (Lamar's Interscope deal also included a label deal for Top Dawg). Dre is one of *Good Kid*'s executive producers and is featured heavily on the album's Twin Sister–sampling lead single "The Recipe" (Lamar also has worked on several tracks for Dre's eternally delayed *Detox*). Lamar smiles broadly when talking about Dre, a fellow graduate of Compton's Centennial High School, who he alternately refers to as his "big homey."

While much has been said (including by Lamar himself) about picking up where his hero Tupac Shakur left off, Dre's patronage cements the extension of that classic '90s West Coast legacy. It's worth noting that the last time Dre ushered a young rapper into the mainstream with such support it was Eminem. So, is the pop world ready for this next evolution?

Ab-Soul believes that what's on *Good Kid* is universal: "It's Kendrick's story, but it's my story; it's not just an L.A. album. Everyone will get an understanding of why my generation is acting the way they are: violence, vulgarity, anguish, and resentment, rebelliousness, and eff the police. He puts it all in perspective—telling the whole story of homies we all had."

While *Good Kid* is autobiographical, like much of Lamar's work, it's allegorical. While he is rapping about himself, his songs are heavy on experiences and feelings that are universal and easily relatable. Lamar is peerless in his ability (he never rides the beat the same way twice) and also in the space that he occupies; he's different from the artists that came before him who were touted as rap saviors. Lamar is not a scold and his hooks are as important as his message. Though, more than all of this, what defines Lamar is that he's haunted and driven by what might have been for him had he not found himself in music; he cannot shake the proximity of Compton, and how the city made him who he is.

Lamar is aware of the power of his influence, but says he's not out to change the world. "The idea of me sparking change; it's got to come from within. I couldn't be saying I want Compton to change. Compton is a beautiful place. You just gotta keep your eyes open."

LANA DEL REY, *HONEYMOON*

PITCHFORK, SEPTEMBER 2015

On the cover of *Honeymoon* is Lana Del Rey, the young star as the idle passenger of a parked convertible Hollywood tourmobile, gazing through face-obscuring shades. As an artist, she's never shied away from the obvious, but the image feels almost *too* on the nose, *too* apt—Lana doing the Full Lana. And yet that's exactly what *Honeymoon* gives us; it is Lana Del Rey's purest album-length expression, and her most artful one.

Accordingly, *Honeymoon* is a dark work, darker even than *Ultraviolence*, and the pall does not lift for its sixty-plus minutes. It's an album about love, but "love," as Del Rey sings it, sounds like mourning. The romance here is closer to drugs—something that's sought for its ability to blot out the rest of life's miseries. On the title track, when she croons "Our honeymoon / Say you want me too," she's as dopily hopeful as Brian Wilson singing "We could be married / And then we'd be happy." The album luxuriates in this bleak space between dream and reality, which stretches endlessly from one melancholy track to the next. It's not until "The Blackest Day," eleven songs

in, that *Honeymoon*'s static depression gives way to apocalyptic ecstasy, as she gasps, "In all the wrong places /
Oh my God," in multitracked harmonies on the chorus.
The moment is *Honeymoon*'s emotional apex, but it still
moves at the pace of a funeral march, and the release it
depicts is that of embracing rock bottom.

The morose orchestral grandeur of the album feels like
an arrival point, and also possibly a dead end: the sentimentality and drama throws back to old Hollywood film
scores. The setting is pitch-perfect and a million moth-
balled years away from the current pop landscape; it's
strange, an artist emblematic of youth culture trading in
such old music. As a vocalist, Del Rey sounds more like
the singer of her pre-Lana Lizzy Grant days here, when she
was performing torch songs in secretarial skirts at A&R
showcases, looking too young to seem so haunted. Her
previous two records felt like earnest stabs at finding a pop
context for that voice, but they were both overwrought,
and *Honeymoon*'s arrangements feel built to rectify that.

Honeymoon acknowledges what listeners are here
for and delivers with big, sad, fucked-up epics. It's rare
to get to a chorus within the first minute, and until that
point it's usually just Lana, maybe a little guitar or some
cinematic strings. The programmed drums of "High by
the Beach" and "Religion" wait nearly a minute to enter,
and "Terrence Loves You" is even sparser. Many tracks
expand sleepily past the five- or six-minute mark, which
is to say that *Honeymoon*'s languor takes the listener's
attention for granted. Which is certainly not a mistake.

While she's obviously a pop artist, *Honeymoon* feels

as though it belongs to a larger canon of Southern California Gothic albums—*Celebrity Skin*, *Hotel California*, *The Hissing of Summer Lawns*. She sings about it all—the sprawl, the toxicity, the culture of transactional relationships, the particulars of the light ("God Knows I Tried")—with a New England accent ("scared" becomes "skaaaahd"). All the gee-whiz irony of previous albums is gone; often she sounds like ABBA's Agnetha Fältskog roused from a nap, sweet but disconnected.

Like Joan Didion's ur-California-girl transplant, Maria Wyeth, Del Rey sings like a woman who "knows what 'nothing' means"—on "High by the Beach," "Freak," and "Art Deco," she sounds beyond longing, like it's been a long time since she felt anything at all. She is cruelly incisive on "Art Deco" ("you're just born to be seen"), a highlight that curdles when the phrase "you're so ghetto" comes out in the chorus. It's one of the few misfires on an album that otherwise feels like Del Rey moving into the temple she's built.

She has been transfixed by, and riffing on, America since the beginning, but *Honeymoon* pushes past easy Kennedy kitsch and undulating flags to mine something more specific. In the opening track, she sings "We could cruise / To the blues / Wilshire Boulevard," and the name check is shrewd. One of L.A.'s earliest thoroughfares, a locus of establishing the city's car culture, Wilshire runs sixteen miles and, as the architecture critic Christopher Hawthorne writes, "can take you from a world-famous piece of architecture to a weed-choked lot, from a realized ambition to an abandoned one, in the space of a few blocks."

In the following verse, she replaces blues with "news" and substitutes "Pico Boulevard," a street that stretches thirteen miles between downtown and the Pacific, bisecting working class Koreatown and running through Ecuadoran, Salvadoran, Russian, and Mexican communities. The juxtaposition is startling and canny. In the space of one lyric, she posits the invisible yet real metropolis running parallel to the gleaming, manufactured one, sketching an arterial map of a city coursing with ambition. It's a reminder of something that was the very issue with Del Rey that irritated some early on—she knows what she is doing. *Honeymoon* synthesizes and justifies ideas she's been vamping on from the beginning into a unified work. She figured where she was going long before she got there; with *Honeymoon* she has finally arrived.

CALIFORNIA DEMISE

Tyler, the Creator and EMA Feel the Bad Vibes

VILLAGE VOICE PAZZ & JOP CRITICS POLL, JANUARY 2011

Tyler, the Creator is stuck inside "Yonkers" with those California hate-fuck blues again. Don't ask him what the matter is—you'll get an album-length spleening in response. He's rap's nouveau old-model bad boy, showing the kids that "breaking rules is cool again," rhyming impolitely about his problems with, well, everything. Many spent the year trying to gauge the misanthropic messiah MC. On *Goblin*, he came across as so ferociously indifferent, it was hard to imagine he could give a shit about anyone at all, including himself.

He's unlike some of the other cool California kids of recent memory, who're writing songs that pick up where David Crosby's sailboat docked. They're obsessed with the various qualities of sand, sunshine, friendship, and/or the waves, and they're too high to take a position on much else. Last year's chillwave wave was the latest iteration of California's musical posi-vibe, all bright smiles highlighted by a deep tan. Chillwave's methodology of easy hooks submerged in reverb and delay served as a constant reminder of being distant and of singers floating in their own worlds.

With decades of this chill cheer as SoCal cultural inheritance, it's easy to see why Tyler's Wolf Gang wants to kill 'em all, let God sort 'em out (and then kill God), or why EMA came blazing for "California" with nothing but middle fingers and buckshot for the left coast. Can you blame them? The thrill of popping that bubble is undeniable. One of Tyler's central talents is antagonism, a puerile needling that knows to go for the jugular and say the exact thing you don't want to hear, flippant and cruel in equal measure. Although plenty of Southern Californian MCs have paired rage with ridicule, Tyler's effusively macho posturing is less *Straight Outta Compton* and more like that of the man who made it his trademark: Henry Rollins.

Historically, California punk has had its share of teen loathers with suicidal tendencies. Alongside Eminem, Rollins is perhaps Tyler's clearest primogenitor, to wit the myopic focus on bad feelings, a hangover of confused, adolescent tumult tangling hard with violent solutions. Tyler's sober indifference isolates him from the other California girls and boys, and the intensity with which he doesn't give a fuck seemingly belies just how much he actually does. It's the most un-L.A. thing he could possibly do.

So much is the same for Erika Anderson—known on-record as EMA—even though she is, in essence, Tyler's inverse. Born-and-bred Midwestern riot girl rides west in search of new liberation in noise, gets grown, and explodes her heart and head open on *Past Life Martyred Saints*. It's a brute-force reveal: she's done with the known archetypes and instead has an album full of blood and "Twenty kisses with a butterfly knife." Self-preservation is not a principal interest; she is gutting her guts, and blunt about the trauma she has known, a far cry from the apathetic yearning that typifies indie rock's notion of a "confessional." Like on *Goblin*, the volatility and capriciousness is unsettling.

When Anderson faces her audience, foot up on the monitor in confident, rock-star repose, and begins wrapping the mic cable around her neck, her methodical calm is what shocks. Her seemingly easy acquaintance with violence makes her shows seem less like performance and more like a visceral expression of how little (or much) she cares. Coaxing howls from her half stack, the tall, beautiful blond calmly coos, "I used to carry the gun / The gun, the gun, the gun." In the underground, she's as much of a "walking paradox" as Tyler. Both artists goad unease for different reasons (EMA's violence is directed inward; Tyler's viciousness outward), but discomfort is crucial fuel for their spectacle. The placement of "Yonkers" and "California" in this year's poll offers evidence that listeners are taking them up on the thrill of their Cali-kid violence, regardless of whether it delights or disgusts.

WILL THE STINK OF SUCCESS RUIN THE SMELL?

LA WEEKLY, FEBRUARY 2009

The story of the Smell, on the surface, isn't exactly spectacular. It's an all-ages venue that's a wellspring for young punks here in Los Angeles, and like most clubs, it's a depot of questionable haircuts and bombastic bands. Yet the Smell is different from the rest: it's a no-booze, not-for-profit operation that is staffed mostly by teenage volunteers. The recent success of some of the exciting bands it fostered—namely No Age—has made the Smell a point of focus for the worldwide underground, a place delivering on punk's often unfulfilled promises of DIY community and inclusion.

The way people talk about Jim Smith, you'd think he was sanctified and risen. The story of every Smell band, every volunteer's gee-whiz excitement, always hinges on Smith, who opened the venue eleven years ago. A labor union organizer by day and dutiful scene facilitator by night, Smith is taciturn and humble. He's got an old-fashioned gallantry to him; he dresses in workingman's clothes and decries little. He has the gravitas of a man living by a code. Smith closes up at the Smell at 1:00 or

2:00 a.m., then goes to work at 6:00 a.m., night after night. Without complaint or even the slightest sense that this unpaid toil brings him anything other than gratification.

If Smith is the Smell's heart, No Age are its arteries. The story of L.A.'s zeitgeist noise-pop duo is braided with the venue's genesis. Given the amount of press and hype the band has garnered in the last year and a half, it's become part of their mythic tale: the Smell as the house No Age built. This is objectively true; talking to guitarist Randy Randall in early October, he lamented that though he and drummer Dean Spunt helped break concrete for the construction of the Smell's second bathroom, No Age was on tour during its completion.

No Age might very well be the coolest band in America right now, and it's easy to understand why. Being a No Age fan feels like more than mere fandom, which is fitting since No Age feel like more than just another band. They stand for hope and big ideas as well as simple ones: have fun, include everyone, be positive, do good work. It's an active rejection of adult cynicism. You could call it anti-capitalist, but there's no indication anyone involved has given it that much thought. These are the same principles that the Smell seems to impart on everyone who passes through its piss-soaked doorway.

In No Age's Dean Spunt and Randy Randall, Jim Smith found his two most dedicated and willing volunteers— seeds of the scene. Like most of the kids who've found purchase in the Smell's hallowed space, they were refugees from the city's rock club circuit. "One of the first places I ever played was the Cobalt Cafe, in the Valley," says Spunt. "They'd do a bill of six local bands and when you walked in they asked you what band you were there to see. Once you got over fifty people for your band, which was impossible, then you got fifty bucks and a dollar a head after that." He adds, "They made you really feel like a kid." Never mind that he still was one.

"The first time playing Smell, it was the anti-version of that." No booze. No tickets. No backstage. No bullshit. No security hassling you. No pay to play. The Smell is anti-club. "At the Smell you were treated as an equal," explains Smith. "The kids that come, they are people, not 'patrons.'"

When Spunt and Randall discovered the Smell in 1998, it wasn't the province of teen punks, but a dingy downtown venue that'd been occupied by the experimental noise scene—Nels Cline and Win Records bands. The two promptly began booking shows for their then-band, Wives, and as Spunt puts it, "we took the place over." They began booking hardcore and punk bills, including an all-woman crust band from the Valley, Dead Banana Ladies, who would soon become scene-queens Mika Miko. Exit old noise dudes, hello excitable tenth graders of the Inland Empire.

Spunt's devotion to the Smell was instant: "The first time I went there I thought, 'I want to be here every day!' and until about a year, year and a half ago, I was. I was there every day. It was *so* crazy and *so* special."

Spunt and Randall joined the cabal of people around Smith who were deeply involved in keeping the place open. In 2002, after the Great White club-fire tragedy in

Providence, the Smell, like many on-the-fringe-of-legit spaces around the country, was closed by the fire marshal. For the next six months, the Smell crew worked to bring the club up to code as quickly as possible. Spunt moved all the shows that had already been booked into a squat where he was living in Hollywood. Almost nightly, there was a four-band bill in his living room, and almost every day the two would be down at the Smell, building and painting, alongside Smith and the rest of the regulars.

Amid the process, the Smell became more than a hangout, it became a place Spunt and Randall were responsible for keeping running. "Anthony Berryman from Soddamn Inssein came down to the video store where I worked," explains Randall. "He told me, 'Jim cannot do this by himself. Listen, you are going to get keys. I don't want to hear that you are flaking on shows you booked or not showing up.' I had to learn how to do sound, how to put the mics up there and run the soundboard, be there every night. Jim would try and pay me, and I would avoid him. He'd try to slip a twenty in your pocket somehow."

"And then we did the same thing to Mika Miko, because Wives were going on tour for four months. They were there every day and playing twice a week," says Spunt.

In the years since the Smell's rebirth, the venue's stakeholders have gone from being just a trusted few bands and regulars to the scene at large. The door was thrown open for everyone to get involved, but it wasn't merely good intentions; No Age began to tour frequently (sometimes with Smith in tow), as did Mika Miko, Abe Vigoda, and longtime Smell booker/compatriot Brian Miller. Randall explains, "Jim figured that it had to get bigger than just us and other bands, it had to be the kids, too." He made a "What Would Jim Do" book that volunteers consult; a dozen volunteers have keys. The Smell transitioned from the hands of a few to any and all willing hands.

"[Jim] really sent it out to the community, that they *have to* do it," says Randall. "People complain that the Smell won't book their band, but then you have to ask them, 'Well, how many shows have you been to? Have you volunteered there?' It's about nurturing the community."

■ ■ ■

Backstage after No Age's show in London in late October, a young blogger has been waiting, impatiently, for the thirty minutes since Spunt and Randall got offstage, to interview them for her website. They are soggy and winded from their set and trying to get it together to walk across the street to play a second, "secret" show for 120 diehards at a 90-capacity sushi bar. Despite the fact that the blogger is openly hostile and has a list of forty terrible questions, they indulge her. With smiles. They are unwaveringly polite. It is the L.A. way to never offend, but their gentleness, removed from the context of the Smell's downtown alley, becomes immediately recognizable as the spirit of Jim Smith. After ten minutes, they have to go. They invite her along—she carries the cymbal stands.

At the packed sushi joint, kids are blowing up balloons,

and the Smell-scenester Vice Cooler is DJing, playing R. Kelly too loud. The band heads backstage—a stairwell to the roof—where they learn the Misfits' classic "Where Eagles Dare." Someone had dialed up the guitar-tab on their iPhone, learned it, and proofed it against the collective memory of the band's friends that have gathered in the stairwell. Five minutes later, Spunt and Randall open their set with it. Ebullient fans scream along: "I AIN'T NO GODDAMN SON OF A BITCH! YOU BETTER THINK ABOUT IT BAY-BAY!" The floor begins to flex wildly under the pogoing people, so, at Randall's insistence, the audience sits down, which sparks a pig-pile pit. The band blazes through a short set with everyone rolling on one another, singing along and writhing on the floor.

At the club show No Age played just an hour before, for twelve hundred composed Londoners, they were a truly fun band. But to see them play a party at this too-small spot, heavy with diehards, is to see No Age at their incandescent, miracle-band best. It is in those moments that they become so much more than a band. To their fans, they are deliverance, a band that walks the walk; an articulation of DIY's foundational principles.

Since its inception thirty-odd years ago, punk has had a spotty history of living up to its best intentions, which is part of its charm. Periodically, there have been bands—most notably Crass, Fugazi, Bad Brains, the Ex, Bikini Kill—or labels (K, Dischord) or scenes that sprang up with radical notions that inspired a paradigm shift. It is a matter of inspiration paired with powerful records or

live shows that are necessary to wrap people up in the big
ideas (or ideals) in the music. These times, scenes, bands
where the pugnacious do-it-yourself dogma is transmogrified into something momentous and empowering. It's a
rare once-or-twice-a-decade thing, when a band shows
its audience they can be more than fans, and that this can
be about something other than entertainment, getting
wasted; it can have deep meaning and political purpose.
It is an alchemical shift, where music becomes exactly
what you believed it was when your heart was fifteen and
pure, and all the hope and time you've invested pays out.
The Smell is home to one of these coalescent moments;
No Age is one of these bands.

While the Smell may have indoctrinated No Age on
how to approach their career and given them an ideological
toehold for their music, it didn't necessarily prepare them
for their current level of success. The band is being held up
as an emblem of positivity in the mainstream music media, hailed as a signal of a new Los Angeles, and the band
is wearing the weight of those expectations. "We want to
play and do our thing but the visibility puts a lot of stress
on people around us, the community of L.A.," says Spunt.
"I have to wonder, like, did we fuck something up?" What
happens in a scene of equals when suddenly one band is
declared king?

■   ■   ■

It's the morning after what should have been No Age's
triumphant return to the Smell. It's been a big year for

the duo; their debut on Sub Pop, *Nouns*, has the underground hyperventilating with glee, and has brought them to the attention of the overground: they have been profiled in *The New Yorker* and played on a late night TV talk show. They have been nominated for a Grammy for their album packaging. Recently, after months of nonstop touring, they had two weeks home for a break, and booked a hush-hush show at the Smell. No Age shows here, historically, have been a crush of sweat and screamalongs. The secret show was moderately attended, but the audience had few familiar faces. Then, after the third song, in a pocket of strange silence, a kid yelled giddily from where the pit should have been, "YOU WERE ON MTV!" Dean and Randy exchanged stricken glances and Dean quickly counted off into the next 4/4 blitzkrieg; a handful of kids pogoed, while the rest gawked silently at the band.

The show had a curious pall for a band that has enjoyed such a fast ride to fame, and it exacted a toll from the already-exhausted band. Randall explains, "What was weird last night was that we were in our home, but there were a bunch of strangers in it. Normally we might yell out to our friends in the audience, but there were so many strange faces."

"It was just weird. It was the Smell, but it wasn't," says Spunt. "Me and Randy were pretty much just hanging alone. It was fine, it was cool, but it wasn't our friends. I wasn't concerned with [the] amount of people. It was just . . . All of our friends were busy—Mika Miko was playing a show, Abe Vigoda was doing stuff, everybody is doing stuff on a bigger level, so . . ." He trails off. As No Age's profile has risen, so has that of some other Smell bands, namely Mika Miko and Abe Vigoda. Lately, the press has portrayed both bands as No Age's retinue rather than the close-knit crew they are.

"After last night, I was bummed. This morning I was trying to get clarity on it and I cried. It's not that I've lost my friends—but doing this was fun because we were doing it all together," says Randall. "Being gone so much, you miss the parties, you miss birthdays, and then after a while I'm not expected to be there, so no one is bummed when you don't show up. I have lost certain community ties, friends." He continues, "Last night I was thinking, 'What makes you think you can just come home and expect everyone to show up?' Who am I to ask for that when I am not there?" He sighs, "The reason I cried was the sacrifices. There's been too many. Too many little things that I didn't know were on the line."

It is Jim Smith, more than anyone, who insists that all the attention on No Age and the Smell is not having a corrosive effect. Despite what naysayers may predict, the Smell isn't losing its community cohesion. While a lot of the regulars insist that shows regularly sell out now—which would have been a freak occurrence in the past—Smith is reluctant to cop to any discernible shift, in attendance or otherwise. "Sure, the Smell is in transition," he says, "but it's always been that way, since the beginning—evolving and growing. Fundamentally, nothing is different. We still operate on the principles by which it was founded. The energy is still there. We have remained intact."

PART VI

STRICTLY BUSINESS

PUNK IS DEAD! LONG LIVE PUNK!

A Report on the State of Teen Spirit from the Mobile Shopping Mall That Is the Vans Warped Tour

CHICAGO READER, AUGUST 2004

Teenagers are the most powerful audience in America, and this summer the Vans Warped Tour—which began June 25 in Houston and ends today, August 20, in Boston—celebrated ten years of unwavering devotion to this principle. At each stop, between ten thousand and thirty thousand teenagers converged on a parking lot, a field, or an amphitheater, wading deep into the froth of pop-cultural commerce that they drive with their fickle tastes. In exchange for the eighteen to thirty dollars that a Warped ticket costs, depending on the venue—not bad at all for five dozen bands—the sunburned throngs got eight hours of accessible punk, hardcore, and hip-hop.

Yet no impartial observer could conclude that Warped is first and foremost about the music. It's about teenagers and their disposable income. Punk in its primal form is of course a deeply anti-commercial genre, but Warped has turned money into the medium of cultural affiliation here, as it already was everywhere else. What's being sold is an entrée into punk, and most of the fans are too new to the music's ideals to understand that they're buying a version of fuck-all rebellion that's been repackaged by businesspeople. Or maybe they do understand, and they come because they think it's the only version left. Warped is a mammoth shopping and marketing experience, a towering conglomerated product of the Clear Channel Age, and though the music is the initial draw, purchases are the way the kids express themselves to themselves, to the bands, and to one another.

Look no further than the Casualties' merch tent, with its twenty-four T-shirt designs, two styles of handkerchief, and three different hats. A day at Warped is about kids saying "I love you" to their favorite bands, with cash in hand—and on a scale that boggles the mind. We're a long way from the Fireside Bowl, which is the kind of punk dive many Warped acts came up playing, sometimes to only twenty or thirty kids at a time. Selling a handful of seven-inches for gas money isn't gonna cut it if you're touring as part of an operation that requires a fleet of ten tractor-trailers, a hundred tour buses and vans, eleven sound systems, a full-time on-site doctor and massage therapist, and a catering service that can handle two hot meals a day for 650 to 800 people. On July 24, the day Warped stopped at the Tweeter Center in Tinley Park, the band Taking Back Sunday grossed $20,000 in T-shirt sales alone.*

---

* I saw a lot of typically wild shit during my few weeks on Warped, but TBS running $26,000 in small bills through a professional-grade currency counter on the dining table of their bus like it was no big deal still sticks out.

I spent a few weeks on the 2004 Warped Tour, doing research for a book and hanging out with my boyfriend, who was performing. The fans' average age seemed to be about sixteen. I remember sixteen as a pretty grim year, but from the safe distance of a decade or so, sixteen-year-olds are completely fascinating. I was surrounded by thousands upon thousands of kids, a rushing tide of adolescent self-concept run riot, of bad tribal tattoos and rapturous infatuations and questionable hairstyles, all reeking of the pungent desire to simultaneously transgress and fit in perfectly.

This un-self-conscious incoherence is a magnificent thing to behold. These kids all seemed to have a flawless idea of who they were, or who they wanted to seem to be, with their carefully arranged ensembles of brand names, slogans, and symbols, and absolutely no idea how they actually appeared. I saw boys milling around a San Diego sports pavilion parking lot, chewing on corn dogs and wearing mesh-back caps reading "My Balls Itch" at 11:00 a.m. on a Sunday. I saw a girl with the name of every act on the tour written in pen down the legs of her jeans, apparently signifying an impulse to identify with simply being at a "punk concert" more than loyalty to any of the actual bands. None of this, of course, was any less honest for being so obviously calculated—even when you're a teenager faking it, approximating a notion of cool, you're still bound to be more real, more transparent, and more vulnerable than any adult.

The second thing you notice at Warped is the din. At any given moment there were at least four bands playing on the sprawling carnival midway of the concert campus. Most festivals make do with a single main stage and one or two distraction stages, but Warped was operating four main stages, four secondary stages, and a handful of stages-in-name-only—usually just a canopy in front of a van or a strip of grass between a set of PA speakers. The Brian Stage and the Teal Stage were for the headliners; when a band on Brian finished its set, another band cranked up on Teal within three minutes. You could watch NOFX, the Alkaline Trio, the Sounds, and Yellowcard back-to-back simply by ping-ponging one hundred feet to the left or right. Next year's headliners apparent (Rufio, My Chemical Romance, the Casualties) played on the Maurice Stage and the Volcom-sponsored stage, also side by side. Shunted out into the general population, next to the merch booths, were smaller elevated stages sponsored by Smartpunk, Punkrocks.net, and Ernie Ball. The Hurley/Kevin Says stage, barely a stage at all, had a ground-level linoleum floor and yellow caution tape strung along the front.

With so many bands playing at once, not even the most dedicated fan could see everything. Like a shopping mall, the concert campus was designed to keep customers circulating, to convince them to check out every tent and booth at least once. Warped has even developed an ingenious strategy to bring the kids in early and keep them all day: the lineup of set times was different at every stop and wasn't announced in advance. Though technically a headliner, Bad Religion might have been playing at noon rather than taking the day's last slot at 7:30 p.m. Thursday might have been slated for 1:00 p.m. or 5:15 p.m., and you couldn't know till you got past the gate. So you'd show up at eleven in the morning and find out that your two favorite bands were going on at noon and 6:00 p.m. What to do with the hours in between? There were band booths and label booths. There were good-cause booths: PETA, breast cancer awareness, Take Action! (progressive activism and "personal empowerment"). And then there were booths for the likes of Slim Jim (free wristbands and meat sticks!), Cingular Wireless (plastic gems and band stickers to decorate your cell phone!), and Dodge (custom racing cars in a showroom tent!). You could get your merch, purse, or person autographed, sign up for dozens of mailing lists, try out a bass or guitar, get your hair shaved into a Mohawk for free, or chew some complimentary Wrigley's Winterfresh gum. You could also buy stuff: sneakers, a skateboard deck, a hot dog, a hemp necklace, lemonade, band stickers or pins, spiked leather wristbands, thong underwear, a furry neon belt, sunglasses, a pizza from Domino's, a shirt that said "I'm sick and tired of white girls."

The hip-hop tent, dubbed the Code of the Cutz Stage, offered the only respite from the ever-present feeling of being marketed to. The dozen or so acts in the rotating daily lineup often left the stage, rubbing elbows with the crowd, or ventured outside the tent, mike in hand—I saw New Hampshire rapper ADeeM (from the duo Glue) holding forth from atop the nearby picnic tables. It's not like there was no selling going on here, but it wasn't the faceless, focus-grouped variety: the Code of the Cutz performers frequently hawked their own CDs and shirts outside the tent after their sets. They were also pushing some of the more aggressive political agendas on the tour. NOFX, masterminds of Rock Against Bush, may pause between songs to wish Dick Cheney a heart attack, and Yellowcard may beg kids to get off their asses and vote, but those gestures seem rote next to Non Phixion free-styling on the human impact of unfair drug-sentencing laws or Immortal Technique calling Condi Rice "the new age Sally Hemings."

On July 20 in Milwaukee, I hung out with a friend who ran the *Alternative Press* autograph booth while he got ready for a Taking Back Sunday signing. (The band's sets were always so mobbed that I never managed to see them from less than three-quarters of a mile away, but I did hear that TBS's kickball team with Thursday—aptly named Taking Back Thursday—was the one to beat on this year's tour.) My friend set up stools, laid out fresh Sharpies, stacked posters into huge piles, and shooed too-eager fans back into the quarter-mile line. In front was a boy in a homemade Taking Back Sunday T-shirt: with colored markers he'd written the date, the band's name, some lyrics, and the name of the venue in careful capitals, and along the bottom edge in alternating colors was a repeated rickrack ribbon of "Taking Back Sunday * Vans Warped Tour * Taking Back Sunday * Vans Warped Tour." The homemade Warped Commemorative Shirt, Pants, or Hat was common enough to be a phenomenon on the tour. That public display of affection, that preemptive sentimentality pivoting on this exact moment, is what emo has instilled in the culture of punk fandom: advance nostalgia for the peak experience.

That's not to say that Warped can't offer genuine peak experiences, even to a twenty-seven-year-old like me. In San Diego, I cried watching Patty Schemel play drums. She's a strong hitter with perfect placement, but more than that she plays with such joy that I could feel it myself. Schemel used to drum for Hole, but she's now with Juliette & the Licks, a new band fronted by Juliette Lewis.

The audience at Warped, unlike a typical ground-level punk show, is about half women, maybe more. But in San Diego there were only seven women performing, spread across three bands. The Licks drew a screaming, girl-heavy crowd every time they played, though this was their first tour and they didn't even have a CD out yet. Between songs Lewis fell into a put-on honky-tonk drawl, yelling bons mots like "Aaawright!" and "This one is for the ladies!" and introducing the band at the top of her lungs ("This is my drummah, Patty Schemel!"). When I saw her, she was wearing a couture T-shirt, a bikini, knee pads, and fingerless gloves, and her makeup was running with sweat. She grabbed her crotch, humped the monitors, threw the horned hand at the crowd, and assumed several different yoga positions. She's like Andrew W.K.'s spirit in Joan Jett's clothes. She's lithe and tough, a real performer; judging by how she moves, she's spent much of her waking life with people staring at her.

In Los Angeles, I watched the Mean Reds deliver what would turn out to be the rawest set I'd see on the tour. The Mean Reds are from Tucson and barely a year out of high school. It was only the sixth day of the tour, and they were already on "probation" for running their mouths onstage about what a sold-out capitalist-pig enterprise Warped is, how it isn't really punk, et cetera. Warped founder and figurehead Kevin Lyman in turn advised the boys to do their homework before letting fly with the rhetoric: Did they think for a minute that he'd invited all those sponsors along for the ride for any other reason than to defray the tour's enormous expenses and keep ticket prices sane? (You might assume a band would give these questions some thought before committing to a couple months on the tour.)

The Mean Reds are off the Richter, bionically crazy, oblivious and obnoxious and out of control. They have all the fire of Nation of Ulysses, but instead of suits and manifestos, they have other people's Klonopin prescriptions and women's thrift-store blouses à la Bob Stinson. They look like scumbags who sleep in the desert. I'm not sure they have any idea what they're doing or how great it is. Halfway through their apocalyptic twenty-five-minute set, I told the guy who runs their label that Anthony Anzalone, the singer, reminded me of Darby Crash. The label guy said, "He has no idea who Darby Crash is." He also told me that the band had gotten into music by listening to Nirvana—and that they were recently the subject of a seven-label bidding war but refused all offers.

By the time Warped reached Minneapolis, a little more than three weeks later, the Mean Reds had been kicked off the tour. Their labelmates the Rolling Blackouts had gotten the boot after their singer pissed next to a stage while another band was playing, and Anzalone pissed his pants during a Mean Reds set in solidarity. The Mean Reds are more like the Warped audience than they know— confused, idealistic, angry, and furiously trying to slap the world awake and tell it who they think they are.

When I saw the band in L.A., Anzalone was filthy, his sweat making bright stripes in the layer of dirt caked to his skin—he'd made a vow that he wouldn't shower until the band was off the tour, which at the time was still supposed to mean another month and a half. He was shirtless, covered in cuts, and wearing swim trunks, boat shoes, and a wrinkled women's vest with gold anchors on it. He rolled in the grass in front of the stage, right under the yellow caution-tape barrier and into the crowd. The security staff watched with alarm as this yawping kid, pink-faced and exploding, writhed at our feet, humping the grass, grabbing ankles, and screaming, "Holla! Playa! Holla! Playa!"

Between songs, he contended with the Winterfresh gum camper-van thirty feet away, staffed by a chipper woman who leapt into the brief lulls in the Mean Reds' set to announce, via her large vehicle-mounted PA, that "fresh breath and fresh music go together!" Anzalone glanced hatefully at the truck and passed the mike, interviewing the girls in the front row: "What does punk rock mean to you? What is punk rock about for you?"

A Latinx fan no older than fifteen with red-streaked hair and matching red bands on her braces answered, "Punk rock is about being who you are and doing what you want." The rest of the small audience, mostly older punks and industry folks, clapped.

CHIEF KEEF, KING OF CHICAGO'S INSURGENT RAP SCENE

CHICAGO TRIBUNE, JULY 2012

Chief Keef does not want to talk to the *Tribune*. It's been rumored that the first piece of advice Kanye West gave the seventeen-year-old rapper was to stop doing interviews, and he has seemingly heeded Ye's word. Nonetheless, his management team pleads and cajoles. "The *Tribune* is bigger than the *RedEye*," says Peeda Pan, one of a fleet of managers who tends to Keef. "It's twelve or thirteen times bigger." Keef crosses his arms and purses his lips. "It's for the cover," explains Peeda Pan, punting. "Jay-Z has done the cover. Kanye's done it." With these references to name-brand rappers, it's hard to discern whether they're being dropped because that's who Keef is modeling his career after, or because he believes he merits similar star treatment. The young rapper shakes his head, almost imperceptibly, no. He is a petulant teen with a superstar's largesse.

It is 6:00 p.m. on Sunday, the final day of the sold-out Pitchfork festival and AraabMuzik is onstage making eighteen thousand people dance. Keef and his crew of sixteen (three managers, his publicist, recently signed rapper Lil

Reese, his sometimes-producer eighteen-year-old Young Chop, a bevy of friends) have just arrived. Keef and Reese are scheduled to make an unannounced two-song cameo appearance during AraabMuzik's set; this will be the biggest hometown audience they've ever played to. As is often customary in hip-hop, Keef and Reese's handlers have demanded payment in full before the two MCs grace the stage. This is not how things usually work at Pitchfork. *Pitchfork* founder Ryan Schreiber is pacing in tight circles, drawing hard on his cigarette and impatiently redialing his iPhone. The person with the money and the contracts is not picking up. For these two songs, Keef is rumored to be collecting his regular show fee of $10,000. According to Schreiber, even at that per-song rate, Keef isn't the most expensive act on the bill today. "Not even close," he says, smiling and shaking his head.

If you do not know who Chief Keef is, you will soon. Last month, the South Side–born Keith Cozart signed a record deal with Interscope Records. The deal also included his life rights for a biopic, his own line of headphones ("Beats by Keef"), and his own label to issue the records of other artists in his crew—effectively making him the youngest label head ever.

He became a phenomena via YouTube earlier this year with the low-budget video for "I Don't Like," a song chock full of bleak, misanthropic rhymes. It also features a few frames of the young rapper with a Glock in his grip, made all the more notable given that for the first half of the year he was on house arrest for a gun charge (he allegedly pointed a gun at a police officer).

Chief Keef is the prince of "murder-capital" Chicago rap, his insurgent popularity raising up the profiles of a dozen other local artists with him; a feat, given that it had been six years since the last Chicago rapper was signed to a major-label deal. Since February, nine acts have announced their signings, with a handful of others in the works. Some, like King Louie, have already put years into developing their career. Others, like Lil Reese, have been signed off the strength of a verse and proximity to Keef. The last rash of outside interest in Chicago hip-hop that even broached this current level was roughly fifteen years ago, when elder statesmen Do or Die and Twista were fresh prospects.

Suddenly, where there was once no ladder up to the national spotlight and modest evidence of the extant Chicago scene, there is a cottage industry of managers, labels, and burgeoning talent putting the city on the map in a real way.

For Larry Jackson, the executive VP of A&R at Interscope who signed Keef, his initial reaction was visceral: "It scared me. And I knew it was going to be huge. It felt disturbingly powerful. Nobody really talks about Top 40 music anymore because the music is like wallpaper—it doesn't make you feel anything. ["I Don't Like"] pushes people."

Jackson says that the reason they gave Keef his own label was in order to grab any other Chicago talent that comes bubbling up. "We did it to widen the net—so that anything that comes within fifty feet of Keef, we can catch it." The label has already inked deals with two MCs who are part of Keef's crew, GBE. Lil Reese and Lil Durk both recently signed to Def Jam; Lil Durk was released this week after serving two months for a weapons charge.

For Interscope and the other labels that were courting him, Chief Keef's legal woes just added credibility to his swaggering image. While part of the appeal of this new wave of Chicago rappers is just that—the newness of it—hip-hop fans are eager to hear the real stories of the street, songs that are a true-to-life reaction to what's happening in Chicago. Industry insiders insist that Keef's gun charge, for better or worse, adds authenticity to the biography he relates in his songs.

"You look at the news and see who is doing most of these killings—he fits that profile," explains Larry "Larro" Wilson, CEO of Lawless, the South Side record label that is home to King Louie and Katie Got Bandz. "Does it help that Keef is on house arrest? Absolutely."

For eighteen-year-old Tavares Taylor, who goes by the name Lil Reese, it all seems a bit unreal. He's known Keef since childhood and the two are still close; they have an air of brotherly collusion between them. Waiting backstage at Pitchfork, Reese's demeanor stands in stark contrast to Keef's; while no less a talent, he still seems like a kid, unaffected and wowed by the attention. Up until two days ago, he didn't know what Pitchfork was or that it was even a big deal until he retweeted their review of his new mixtape and saw they have nearly 2 million Twitter followers. Backstage, he is listless, he wants pizza before he hits the stage but doesn't know where to get it; his manager

J-Boogie presents him with the show contracts, which Reese signs atop a garbage can lid. The biggest difference between Keef and Reese seems to be that Reese didn't expect this fame.

For Reese, the main thing that has determined his life and music is also the same thing he most wants to communicate to the rest of Chicago and the world. "I never felt safe. Still don't." J-Boogie begins herding the dozen-plus teenage boys toward the stage: "It's time." Reese and Keef walk side by side in spotless head-to-toe white outfits, collars popped.

In these two young artists, Chicago has finally gotten the pop ambassadors it deserves; they are swaggering teenage wonders tapping into the zeitgeist like experts, telling their truth in blunt, steely lines. The first measure of "I Don't Like" booms and approximately eighteen thousand pairs of hands reach for the sky. The duo are met with screaming as they walk out from the wings. For the ten minutes they are onstage, they are magnetic, Keef's incandescent, and suddenly they are done. Walking offstage, he finally agrees to be interviewed. Asked how it feels to have just played to his biggest hometown audience yet, he replies without pausing, "This? This ain't shit."

HOW SELLING OUT SAVED
INDIE ROCK

BUZZFEED, NOVEMBER 2013

It's 2:00 p.m., the Friday before Christmas 2012, on the twenty-first floor of the Leo Burnett Building in downtown Chicago. Young executives, creatives, admins, and interns are all packed into a large meeting room, giddy and restless; today is special. Canadian sister duo Tegan and Sara step onto a foot-high stage and play three songs—including the first two singles from their seventh album, *Heartthrob*, which they will release the following month. The fluorescent lights stay on, the city's skyline splayed out behind them. Afterward, nearly all of the two-hundred-odd employees in attendance will stand in line, phone at the ready, to pose for pictures with the band, just like fans after any concert.

Tegan and Sara, who eventually cracked the Top 20 with *Heartthrob*'s "Closer," need to win over this audience just as they would at any concert. A track in the right commercial could bring about the kind of attention that magazine covers and radio play alone can no longer garner. Commercial placement, also known as a "sync," has evidenced itself as the last unimpeded pathway to our ears—what was once considered to be the lowest form of selling out is now regarded as a crucial cornerstone of success. And as ads have become a lifeline for bands in recent years, the stigma of doing them has all but eroded. But with desperate bands flooding the market, the money at stake has dropped precipitously. Even the life raft has a hole in it.

"A tiny sliver of bands are doing well," says the duo's Sara Quin. "The rest of us are just middle class, looking for a way to break through that glass ceiling. The second 'Closer' got Top 40 radio play, we were involved in meetings with radio and marketing people who said, 'The next step is getting a commercial.' I can see why some bands might find that grotesque, but it's part of the business now."

■ ■ ■

Fifteen years ago, the music industry was still a high-functioning behemoth pulling in $38 billion a year at its peak, able to ignore the digital revolution that was about to denude it entirely. Starting in 1999, sales of recorded music fell an average of 8 percent a year; 2012 was the first time since then that sales went up—0.3 percent. Last year, it reported $16.5 billion in global revenue. America accounted for $4.43 billion of that—approximately the same amount spent by AT&T, Chevy, McDonald's, and Geico on ad buys in the United States alone.

Back in the early nineties, when the music industry was thriving, commercials weren't a way indie bands got ahead—the punitive value outweighed the relatively small financial gains bands made for licensing a song to a commercial campaign. Band manager Howard Greynolds, who looks after the careers of Iron & Wine and Swell Season, was an employee at indie label Thrill Jockey when two of its flagship bands, Tortoise and Freakwater, each licensed a song for a 1995 CK One campaign.

"I remember people calling us saying, 'I can't fucking believe they did that, I can't support this band anymore!'" says Greynolds. "We were overly transparent then, we told people, 'Listen, this five thousand dollars bought them a van—*fuck off*.'" A few years later, another Thrill Jockey band, Trans Am, were outspoken about turning down a rumored $100,000 deal to license a song for a Hummer commercial. A generation ago, refusing these kinds of offers was a way for bands to telegraph where they stood, the sort of thing that showed their allegiance to underground values.

It's been nearly thirty years since Lou Reed hawked Honda scooters with "Walk on the Wild Side" and twenty-six since Nike used (and was summarily sued for using) the Beatles' "Revolution" to sell sneakers, but the diminishing of outrage has sped up over the last decade. Volkswagen used Nick Drake's "Pink Moon" and a half dozen Wilco songs, Apple placements are gold medals rather than albatrosses for relative newcomers like Feist and rock royalty like U2 alike, and no less an anti-commercialism scold than Pearl Jam got in bed with Target in 2009. Such moves are commonplace now.

Greynolds says what expedited this change wasn't just

the huge drop in record sales, but as layoffs swept through the record industry, contacts from labels and distributors went to marketing, advertising, and brands. "All of the sudden those were the people at music houses," says Grey-nolds. "People from your world. They might be feeding you a line of shit, but there was trust. They were different."

These new players within the advertising industry proved to be capable navigators of the ad world as well as the music underground. They could help forge lucrative connections between brands and cash-strapped bands—and their fan bases. Decades of posturing and sanctimony were rendered moot once artists realized that corporate gigs were the only paying gigs in town; they quickly became a justifiable evil.

Sitting in his not-quite-corner office, two floors below where Tegan and Sara played their lunchtime set, is one of the most important gatekeepers of these coveted career-making opportunities: thirty-eight-year-old Gabe McDonough, Leo Burnett's vice president of music. Within the music industry, some believe McDonough and execs like him now play the role once occupied by major-label A&R guys—the talent seekers whose attention can mean the difference between music being your living or your basement hobby. He handles everything from music supervision for commercials to pitching artists' tours for corporate sponsorships. His reputation was made early in his career for "breaking" Santigold with a Bud Light Lime spot and placing Brazilian pop oddities Os Mutantes in a McDonald's commercial—a spot that *Adweek* named one of the five best uses of music in a commercial ever.

That was five years ago. McDonough's pre-agency cred originated as bassist in Chicago indie-rock band Boas (most of the band went on to form Disappears), and he's seen as a savvy translator between the creative and corporate sides. His most recent coup was getting Lorde's "Royals"—her first sync—for a Samsung campaign.

McDonough is effusive and modest, reluctant to claim credit for even the things he is often credited for. Tacked on the wall above his desk is a small slip of paper with a Warren Buffett quote: "It takes twenty years to build a reputation and five minutes to ruin it." Dressed in an anorak and expensive jeans, he looks as if he's in a successful Britpop band. On his desk are a stack of cassette tapes from a producer at a Los Angeles music house and a spray-painted vintage Walkman—a promotional item from another.

"Selling records was how [artists] made money," says McDonough. "With that gone, it's just never going to be the same. It's certainly not something that licensing music is going to remedy." But artists, labels, and managers may beg to disagree: A one-year license for an existing song by a smaller band runs from $10,000–$25,000; an original composition can run $25,000–$30,000. A marquee-name band, for a year-long national campaign, could get $150,000 for existing work, or up to $300,000 for an original composition for a multi-year campaign. While licensing an album cut has the potential to break an album and make a career, thirty seconds of original music pays the same as months of intensive touring—and often anonymously.

"Five years ago, more bands said no, but even five years ago, no was the exception," says McDonough. "A band that turned me down five years ago just came in and played in our office last week." There are few bands that are no longer gettable; many are eager to take whatever money is on the table. Now when McDonough goes to a band with offers of whatever the client is interested in spending, "it's almost always yes."

McDonough insists that getting that perfect song into that right spot is a loose science at best. For a band that is teed up for such an opportunity—like Phoenix's breaking through a Cadillac commercial, or fun.'s "We Are Young" in a Chevy Super Bowl spot—it can mean significant sales and radio play, as well as fast-tracking them to the mainstream. It shows they are an even more viable partner for brands. McDonough explains that the synthesis, when a song gets people talking about a commercial, cannot be manufactured. "You can't talk someone into, 'Strategically, this is the right piece of music for this spot.' The first thing people want is something that makes their commercial look great."

Though licensing a song to an ad is lucrative for an artist, McDonough says that the benefits of this relationship are even more valuable for a client. "Eight out of ten of the most-followed people on Twitter are musicians. Nine out of ten of the most-viewed things on YouTube are music videos. What's the value of having [a musician tweet] about something to twenty million followers? That's more than a primetime ad buy on NBC you could spend gazillions on. And musicians are finally starting to realize that this is worth more than any song [they] could write. *That's* money."

For bands and artists seeking commercial dough, the point of entry into the ad-world fray can come through music houses like Black Iris, which are commissioned by ad agencies to compose songs for their clients' campaigns. While the vast majority of music houses are standard-issue "jingle houses" that may draw upon prerecorded libraries of music, there are approximately a dozen that posit themselves against the old stereotype. Comprising musicians who've come from bands in the independent music scene, they hire and/or license music from musicians who are from that same underground. Their stock is in being "music people" and their close associations—which cool scenes, producers, and artists they have a connection to.

Daron Hollowell started Black Iris with two friends from Richmond, Virginia, after the demise of his band, 400 Years. Hollowell, forty, spent the early '90s sweating it out in basement shows on the hardcore circuit. For him, the revelation of doing commercial work was what it offered artistically. "There's the idea of writing something beautiful that somebody may never hear or [that may never] see the light of day—I don't know if that's any better than the other side of the scenario." Hollowell says he still has personal music projects on the side, but, "I'm not sure I'd want to be in a band, put a record out every year and a half, and go on tour. I have freedom from that."

Black Iris—as well as enterprises such as Heavy Duty, which boasts HAIM and Vampire Weekend producer Ariel Rechtshaid as a partner, and staff writers with songwriting credits on nine songs on Sky Ferreira's just-released debut album—has a cool cachet with ad agencies because of its ties to certain artists with which it works closely. It can offer entry to certain scenes and sounds companies want to transact with; many of the music houses also have other creative sidelines, and for others, advertising work is the sideline. Black Iris has a singles label, White Iris; Hollowell admits to using this like a business card when meeting with ad creatives.

In a dark production suite in Black Iris's L.A. office, composer Rob Barbato is recording two demos for a commercial for a major national financial institution. An agency has commissioned original demos from Black Iris (and several other houses) for the spot. Barbato works quickly, switching between finessing a twee, acoustic pop track and a terse, synthetic one with a loop that mimics a boys' choir. After a few takes of whistling, his boss Hollowell pops his head in and interrupts—the singer they've hired for the spot is on her way over.

Prior to this, Barbato worked as a musician—first as a member of Darker My Love, later as Cass McCombs's sideman, and even doing a stint in the Fall. He went to Berklee College of Music, but instead of Barbato pursuing studio work like his classmates, Darker My Love got both a recording and a publishing deal. He quickly became uncomfortable, however, with the artistic compromises that were expected in exchange for advances the band was given. At twenty-three, living on the road was his dream; by the time thirty rolled around, he wanted stability that touring couldn't provide and began working as a freelancer for music supervisors Beta Petrol, before coming in-house at Black Iris last year.

"Everyone is constantly asking me about it," says Barbato of his musician friends, who are eager to commodify their songcraft at a higher rate than indie rock pays. He tries to help the ones who are genuinely interested whenever he can, but composing for commercials means being an engineer, a dexterous composer, and a multi-instrumentalist—it's not for everyone. Barbato, and every producer and music supervisor interviewed for this story, says the common misconception is that writing music for commercials is easy because it's only fifteen or thirty seconds of music, and musicians regard it as a lesser art.

Other underground musicians are just happy to dabble—playing or singing on a demo for a spot can bring one hundred to two hundred dollars—though some older musicians and those with a particular DIY credibility still insist on keeping their names off of it. Barbato has done spots with members of bands whose names would be familiar to anyone who's read *Pitchfork* in the last five years, who take pains to keep their corporate toil anonymous. Barbato understands that, but he's emphatic that to differentiate between commercial music and indie rock is to draw a line that does not exist; it's simply a matter of degrees.

"If someone in the independent-rock world thinks

that this is bullshit, they should take a look at themselves. They're doing the same thing; they're writing albums that people stream thirty seconds of on fucking *Pitchfork* and then people are like, 'Oh, I like your album.'"

The real difference between a preening, indie-rock band and a commercial composer is that Barbato is pulling down a low six-figure paycheck annually, and he still has the freedom to entertain purely creative pursuits like producing albums. Aside from his salary, Barbato gets royalties if his original composition makes it into a client's spot. When he was a freelance composer, if a spot made it into a national ad, he'd net a few thousand bucks—more than he ever made playing in successful bands. Some of Black Iris's core staff originated in the Richmond hardcore scene; almost all of its employees and freelancers—including members of Fool's Gold, Eric Pulido of Midlake, and Andy MacFarlane of the Twilight Sad—still play and tour in bands.

Barbato is setting up the studio to track vocals with a female singer, a known-name solo artist in indie rock. She's done demo work for Black Iris periodically and is looking to get back into it; she's broke until her album comes out this fall. (She asked not to be identified.) Though she is signed to a prestigious indie label with worldwide distribution, she's barely scraping by and has been saying yes to whatever opportunities arise. Today, it's harmonizing on a bank commercial for one hundred dollars while in Los Angeles to play Coachella.

She curls up on the black leather sofa in the control room and Barbato plays her the track a few times so she can pick up the melody. "So, kind of a Shins-y thing?" she asks. He nods. The song is sweet, pretty, California folk pop, with a little ukulele. If stretched to song length, it'd be getting raves from music sites for being so instantly memorable.

Barbato sets her up with a mic in the neighboring tracking room and the singer runs through her clarion aahs a few times until she nails it. Barbato gets a few takes and gives her the thumbs-up. They got it.

Lunch arrives, and Barbato, Hollowell, and the singer catch up over their salads. She's put her stuff in storage, she's trying to figure out what she's doing with her life and her career. She's tried her hand doing freelance composition for spots—the money for that work is better—but she admits she doesn't fully have the knack for it; composing often involves quickly revising a piece of music several times to meet a client's specifications. She is eager for session work like this, which is easier for her to fit into her schedule.

On her way out the door, the singer asks, "So, should I just invoice you, then?"

"Yeah," says Hollowell.

She flashes a big smile and reminds them of her availability for next week before she waves goodbye. Neither track would ultimately wind up being awarded the spot; the client ended up licensing a preexisting track from another artist.

Beta Petrol's founding partner Bryan Ray Turcotte is perhaps the ultimate poster child for outré artists seeking credit in the straight world. The small firm specializes in music supervision for film, TV, and commercials, and Turcotte is known to be one of the foremost punk collectors in the world, having amassed a stunning amount of memorabilia, art, and ephemera. On display in his office is a Cannes Lion he won for a Nike spot, as well as the original mold for Devo's flowerpot hats.

Turcotte is the author of punk-art tome *Fucked Up + Photocopied*, and the Beta Petrol office houses two employee-run labels—one issues vinyl only, the other cassettes. Turcotte's meeting immediately prior to this interview was with Gee Vaucher of British anarchist-punk heroes Crass about a series of exhibitions Turcotte is curating with Los Angeles's Museum of Contemporary Art. Beta Petrol's ad-world business is tangled in its creative endeavors, serving as the money hose for artistic pursuits. But Turcotte knows commercial work is the only lifeline some bands have and sees it as a way to help keep artists going for another album, another tour.

When Turcotte started out twelve years ago, many artists considered commercial work to be gauche, but a big part of the problem, says Turcotte, was the (corporate) messenger. "They don't know how to talk to DIY artists about what it means," he says. "It was just, 'We want your song in perpetuity.'" It was a natural place for Turcotte, a former musician, to serve as a go-between.

"It was an uphill battle. Some bands were not going to do it at all." Over time, Turcotte found bands that would. Then it was a matter of working the corporate side to finesse the licensing rights, whittling terms down to what was actually needed rather than blanket licenses. The next steps were unconventional work-arounds; Turcotte would often circumvent managers, publishers, and labels—people who had a piece of the artists' pie—in order to appeal directly to an artist about why the spot was right for them. (Turcotte once called Lou Reed at home about the use of two Velvet Underground songs; the ploy worked.) And all of this was fueled by a Robin Hood philosophy that is, in its own way, punk rock.

"I got into the business to put the money where it should be—in artists' hands," says Turcotte.

"It was more money than we made in a year," says Matt Johnson of Matt and Kim, a band born of Brooklyn house shows, explaining that their advertising windfall also gave them a mainstream career along the way.

Before that, the duo, who are a couple, were touring constantly and hovering around the poverty line. Though they had trepidation about what doing a commercial would mean, it was limited to fear of backlash from within the DIY scene of which they were a part. In 2008, they'd licensed "Yea Yeah" for a Virgin Mobile campaign; negative reaction was limited to a few Myspace comments. The following year, when Beta Petrol wanted their single "Daylight" for a Bacardi spot, the duo's initial impulse was to take the money and run.

"We thought, maybe no one would ever see the ad, or even recognize the song," says Johnson. The money would buy them a van, though it was enough to have bought them a house. They said yes, and quickly began to regard it as much of a Matt and Kim commercial as a Bacardi one. "I have a gold record for that song, and it wouldn't be here if it had never aired."

For some artists, taking a check from Bacardi, Pepsi, or Red Bull is an easier transaction than dealing with labels in that it's cut-and-dry—everyone knows what they're getting.

"What artists need are resources to make music, go on tour, make videos, grow their networks, and expand their audience," explains Adam Shore, who manages Best Coast, who have soundtracked commercials for Windows, Payless, and JCPenney (and recorded their debut album at Black Iris's studio). While bands need the same things they always have, record labels are at a loss for how to create revenue and provide reach. Larger deals (and larger advances) come at the expense of selling off an artist's rights to everything—publishing, merchandising, tour revenue.

Meanwhile, a commercial sync has more reach, nominal terms, and bigger paydays. If ad execs are the new A&R, then it only serves that brands are the new record labels, yet "brands can provide these better than labels ever could, at minimal cost and effort to them," says Shore. "Plus, they don't want to own your albums."

Turcotte explains it this way: "You can be very successful being a small band that has control of its destiny versus a bigger band that has to answer to a [record label]." Compared with record deals, which have become insidious and vast as labels seek greater dominion in order to profit, licensing a song for a beer commercial is practically free money. It's a choice at a time when options are rare. "When we started, you could control where your music was or wasn't," says Quin, "but now that feels impossible."

In recent years, as bands and managers have seen that ads can be a proven method of discovery for new artists, it's become much easier for Turcotte to get songs. "I'm seeing baby bands talk about advertising the way that baby bands used to talk about getting signed, which is very interesting to me," he says. "It's like the in-house music producers are the new A&R guys, and the bands want an ad, just the way they wanted a record deal. That's what they aspire to have. And that's something I could have never expected because I never thought that it would have that much power."

The evolution has also happened within the business itself. A song can put nuance to a brand identity; an artist's identity—what their art has made us believe about them and why—can be just as easily linked to a product. That has long been understood, but perhaps what has evolved since "Buy the World a Coke" went from soda-pop jingle to *Billboard* Top 10 pop single is just how much meaning a band, a song, and their fan base can impart in this cosigning.

Johnson admits that while syncs are how Matt and Kim make their living now, he is mindful of corporate credibility—the duo recently turned down a spot for a breakfast product (the spot ran with a song composed to sound nearly identical) as well as spots that a friend's band later said yes to. What won't they do? "Yogurt," says Johnson. "Cheesy commercials with the mom—it's not artistic. We'd have a hard time keeping our edge as a band."

Almost a year after Tegan and Sara played their Leo Burnett lunchroom gig, they've finally landed their first national spot—stemming from a different agency gig they did this past summer, placing "Shock to Your System" in a JBL campaign that begins in November. Some within their promotions team are worried that after all this effort, a commercial spot that introduces an album track won't be the thing that seals the deal. Says Quin, "If people can't connect that song to you—your name, your face—then it's all for naught."

Still, McDonough is emphatic that even a saturated market is better than nearly any option an artist could have: "Ads are not the answer; it's just a piece of the puzzle." Now that so many bands are trying to get their piece of it, the value on sync licenses have come down. "*Way* down," he clarifies. The trend is away from original compositions and toward existing tracks, which are always cheaper. "Two decades ago, there was crazy money," McDonough says. "The money now is not life-changing for anyone."

For all the freedom and choices an infusion of ad money can provide, or the signal boost a well-placed spot can provide, it comes at a cost. Success can change things, just as sure as a platinum record once did, and access to lump sums can affect which direction a band is facing as a corporate client becomes the only paying audience they have.

While advertising cannot save or replace the music industry, there is one undeniable fact, says McDonough: "These big companies are the last people paying musicians what they are worth."

NOT LOLLAPALOOZA

Rollin Hunt, Screaming Females, and Abe Vigoda

CHICAGO READER, AUGUST 2007

This weekend the throngs will decamp for Lollapalooza to experience a vertiginous array of mediocre-to-terrible bands (and a couple good ones) in the company of tens of thousands of half-drunk strangers. Seeing a show outside in the Chicago summer dusk is a welcome reprieve from standing around in a smoky club, but the idea that mega-festivals somehow create ad hoc communities out of their mega-crowds—an idea likely owed to Woodstock—is ridiculous. The only thing everybody at Lollapalooza has in common is the willingness to be painfully gouged for a ticket. Even crowds that might seem a bit more like-minded (say, at Pitchfork) make for a grim and dystopian scene: mini mountains of litter, security guards, sunbaked Porta-Johns. And when you see bands from hundreds of feet away, they seem unreal—specks on the horizon, or larger-than-life cartoons rendered in Jumbotron pixels and playing hard to the cameras.

As much as I love being able to eat funnel cake and

watch M.I.A. at the same time, it can't make up for all the things about festivals that are fundamentally wack. This summer I've made it my mission to forsake the colossus for basement shows, hoping to find exciting new bands and join their tiny fan base.

The first time I saw local songwriter Rollin Hunt, he was wowing a crowd of a dozen or so at Ronny's, trembling before the mic with his eyelids squeezed shut. "Wow. He's really special," I whispered to my friend. "Yes," she said. "Very." Hunt was in the middle of a song about going out for a walk and spying on a couple getting hot and heavy in their bedroom. And antelopes.

Onstage, Hunt is terminally shy, like he's cowering from his own voice—it seems like he's used to doing this sort of thing in private. His small, crackly vocals and the songs' ramshackle instrumentation constantly get away from each other. For me, the mystery of Rollin Hunt is whether he's oblivious to how wide off the mark he's gone. Is he on this strange path by conscious choice, or did he simply pursue his love for the Beach Boys and '60s girl groups and just happen to produce his savant-garde doo-wop? His work is so beautifully awkward that it's hard to believe it's all part of a deliberately crafted persona.

Hunt's self-released ten-song demo, *Dearly Honorable Listener*, is closer to outsider art than lo-fi indie rock. It's a marvel of rawness, recorded so poorly that you have to turn your stereo almost all the way up to hear what's going on—you get about 60 percent background hiss and 40 percent music. Live, Hunt is often accompanied by a shambling little backup band, but on disc it's just him, his not-quite-in-tune guitar, and sometimes a drum machine. (At least I think it's a drum machine—often it sounds like someone throwing rocks into a bucket.) The songs begin and end in strange places, like he either ran out of tape or started playing without telling whoever was supposed to press the record button. He has a hard time keeping up with the drum machine, which sometimes drops in jarringly in the middle of a verse, and he multitracks vocal harmonies through what sounds like a baby monitor.

Hunt's ambition as a performer nearly destroys his sweet, fragile little tunes, mostly because it completely outstrips his basic competence, but they end up amazing anyway. His lyrics are crowded with small scenes and unpredictable tangents: one song is about "juice in the air," another about "George who runs the Holiday Inn." His genius turn is "Pamphlet," where he proposes a solution to his relationship problems in a romantic ditty that sounds like a cross between early Smog and a truly touched Frankie Lymon: "I need to make you / A pamphlet / That tells you everything you need to know / About my feelings." It's clunky, unpolished, and intimate, and that's what gives it its magic.

When Screaming Females hit Ronny's in mid-July, they had a paying crowd of six. I'm not counting the people in the other band or the sound guy, who was playing *Tetris* on his cell phone. They were halfway through a two-and-a-half-month U.S. tour with stops at plenty of basements and punk spaces—a few days earlier they'd played a house show in Elgin. But though these three under-twenty kids from New Jersey are almost entirely unknown, word is spreading fast. Front woman Marissa Paternoster is the teenage girl-guitarist messiah, and miracles and conversions come with the territory; show by show, she's turning the uninitiated, myself included, into true believers.

We may be witnessing the dawn of a new age of femme shredders (Marnie Stern, Aimée Argote of Des Ark), but Paternoster isn't waiting around to see if anyone else is following her. On a defiant, punk-fast version of Neil Young's "Cortez the Killer," she carved into the song until practically the whole thing was a solo. Screaming Females have just self-released their second album, *What If Someone Is Watching Their T.V.?*, and it can match any (decent) Dinosaur Jr. record, pound for pound, in teen malaise and ripping solos. Paternoster's got some blues boogie in her riffing, a little Billy Gibbons in her muscular punk. She's a deft songwriter, but she doesn't like to let more than a minute or two go by without stepping on a stomp box and firing one off. She ended the set in a cloud of screeching feedback, hunched over her guitar and pounding on her pedals with her fists. I don't think anything like her has happened to punk before, and I'm glad it finally has.

Two weeks ago, the posi-kidcore band Abe Vigoda brought L.A.'s Evolution Summer scene to a pair of Chicago basements: the first night, they shimmified nineteen stinky kids and a beer-drunk dog at a party in Pilsen, and the second, they did a last-minute set at People Projects as the token dudes at a Ladyfest benefit, playing for maybe twenty people, half of them festival volunteers. In Pilsen, they kept it short and sweet, with six songs in less than fifteen minutes: "We've gotta make it quick before the cops show back up," explained guitarist/chatterbox Juan Velazquez. The PA kept feeding back and you couldn't hear the singing, so the band turned off the mics and just shouted along; none of us really knew how the songs went anyway, and everyone was too busy dancing to care.

The B-side of Abe Vigoda's recent "Animal Ghosts" seven-inch, "All Night and Day," hasn't left my turntable since I dropped it on. Their tribal thunk and sideways funk make for a kind of dance punk nobody else has dreamed up yet. Full of jostling guitars that manage to be both precise and playful, their sound has a kind of cloistered innocence—it knows nothing of disco. Calypso would be more like it, given the deep love these guys have for the woodblock. Abe Vigoda's antecedents are hard for me to pin down: maybe dub, maybe New Zealand pop, maybe some band they hang out with in Chino that I don't know about. No matter how you slice it, their show is a cynicism-destroying good time.

Fans are supposed to believe that they're enjoying some sort of meaningful collective experience at a big festival, with modern rock blaring from a bank of speakers the size of a condo complex. But such a grand scale actually tends to dissolve community—the anonymity and impersonality of an enormous event sometimes even encourages people to act shittier than they otherwise would, since they don't feel accountable to anyone around them. At a basement show, though, where the bands aren't whisked to the stage by golf carts to make a thousand dollars a minute, people are gonna get pissed if you leave your chewed-up corn cobs and beer cups lying around. You can smell the band. You can give them seven bucks for a T-shirt and know that the money is going to get them a tenth of the way to Iowa City. In the basement, you can feel the band's humanity as well as your own.

PART VII

DESIRE,
POWER,
PLEASURE

LIZ PHAIR, *EXILE IN GUYVILLE,* EXPANDED REISSUE

ROLLING STONE, MAY 2018

Before I ever heard Liz Phair, I heard about Liz Phair. The Midwestern indie-rock gossip train had traveled from Chicago, her hometown, to the Minneapolis record store where I worked, in high school, weeks before an advance copy of her 1993 debut, *Exile in Guyville,* did. Listening to the men I worked with call her an amateur and a slut because she'd written a song called "Fuck and Run" and reportedly appeared topless on her album cover taught me a crucial early lesson: the men who run this scene will hate your ambition either way, so you might as well just do whatever you want.

It's hard to overstate what *Guyville* meant at the time. Today, echoes of its direct, finessed, feminist interiority can be heard in similar work by young artists like Mitski, Phoebe Bridgers, St. Vincent, Snail Mail, and others. In 1993, Phair was at the vanguard. Her double-album *debut* was audacious; her clear-eyed and candid presentation of her own sexuality and gendered experience of the music scene even more so. Musically, its versatility showed Phair as an auteur with the creative vision and chops to back up her ambitions. *Guyville* was styled and dynamic from start to finish, from the single "Never Said," a wry anti-kiss-'n'-tell anthem with a soaring, multitracked harmonic "I," to the more subtle, but no less complex, "Stratford-on-Guy," where Phair sings about flying over Chicago, imagining a cinematic upgrade of her life, pretending she's in a Galaxie 500 video. The subject matter was certainly striking, but the bigger deal was her double album of flawless songcraft.

Guyville's lyrics presented a woman in love with who she was and was becoming, making her secret dialogues—and her internal ones—visible in a space where most often only white, cis-heterosexual men's voices counted and endured. The impact was tangible, massive, and, to an extent, disoriented the independent music scene. Phair became the first female artist in nineteen years to claim the number one spot on the *Village Voice* critics poll. Alongside Green Day and Nirvana, she was one of the principal acts to clear a path from the underground to the mainstream in the first half of the nineties. Now, twenty-five years later, Phair is back, touring behind a new deluxe edition of *Guyville*, and being feted with nearly as much media attention as she commanded upon its original release.

■ ■ ■

In 1993, even as riot grrrl bands like Bikini Kill were shaking up the punk scene, *Guyville* felt like a bomb drop. A season of rhapsodical zine mentions for Phair's elusive, stripped-down Girly-Sound bootleg demo cassettes (all included in this reissue) preceded the release of *Guyville*, which she claimed was an answer-back to the Rolling Stones' 1972 monolith, *Exile on Main St.* Phair's debut arrived fully fleshed; it was a winking bit of rock 'n' roll subterfuge clad in sui generis melodic invention. If this was her answer to *Exile*, then, as Robert Christgau once suggested in a review of Prince's *Dirty Mind*, "Mick Jagger should fold up his penis and go home."

From the opening rush of "6'1"," the album came on like regular indie rock. Yet over the course of *Guyville*, Phair indexed the psychic price of being a get-along girl in a rock scene historically dominated by men. Her songs were full of inside observations that made clear she was keenly aware of how she was seen, that her ingress into this hallowed guy space transacted on her charming silence, her smile, her good looks, her obedience. "I sing like a good canary," she sang. In interviews, Phair would explain that Guyville is anywhere people are pushed to the margins: "Guyville is everywhere." The call was coming from inside the house.

Phair's relationship with indie rock was much like the relationship with men she depicted in her songs: they knew, but she knew better.

Producer Brad Wood worked to create a sound that was distinctive and wholly her own, identifiable from the first chord. Phair's plain alto ranged from crystalline to a little hungover, her delivery conversational, often sounding like she was smiling when she sang. Her strummy-guitar-driven sonic lineage went back to the

Feelies, with the occasional experiment like "Canary," where a discreet personal history of obeisance unravels over a treated piano, overwhelmed in sustain, an inkling of the psychedelic space she'd pursue on *Guyville*'s 1994 follow-up, *Whip-Smart*. It was unfancy and sonically familiar, and yet because of its gendered grievances, musical polish, and the powerful persona at its center, it was unlike anything we'd ever seen.

■ ■ ■

The woman Phair presents on *Guyville* is one with nothing to lose. She's exhausted by the ambient sexism that surrounds and mutes her ("I practice all my moves / I memorize their stupid rules," she sings on "Help Me Mary"). She examines her assigned place in the social hierarchies of the post-collegiate rock world, rife with intimate indignities and public negation. Her only reasonable mode of recourse was to blow up her spot rather than play along with underestimations of her capacity, talent, intellect, and desire. Though it's worth noting that for a pretty, well-educated white woman, her risk was relative.

While songs like "Never Said," "Mesmerizing," and "Help Me Mary" laid bare what these boys' cool rules and confidence masked, they are incidental characters; Phair was her own muse, *Guyville*'s self-possessed center ("I loved my life and hated you," she sings on "6'1""). Phair's "I" is far more central than any "he" or "we" (she strikes first-person approximately 150 times over the course of eighteen songs). She isn't dazzled by their conception or construction of power, she's driving headlong into her own. And just as Joni Mitchell's *Blue* or Jackson Browne's *Late for the Sky* had done for a generation of songwriters in the '70s, *Guyville* further permitted songs to feel at once direct and interior. It demanded that its listeners interrogate their assumptions about what young women truly desire and *really* think about.

Like Mitchell, Phair was miscategorized as "confessional"—as if the work tumbled out, unfiltered, from a sentimental diary page. Yet *Guyville* is nothing if not a calculating work created with acute knowledge of the audience it was destined for. The woman (or women) Phair illustrates so intimately made the songs relatable and accessible. Maybe you'd never been a Midwestern good bad-girl, or some man's blond mirage, but anyone knows what it means to long for others, to dream of self-actualization. Liz Phair treated girl life as intrinsically interesting and complex source material. *It was.*

Guyville's candor and sexuality, heard most strikingly on "Fuck and Run" and "Flower," were seized upon and sensationalized by the press. As Phair admits in recent interviews, *"How could they not?"* In the early nineties, indie rock's relationship to eroticism, pleasure, and bodies wasn't just ironically distant, it was estranged and utterly fuckless. Phair's Matador labelmates Pavement were doling out lines like "My eyes stick to all the shiny robes / You wear on the protein delta strip"; Jesus Lizard frontman David Yow routinely did "dick tricks" mid-set; Jon Spencer's Elvisian swagger was what passed as panty-moistening sexual charisma. And then, suddenly, here's Phair, landing hard emphasis on the *t* in "cunt" in "Dance of the Seven Veils," only to chime sweetly, "You can rent me by the hour." Sure, Sonic Youth's Kim Gordon had played out similar narratives, but there's a galactic expanse between her "Kiss-ability" and Phair leveling "everything you ever wanted / Everything you ever thought of is / Everything I'll do to you / I'll fuck you and your minions too," like a threat. This was the real *Songs About Fucking*.

That realism was doubly new because Phair didn't entirely fit previous images of rock sexuality. The thing about archetypical "bad girls" in punk and indie rock, until Phair, was that you could usually see them coming. They were fantastically tough, reckless, and a little scary, witchy with foghorn voices—Lydia Lunch, Courtney Love, and Kathleen Hanna are the prime examples from that era. Phair looked scrubbed and collegiate, flashing a big smile as she gazed up from her guitar in a posed Polaroid in *Guyville*'s inside sleeve art; on the cover, she was baring teeth and a tit. The images posited something gloriously confounding, as if to say, "I am both, I am everything, maybe I'm any girl you know."

There's no question that the sustained power and musical potency of *Guyville* merit another deluxe, anniversary-pegged reissue, but this is the first to unearth all three of Phair's pre-*Guyville* Girly-Sound tapes, which she recorded in 1991. The earliest are bedroom demos in the truest sense, her voice quiet so as not to disturb her roommates; it's occasionally overpowered by her guitar. Recognizable stylistic themes soon affix themselves—overconfident, aging men as a stand-in for America, class, her adoption, men who want things she doesn't want to give. It's no surprise, given how developed *Guyville* is for a debut, that Phair's playful arrangements and lyrical incision were there from the jump. Her voice expands from singsong to confident as she figures out just what it can do. Some of the demo songs routinely run to the five-minute mark; Phair sounds like she has a lot to say and is eager for her creation to hit the tape. When she jumped to the polished, produced work of *Guyville* and buried the lo-fi amateurism, it was hardly a stretch; she'd simply grown into her ambition.

Due to Phair's songwriting and enduring cultural salience, and Wood's production, the album has aged better than the work of her peers. Phair was initially derided for being too pop, but that's what gives *Guyville* both timelessness and grace. There was a generation of bands born at the same time as *Guyville* who took Slint's 1991 epic "Good Morning, Captain" as their grail; they were mostly Midwestern boys who made long, primarily instrumental songs and veiled their emotions in nautical metaphors. Precision and heroic virtuosity were exalted above all else, but it was important not to seem like you were trying too hard. When *Guyville* came home to roost, it became clear that while these dudes had been down at the Rainbo Club arguing about La Monte Young records in the bar light, Phair had been holed up, putting in work on a record that would outlast their collective careers.

Which is to say *Guyville*'s most withering indictment

of the indie rock scene isn't Phair's sizing up of these men's faulty self-conception or their fuck-and-run propensity, but what she calls out on "Help Me Mary" when she offers an interventionist prayer: "Weave my disgust into fame / And watch how fast they run to the flame." Decades from *Exile in Guyville*'s initial rapturous critical reception, the list of men who claim (or have been assigned) linchpin status in Phair's artistic development has only grown; the sundry oral histories of the album are packed with men, elbowing forward to claim, "It was I" who loaned her that guitar, booked her on that bill, or noticed a potential she, naturally, wasn't even sure of herself. This box set deadens those dubious claims, underscoring what fans already knew: *it was all her, all along.* Its gift is letting us hear a great artist become forged, and become herself, song by song.

CAT POWER IS DOING JUST FINE

THE CUT, OCTOBER 2018

When I told some journalist friends that I was going to interview Chan Marshall, both their immediate reactions were the same: *"Is she okay?"*

Since Marshall first launched herself into collective consciousness with her 1996 album *What Would the Community Think*, speculative diagnosis of her mental health has seemingly become a pastime for her fans, critics, and detractors alike. Marshall is presumed "okay" if she's satisfactorily performing the part of indie rock icon, soberly upholding the social contract between audience and artist. She is presumed "okay" if the pain and vulnerability she exhibits onstage remain entertaining and not difficult to identify with. If she's discreet about her issues with health or sobriety, she is "okay." If she has canceled a tour to take care of her mental or physical health, as she has done after releasing 2006's *The Greatest*, and *Sun* in 2012, she is "not okay"; if she has rambled and gambled the audience's patience at her shows, she is "not okay"; if she is curt or lax about her boundaries in interviews, she is "not okay." All this gestures toward concern for

Marshall, but it's ultimately predicated on just how good a show pony she can be. Marshall is a singularly gifted American artist, whose work powerfully communicates grief and disillusionment, work she is celebrated for unless her darkness gets, well, *too dark*.

Given all of this, it's unsurprising how often Cat Power songs lament, as does her new single, "Woman," *you think you know me but you don't*.

■ ■ ■

It's a rainy early September afternoon and Marshall is back in New York for a few days to promote *Wanderer*, her tenth studio album as Cat Power. *How okay is she?* When showing me to the bathroom of her Lower East Side pied-à-terre, she gave me a tour of the closet-sized facilities, offered me an array of hand towels (one is hers, the other her roommate's), and pressed a fresh bar of soap to the sinktop, announcing, "And here you go" with the peach-sweet instructional charm of a stewardess. Before our interview, she showed me pictures of her toddler son, Boaz, on a playground near their home in Miami, the fronds of distant palms ringing his towhead like a halo, her smile huge. Marshall vapes, speaks her mind freely, if somewhat elliptically, and uses eye contact like punctuation to underscore her point. She offers me more water with the regularity and solicitousness of a great waitress. She's a confident and charming grown-ass woman of forty-six, and if her okayness was any of my business at all, I'd say she's perfectly goddamn fine.

"There are streets that I don't walk down anymore."
Marshall is sitting on her quilt-covered daybed, leaning
toward her open bedroom window as she exhales cigarette smoke, waving it out with her hand like a bad teen
hoping not to get busted. "There's nothing for me there
anymore." Marshall has maintained this room in her
friend's rent-controlled apartment for more than twenty
years, since she was a young artist fresh up from Georgia,
subsisting on odd jobs and $1.80 breakfasts (with coffee)
from First and First Cafe. She credits the cheap rent as
what allowed her to foster her career and has never given
it up, though she's lived full-time in Miami for the last
few years. The room is like a cool-girl museum piece:
crocheted lace curtains, a bust of a Native American
chief, repurposed glass perfume decanters, faded framed
Polaroids of a lost love, books on Buddhism and love,
naive art on the wall, Fender amps, and feathers. Yet there
are small, augmenting clues of another life—her son's
Clifford the Big Red Dog books haphazardly stuffed
between two vintage Silvertone guitars. Rearranging the
plush velvet pillows behind me, I locate what's poking
me—a figurine Woody from *Toy Story* that also belongs
to Boaz.

As evidence of New York's continual change, sure,
there's "Starbucks covering some cool eighteenth-century
shit," but most everything has transformed now, Marshall
insists. "There are friends that aren't around anymore.
Ludlow Street is gone. The bag of peanuts that I'd give to
the squirrels, that were always in the bodegas—the bag of
peanuts aren't there anymore, only sour worms candy."

Marshall lets out a little laugh, half mocking her own wistful nostalgia for a Manhattan lost in the upgrade. "I got a waffle from Veselka, and took my boy to Tompkins Park, [the squirrels] just didn't want that waffle." She's careful to qualify her nostalgia. "I don't go back to the past too much, 'cause there's always so much growth to people's lives," but it's clear she's talking about her own as much as anyone she ran with back in the day.

Marshall has been labeled "a survivor" on each successive Cat Power album since approximately 2006; multiple tours have been called comebacks. Her album releases have tended to follow or coincide with personal cataclysm—breakups, hospitalizations (*Sun*, *The Greatest*), dark spiritual visitations (*Moon Pix*). The travails of releasing *Wanderer* are as totemic to Marshall's cast-iron will and righteous artist instinct as anything on the album itself. Her previous album, *Sun*, debuted at number ten on the *Billboard* charts—a first for Marshall—but that day she was in intensive care, by her own account "fighting to stay alive," one of several hospitalizations before she would be diagnosed with an autoimmune disorder that year. The success at hand didn't even register until months later, says Marshall; she'd canceled the European tour in order to recuperate, but was back on the road soon enough, and felt the pressure to make her record the hit that she says her label, Matador, was pushing her to deliver. "They had said that I needed a top producer, famous band. And I chose to become very stubborn and did everything myself," she explains. "I did my very best, I worked so hard on it. I was so proud of it. I was so happy with everything I had created, and out of thin air." Marshall still carries the sting from discovering, months after the fact, that upon hearing she was hospitalized they pulled all the marketing on *Sun*, which the label denies. "They weren't betting on the horse to win." She says she fundamentally misunderstood the transactional nature of her connection to the label as something close to kin. "Just because somebody told me I was their family, I didn't need to believe them. It was business to them, and they knew it was business. But I didn't."

Keeping up appearances of "okay" decimated Marshall's health. "I was on tour for a year and a half with [*Sun*], and was still sick all the time, and hiding it. And just thought, 'Well, if I'm going to die anyway, why am I singing? What is this fucking doing?'" By September 2013 she was exhausted, deeply inspired by the Occupy movement yet disenfranchised from her own work, and isolated by the trauma of a near-death experience and chronic illness. "I felt so invisible. I felt like I maybe had died. Not physically died, but the Cat Power thing. Like myself, as an artist. I felt like I had died. It was as if I didn't know this person I was now, because I had gone through something life-changing. I was on slate one. I was on page one, and I felt invisible, because I had no idea." And that is when Marshall discovered she was pregnant. "Instantly I knew exactly what I had to do. Instantly I understood that now it's time to play the protection ball game, and no one fucking wins this game but me," Marshall explains. "I moved back to Miami. I found a house for rent. I got all my fucking music gear out of storage." She toured until she was seven months pregnant, came home, baby-proofed her new house and set up a home studio at the same time. Her recording engineer moved from France into the spare room. "I had my child. Went on tour when he was two months old. When he was three months old, I started working."

The trad storyline is that motherhood *remakes* a woman, and more particularly if she's an artist. It's an archetype culture is hungry for: babies tempering one's selfish practice of art is taken as proof against any ambivalence toward motherhood. The demands of art-making are not seen as aligning with motherhood, for motherhood is defined as an all-consuming act of sacrifice, and art-making as a fundamentally selfish pursuit. As Adrienne Rich wrote, the suffering of the mother is the primary way culture identifies a woman as a mother. Marshall, a single mom who tours with both her toddler son and a traveling nanny in tow, is having none of that. For Marshall, the difficulties of parenthood are relative. "He has my great-grandmother's first name [as his last name]—Sarah. I thought of her all the time—cotton-picker, alone with five kids, with no electricity." On the album's cover, she holds both Boaz and her guitar close to her against a barren desert background. While her son's place is important, she resents the idea that his arrival rearranged her artistic DNA. "The question is usually, 'How has your son changed your songwriting, and changed you as an artist?' He hasn't changed my songwriting; as an artist, he hasn't changed me. But as a human being, he's fortified something."

For all the dynamics of her Cat Power career arc, one could miss the real throughline of it—the power in Marshall's vulnerability, the sheer tenacity and force of will that has powered her work, a twenty-five-year career defined by her fortitude. With *Wanderer*, there is really no missing it—the album is a testimony to her autonomy and confidence. The album is as to-the-bone as anything she's ever made; *Wanderer* is Cat Power distilled, an unadorned, few-fucks-given essence. Marshall's soft Georgia drawl has grown a little huskier and raspier, but her familiar themes—of god's grace, American might, familial bond, nights both good and bad, odes to cool girls, romantic disillusion, the desire to stay/leave—remain. "Woman" feels like a dare—"I'm a woman of my word / Or haven't you heard / My word's the only thing I've ever needed," she sings, and calls her cage her weapon. The song ends like a mantra, with Marshall duetting with Lana Del Rey, their voices entwined in incantation, "Immawoman / Immawoman / Imma wo-o-oman." Marshall sounds like a woman who is sure of all that she is, with little pity for those who can't grasp her depth or power.

Over the course of a year, in between Cat Power tours, while Marshall put the elegiac folk-blues of *Wanderer* to tape in Miami and then L.A., she says her life and purpose became clarified by a sense of mission: "This new life, these new songs, I'm going to protect them. I'm not going to fight anymore with [Matador]. I'm going to make whatever comes to me, and that's that, and that is art. I have to trust art because *I'm here*. I was so with my own child, and my own fucking songs, that I wasn't going to let any outside influence in. Just to make art! That's all." Then, days after she delivered the record to

Matador, her home for seven albums and twenty years, they rejected the album and Marshall was suddenly and unexpectedly on her own.

The rejection galvanized her. "The seventy-year-old me, who I have yet to meet, was like, 'You ain't got no time for this shit. *You fucking fuck those motherfuckers.* You got your kid here. Keep working, do what you do. Life will continue. You're going to be okay,'" Marshall explains. Despite all the evidence of just how much her music mattered—her fan base, her awards, collaborations with legends like Teenie Hodges, being the face of Chanel, raising substantial funds for causes she cared deeply about—Marshall wrestled with doubt, wondering if this tumult was all the result of failings of her art. She mapped out an ever-after that didn't involve her being an internationally acclaimed independent artist. "I'm an amazing waitress. I can cook really well. I'm good at cleaning house. I know how to do shit with my hands." Marshall laughs and shrugs. "When you become a parent, those kinds of thoughts are more normalized in your thinking pattern because you have a little child that you need to provide for." The "bitchy" arguments of her seventy-year-old self won out, and Marshall pushed on with *Wanderer*.

Amid Marshall's nimbus cloud of doubt came an unexpected break from a longtime fan, Lana Del Rey. In the wake of Del Rey's 2017 album, *Lust for Life*, she thanked Marshall and publicly held up Cat Power as an influential template for her own work; she also invited Marshall as support on her European tour. The two bonded over long evenings talking about their lives, their romances and friendships with men, their fathers. "Us having these conversations, I was like, 'Dude, do you want to sing on this song with me?'" Marshall said. The song was "Woman," which would become the lead single for Cat Power's debut album for Domino Records. "Woman" was a song Marshall had been working on and struggling with since her first session for *Wanderer*, but it didn't feel quite right to her and she'd left it off the version of the album she'd presented to both Matador and her new label, Domino. Del Rey's camaraderie and conversation made Marshall realize what the song needed was another woman's voice to change its bearings. "Lana is singing with me, loaning her credibility as a female who sings about darkness. It's not sad Cat Power singing about her experience of being a woman. It's *we are multidimensional beings*," says Marshall as she works the ashy smudges of eyeliner off her fingertips, rubbing them on her navy jumpsuit. "All these other projections that had been on me from the press, the ex-label . . . Having another female opened the door for the listener to understand that I wasn't alone in it. The subject wasn't *me*, it was *us*."

BODY/HEAD, *COMING APART*

SPIN, SEPTEMBER 2013

Kim Gordon is getting the last word. As each member of Sonic Youth has gone solo successively since the band's shocking 2011 breakdown, we've gotten a dissonant postmortem, a better understanding of how the quartet's parts made the whole. So *Coming Apart*, her debut double-album, with guitarist Bill Nace, as Body/Head, feels like a glorious revelation of her strengths: it makes clear she was the *soul* of Sonic Youth, now standing free in sharp relief against that body of work, reframing what everyone thought they knew about the band.

It's hard not to view *Coming Apart* through the prism of Gordon's transformation these past two years: after decades of seemingly ceding the spotlight to former husband and bandmate Thurston Moore, a recent *New Yorker* profile recasts her as an empty-nesting cool mom with a chicken in her oven, Tim Riggins in her head, hip-hop on her stereo, and a philandering ex in her past. Refusing to bear the myth of her union any longer, the sanctity since spent, Gordon spoke freely of Moore's infidelity; he posted "Get Over It," seemingly in response, on his new band Chelsea Light Moving's Facebook page. Everything falls apart. Their marriage was special; their divorce seemingly was not. She spoke of figuring out who she was now, outside of this band and marriage that defined her, outside of the daily duties of motherhood, returning to her art.

Perhaps this explains why much of *Coming Apart* is about women's traditional roles—their duty, their identity. Gordon sings of the murderess, the mistress, the actress, the "good little housewife" who beckons us to her sofa and asks, "Do you want ice?" The songs are threaded with desperation and desire, detailing their service of and proximity to men's power—both the possession and loss of it. Gordon's Sonic Youth work often had a corporeal focus, approaching a woman's body as contested land ("Swimsuit Issue," "Tunic"); here, the songs combine external narratives—a woman using her body in the world, where she accrues value through men's desire or ministrations—with internal strife. We get private reflections of soft gazes, drifting bodies, lifted legs, offered hands, the desire to remain whole. "I don't want anything," she sings on "Actress"; "I want to touch," she intones on "Frontal." It's an album of connection and disconnection—between the body and the mind, and between the body and the world.

Nace fits seamlessly into this feminine cosmos. Gordon has aptly described him as having "girl energy," which makes him the perfect squalling accompaniment to the heavy themes. Kim has suggested that SY fans will be disappointed by Body/Head, but she's wrong: the duo crafts careening noise and jutting, sensual drones, and while they riff on pop forms, they're free of verse and chorus structures. The album itself feels improvisational, but not loose; recorded live, it features very few edits or overdubs. Nace has the same ecclesiastical regard for Merzbow as Gordon's previous musical partners, but the duo's symbiosis is distinct here, the way Nace undergirds and reacts. Their guitar dialogue sounds colloquial, intuitive.

This is mostly Gordon's show, of course, though occasionally Nace dominates, filling every bit of space with guitar-howl. Other times, Nace contributes a single showy bit, like when he launches a pack of feedback fireworks on "Can't Help You," while Gordon coos a punk redraft of Van Morrison's "Astral Weeks": "Take my hand / Take it to the boss sea . . . lay down easy." To be born again? Maybe. *Coming Apart* seems bent on a kind of transcendence, an act that changes how one orients themselves in the world. On "Actress," she sings of an eager character who wonders, "That dress / Will it make me a star?" "Last Mistress" features a formless man shaped by a woman; "Frontal" describes someone made weak in the presence of another.

The album doesn't have much of an arc; it goes dark and stays there. It's true that the first two songs have a static, meditative quality, but then, seven minutes in, comes "Last Mistress," whose title alone feels like a bit of a bombshell given the TMZ-grade intel on the end of her marriage. ("The last"? Does that mean there were more?) The guitars build tension while she sings, "The last mistress / Pissing like a dog / Territorial marking," accenting it all like some comic-book pooch: "Woof! Woof!" Then comes "Actress," a song of transactions: she wants stardom, and our desire, our gaze, is what makes that possible. Gordon shouts the "HARD! HARD! HARD!" refrain, landing on the "huh" to the point that it sounds like panting, suggesting desperation and carnal mashing. Is it a command? A description? Her delivery of the line is flat, but with a theatrical flourish, a simulacrum of porn dialogue, a comment on the fantasy and a culture that requires women to fulfill the fantasized roles, to be actresses in their everyday lives.

Coming Apart's halfway point, "Can't Help You," is a short respite, a refusal to be dragged down, and dovetails into two tracks referencing songs popularized by Nina Simone circa 1968: Simone's *Hair*-borne medley of "Ain't Got No / I Got My" is reborn here as "Aint," whereas "Black" is a riff on the standard "Black Is the Color of My True Love's Hair," though it also owes a debt to the strangulated Patty Waters version, as Gordon spends a singsong thirteen minutes mewling, "I love the ground on which he stands" with feral, cloying lovesickness. She seems to be mocking true love as she bellows, sending up romantic young naivete as the guitars go ugly. That discomfort is only topped by the album-ending "Frontal," seventeen minutes of desire and domination, while Gordon keens, "You would've killed me / Had you not raped me" over and over, followed by a vow of resistance: "You're not gonna cut me in two."

At no other time in her career has Gordon been so forceful, so in her own power. As often as Sonic Youth broached narratives of women's lives and struggles, it's

hard to imagine them ever doing a song like "Frontal."
Perhaps that was all ramping up to this: Kim Gordon in
her actualized prime, untethered and in true service of
her art, going as deep and dark as she can in a song, in a
sound, the ferocious phoenix diving back down into the
smoldering ash because there is nothing left to lose.

JOANNA NEWSOM, *YS*

CITY PAGES, NOVEMBER 2006

An acquaintance wrote to me the other day, complaining about Joanna Newsom's newest album, *Ys: She's really showing off.*

Exactly! I replied. It's pretty great, isn't it? Finally, an artist with the confidence and vision to abide by the wonder with which she dreams. *Ys* is a work of faith, the labor of a musician who believes in the possibilities of the album as a medium.

Two years ago, Ms. Newsom came outta some Northern California nowhere with a debut, *The Milk-Eyed Mender*, which went gangbusters. The harpist was no hirsute dude with choogle to prove, but nevertheless the nouveau freakfolk scene still rode her coattails into the media spotlight. The Mills College graduate was portrayed as a sprite, caricatured as a forest maiden, her big harp shouldered like a cross, both literal and figurative. Her voice was strange and boldly squeaky. She sounded like a precocious child at times, as her voice exploded in sudden blooms and quickly disappeared into a hush. Her songs

243

were hers alone, set to the delicate gallop of her harp and the hiccup of her voice.

In comparison to that spartan debut, *Ys* is massive. It finds Newsom backed by a thirty-four-piece orchestra of big-name session players, with arrangements by Van Dyke Parks (you may remember him from his work with the Beach Boys). Seesawing strings add depth and hue as glowering French horns rise to solemnly follow the lyrics' lead; the result is regal and ornate. Newsom peacocks her talent and her voice, lays hard into her coos, and phrases sometimes begin with a startled squeak, as if she is peeling out, anxious to put the romance of her words into motion.

As on *The Milk-Eyed Mender*, she favors alliteration and uses the natural world as her put-upon stage; but here on *Ys*, her songs are more linear and complex. Epic story poems are laid in seven-, nine-, and sixteen-minute stretches; language, though ornamental, serves the story (and, moreover, the song). She stretches and thumps her long *a*'s and *e*'s, tugs her *r*'s, bunts her *t*'s; she flips knotty rhymes while mixing consonantal and vocalic alliteration in order to make a punctuating rhythm, a trick she admittedly cops from Shakespearean sonnets ("While, elsewhere / Estuaries of wax-white / Wend, endlessly, towards seashores unmapped"). The album is vertiginous and begs careful repeated listens, aided by the lyric book (as well as a little after-the-fact googling). Rather than weighting the songs, her arcane argot merely matches the majestic expanse of *Ys*.

For all of *Ys*'s proper lace and poesy, Newsom's lyrics

belie a certain tumult and struggle, an escape from that which binds. Sporting birds go free, penned animals paw at their gates, a dove puppet turns real and takes to the sky, horses break loose, and broken hearts betray their keepers. Seas separate and love divides, and not all meet again; throughout the album, martyrdom is maintained as a parcel to love. Many of the songs are draped in longing: for knowledge, for another, for a taste of the other side. But even when freedom comes, it is bittersweet, each emancipated breath a reminder of how long one has lived without it.

In the wresting free, the narrator and her characters encounter their true natures, and those moments yield some of *Ys*'s best lines. Singing on "Sawdust & Diamonds," Newsom sounds fiery (if not a touch disgusted): "I wasn't born of a whistle or milked from a thistle at twilight / No, I was all horns and thorns, sprung out fully formed, knock-kneed and upright." The words are spit with intent and sure purpose, fiercely raised, like a sentinel of self.

On "Monkey & Bear," a melancholy fairy-fable with a monkey anthropomorphized as a jealous boyfriend, the two characters set out for a master-less life in the mountains. But he implores the bear to keep her harness and costume on, so she can dance and support the two of them. When the bear sneaks away to wash her costume off in the river, she reveals the "threadbare coat" underneath: "You'd see spots where / Almost every night of the year / Bear had been mending / Suspending that baseness / Now her coat drags through the water / Bagging, with a life's worth of hunger." By the time the song rises to its urgent conclusion, with a line about the bear burying its teeth, you come to hope that they land in that pimp monkey's neck.

Through all of this, Newsom proves herself a singular talent, not just as the golden-girl anomaly of the underground, or as a harpist nonpareil, but as an artist and gifted writer unafraid of mapping her vision to its very edges.

FIONA APPLE, *THE IDLER WHEEL IS WISER THAN THE DRIVER OF THE SCREW AND WHIPPING CORDS WILL SERVE YOU MORE THAN ROPES WILL EVER DO*

SPIN, JULY 2012

The half dozen years we've waited since Fiona Apple's last record, *Extraordinary Machine*, is roughly equivalent to a Pleistocene Epoch in chart pop. Which nearly qualifies *The Idler Wheel* as a comeback, and certainly makes it a full reintroduction. The question lingers: Will she suddenly seem all grown-up, mellowed with age? Is all that writhing and wailing relegated to her years of teen tumult? Will she be sage and reflective? Is she even subject to that typical turning-thirty sea change, and what, if anything, will wash up?

Plenty. Her fourth album relentlessly reassures us that she's the same beloved Fiona, still wilding and Weill-ing out. Who's complaining (besides her)? Any other version of Fiona would be boring, and if you want somnolent piano pop from a satisfied woman, put on an old Norah

Jones record. On "Valentine," Fiona's only almost-upbeat song here, she puts it plainly: "I stand no chance of growing up."

The pleasures of *The Idler Wheel* are myriad; the thrill is often vicarious. Fiona, gnashing in her pathos, having long since dropped the outward-calm mask most of the rest of us wear, lets her neuroses fester before taking them out into the light. Her ballads revel in the out-of-balance, ultra-needy aspects of herself: On "Jonathan," crushed and confused by the complexities of adult love, she mewls to her lover to "just tolerate" her. Other people send her reeling, but much of the album is about how reeling is her default mode, and as she sings on "Valentine," she's made her peace with it. You don't want to live through this, per se, but there is something liberating about bearing witness to a woman so unrepentant about feeling fucked-up.

Things start off sweetly enough, though. Album opener "Every Single Night" functions as an indexing of sorts, ticking off the pathology of her anxiety, like Joan Didion quoting from her own psychiatric evaluation as a prelude to *The White Album*, giving a backstory to her systemic unease. As Fiona sings it, the rot stems from her poison mind, then heads south: "Trickle down the spine / Swarm the belly / Swelling to a blaze." The song quiets down with sweet pointillist figures on a celeste, then roars up with whomping bass and her voice rising to a holler, shuddering from the exertion, pondering the immutability of self while channeling Popeye: "What I am is what I am / 'Cause I does what I does." She sounds defiant, soulful.

The Idler Wheel strips her music to its marrow, leaning acoustic and bang-on-the-kitchen-table percussive. It's jazzed with long, beatless bits bound by crashing, whirring, and whinnying; she's long since gone Pirate Jenny on the Top 40 world that first beckoned her. This homemade quality creates a feeling of genuine urgency, with Apple and collaborator/drummer/coproducer Charley Drayton grabbing hold of whatever was handy and rattling, strumming, and/or pounding it. The album is sinewy and lean; for all her talk of being at the mercy of her neuroses, perhaps they propel rather than distract her; she's clearly dialed in here. "Left Alone" is her "Beast of Burden," picking apart why love just can't get made, but instead of rhetorically demanding "Ain't I rich enough?" of some pretty, pretty girl, she's got a more complex issue: "I can love the same man, in the same bed, in the same city / But not in the same room, it's a pity."

For the first time in Apple's career, the central story is her voice; it tells us more than the words it delivers, and she draws on its rawness, splays it right where it catches. She'll groan in agony in lieu of a hook, but suddenly snaps up to honeyed high notes, just to show that even when she sounds undone—as when she heaves "Gimme! Gimme!" on "Valentine"—she's far from loose. Because while these visceral throes are breathtaking, the real excitement lies in those little flashes where she shows just how in control she is—the tells of virtuosity and precision. "Daredevil" starts out deceptively rudimentary, but slowly builds in melodic complexity. And "Werewolf," an ode to bringing out the worst in a lover, begins as a simple progression in a low, warm Carole King spot on the piano, proving that Apple can handle a plainly perfect, three-minute pop song with a key change and hooky chorus. But then she sings her fantasy true, stringing out the track until it veers from confident to creepy, ultimately reaching the final utterance: "Nothing's wrong when a song ends in a minor key."

The Idler Wheel is an unvarnished joy, uninterested in dazzling listeners with clever pop, opting instead to push Apple's muse to within an inch of its life. The unexpected triumph lies in her total command of the anarchy that results. The demons remain, and her talent prevails.

NICKI MINAJ, *PINK FRIDAY*

SPIN, MARCH 2012

"This is for the hood / This is for the kids," offers Nicki Minaj on "Champion," one of her second album's half dozen tracks of rap perfection. She also suggests that it's for "single moms" and "the hood," which still leaves out her various other constituencies: pre-tween girls blinged up in Silly Bandz™, the crowded 2:00 a.m. dance floor at Manhole, those lamenting the lack of pop-rap irreverence post-OutKast, and anyone who wants to see a girly-girl MC Godzilla-ing her *muy macho* peers. Which is to say that *Pink Friday: Roman Reloaded*, like a Whitman's Sampler, has something chewy for everyone.

She's showing us all sides here; singer, MC, and theater geek, complete with a few alter egos. *Reloaded* is separated into the Rap Half and the Pop Half, a nearly seventy-minute monolith front-loaded with devastating proof of her skills as an MC that transitions into her pop-diva bit via ten tracks of sparkly Top 40 precision. Such a strict divide is a good idea: switching back and forth between rappy-rap broadsides and Ibiza-ready dance-floor tracks would leave this sounding more like a mix CD than an album, and having a treacly bit of Chris Brown do-me diarrhea ("Right by My Side") sidle up next to the mania and jungle drums of "Roman Holiday" wouldn't serve anyone's best interests.

Her rap offerings are nearly flawless. See the frosty "Beez in the Trap," Minaj's staccato throwback flow flaunting the borough lilt of her voice and annihilating the rest of the record in the process. "Roman Holiday" is high camp, the closest hip-hop's gotten to its own "Bohemian Rhapsody," full of manic crescendos and twitchy verses that verge on the ridiculous, but always shift toward the triumphant. The rest is exactly what you want post-"Monster": the self-described Harajuku Barbie detonating on posse cuts. Though Jeezy, Weezy, Nas, and Drake do their thing, she wrecks any good-for-a-girl doubts that still lingered. "This is the official competitor elimination," she raps on "Champion," and indeed it is. She says she's the female Lil Wayne, but considering his recent singles, he's more the microwavable appetizer to the real meal of Minaj's hot-pink rap exorcism.

Nicki Minaj is pop's superheroine, her image a Hulked-out perversion of female perfection so saccharine it's almost grotesque, all nuclear tits and neon pink. She undercuts the caricature by screaming "Suck my dick!" no less than three times here, which makes bon mots like "It's Britney, bitch" seem a little wan. If it wasn't clear before, she *is* the future, and she's here to fuck with us. Which is why it feels good to believe in Nicki the rapper: her spitter mode puts the impossibility of the whole package into fabulous relief, the defiant glory of the contradictions, the shredding of our expectations. She's chart-savvy, but it's still art.

With such a gratifying front end, it's easy to dismiss *Roman Reloaded*'s subsequent pop tracks as a paying of the piper: the too-perfect, Dr. Luke–produced songs are her penance for sneaking deranged yodeling ode "Roman Holiday" in there. While such dexterity is part of her appeal—she can sing the hook *and* slay on the verse—it's hard not to think of that duality as a hindrance, highlighting her ferocity as a rapper but exposing that, as a singer, she's just a typical girl. Which rings false, because we're already so well acquainted with her riotous Day-Glo style; we know the real Minaj story. Her pop simulacra, with their steamroller synths, Guetta throb, and pant-along verses, are a lesser representation of her talents. How you feel about Nicki the singer depends on how you feel about, say, Katy Perry; same diff. There is nothing to get lost in on the bad-boy romance "Beautiful Sinner," no destroy-all-comers spirit to rile you. A criminal lack of Minaj-ness.

The upside is that even when Minaj is dialed to "mediocre," she's never close to terrible. "Starships," her fun first single, might be your ringtone until June, but until she raps out that verse, she could be anyone. Which is probably the point, but it's asking you to forget that Minaj the MC is singular, the prodigal daughter returned to save all who want to believe.

PART VIII

PERSONAL/ POLITICAL

EMO

Where the Girls Aren't

PUNK PLANET #56, JULY 2003

A few months back, I was at a Strike Anywhere show. The band launched into "Refusal," a song that offers solidarity with the feminist movement and bears witness to the struggles inherent to women's lives. It is not a song of protection, there is no romantic undertow, it's just about all people being equally important. Everyone was dancing, fanboys and girls at the lip of the stage were screaming along—like so many shows at the Fireside Bowl. By the first chorus of the song, I was in tears. I had reached a mournful new awareness: I'd been going to three shows a week for the last five years and the number of times I'd heard my reality, or the reality of women I knew, acknowledged or portrayed in a song sung by bands fronted by men was at zero and holding. The ratio between all the songs I had heard at the shows I saw and sentiments that affirmed my feminist struggle was staggering. "Refusal" was the first.

It's no wonder why my girlfriends and I have grown increasingly alienated and distanced from the scene, or have begun taking shelter from emo's pervasive stronghold in the recesses of electronic or experimental music. No wonder girls I know are feeling dismissive and faithless toward music. As it stands, in 2003 I simply cannot conjure the effort it takes to give a flying fuck about bands of boys yoked to their own wounding, aka the genre known as emo. These songs and scenes perpetuate a myopic worldview that doesn't extend beyond boy bodies, their broken hearts, or their vans. Meanwhile, I'm left wondering, how did we get here?

In the late '80s, as hardcore and political punk's charged sentiments became more cliché and settled into the armchair comfort of the Clinton era, punk stopped looking outside of itself. Instead, it stripped its tough skin and examined its squishy heart. Political rage gave way to romantic ambiguity. Forget the bomb and the impact of trickle-down economics, emo recalled elusive kisses and tender-but-masculine emotional outbursts. Mixtapes across America became laden with relational eulogies, hopeful boys with their hearts pasted to their sleeves, singing of pillows soaked in tears. Romance of the self was on.

Perhaps we lost the map, or simply stopped consulting it. There was a time when emo seemed reasonable, encouraging, exciting; it was revivifying in its earnestness and with its personal stakes. These new bands modeled themselves on stalwarts like Jawbox, Jawbreaker, Sunny Day Real Estate, bands who wrote songs about women who had names, and gave details to their lives. Jawbox's most popular song, "Savory," was about recognizing male heteronormative privilege, about the weight of objectification on a woman ("See you feign surprise / That I'm all eyes"). In Jawbreaker songs, women had leverage, life, spirit, and agency. Sometimes the women were friends or a sister, not always a girl to be bedded or dumped. They were unidealized, realistic characters.

And then something broke—and not just Chris Carrabba's sensitive heart. Albums by a legion of romantically wronged dudes suddenly lined the record store shelves. It seemed every record was a concept album about a breakup, damning a girl. Now emo's contentious monologues—these balled-fist, Peter Pan, mash-note dilemmas—have gone from descriptive to prescriptive. All of this proves this is a genre, a scene, made by and for boys. The stakes of this are real: as these bands have gained prevalence in mainstream media and climbed the *Billboard* charts, emo has emerged as yet another forum where women are locked out, able only to observe ourselves through the eyes of others.

Girls in emo songs today do not have names. Women are not identified beyond their absence, their shape is drawn by the pain they've caused. Their lives, their day-to-day-to-day does not exist, women do not get colored in. They span from coquettish to damned and back again. They leave bruises on boys' hearts but leave no other mark. Their actions are portrayed solely through the detailing of the neurotic self-entanglement of the boy singer; their region of personal power, simply, is their impact on his romantic life. They're vessels redeemed in the light of boy-love. On a pedestal, on their backs. Muses at best. Invisible at worst. Proof is in the pictures on the covers of records: they are sad-eyed and winsome and comely, the fantasy girl you could take home and comfort.

It's evident from these bands' lyrics and shared aesthetic that their knowledge of the stakes of women's lives is notional at best. Emo's characteristic vulnerable front is limited to self-sensitivity. Every song is a high-stakes game of control that involves "winning" or "losing" possession of the girl (see Dashboard Confessional, Brand New, New Found Glory, and Glassjaw albums). It offers no empathy or parity to the women involved.

■ ■ ■

On a dance floor in Seattle, a guy I know decides to plumb the topic:

"I heard you're writing a column about how emo is sexist."

"I am."

"What do you mean, 'emo is sexist'? Emo songs are no different than all of rock history, than Rolling Stones or Led Zeppelin."

"I know—I'd rather not get into it right now."

"How are songs about breaking up sexist, though? Everyone breaks up. If you have a problem with emo, you have a problem with all of rock history!"

"I know. I do."

To paraphrase Nixon sidekick H. R. Haldeman, "History is wack."*

---

* My friend JR and I had a running gag of attributing impossible quotes to Nixon's former chief of staff.

There must be some discussion, at least for context, that *men writing songs about women* is practically the definition of rock 'n' roll itself. And as a woman, as a music critic, as someone who lives and dies for music, there is a rift within me. How much deference can I afford? How much am I willing to ignore in these songs simply because I like the music?

Can you ignore the lyrical content of the Rolling Stones' "Under My Thumb" because you like the song? Are you willing to? Or the dead and/or brutalized women that amass in Big Black's discography? Is emo exceptional in the scope of the rock canon either in terms of treatment of women or in its continual paean to its own trouble-boy cliché image? Is there anything that separates Dashboard Confessional's condemnation of his bed-hopping betrayer and makes it any more egregious than any woman/mother/whore/ex-girlfriend showing up in songs by Jane's Addiction, Nick Cave, the Animals, or Justin Timberlake? Can you compartmentalize judgment of Zeppelin because the first eight bars of "Communication Breakdown" is total fucking godhead? Where do you split? Do you even bother to care, because if you're going to try and kick against it, you, as the dude on the dance floor* says, "have a problem with all of rock history," and because who, other than a petty, too-serious bitch, dismisses Zeppelin?! Do you accept the misogyny of the last few decades of popular music and in your punk rock community as just how it is?

---

* This originally read "dancing friend"; I have changed it because that man was never my friend.

Who do you excuse and why? Do you check your politics at the door and just dance or just rock or just let side A spin out? Can you ignore the marginalization of women's lives on the records that line your shelves in hopes that feigned ignorance will bridge the chasm? Because it's either that or purge your collection of everything but free jazz, micro-house twelve-inches, and the Mr. Lady Records catalog.

It's almost too big of a question to ask. I start to ask this of myself and stop, realizing full well that if I get an answer I might just have to retire. Or turn into the rock-critical Andrea Dworkin and report with resignation that all music made by men propagates and perpetuates the continual oppression and domination of women. Sometimes I feel like every rock song I hear is a sucker punch toward women. And I feel like no one takes that impact seriously, if they notice it at all. It is "just" music.

My deepest concern about the lingering effects of emo is not so much for myself or for my friends (we have some refuge in our personal-political platforms and deep-crated record collections), but rather for the teenage girls I see crowding front and center at emo shows. Emo is the province of the young, and this is their introduction to the underground. Their gateway may have been through Weezer or the Vagrant America tour or maybe Dashboard Confessional's *Unplugged*. They seek music out, wanting to stake some claim to punk rock, looking to the underground for a way out, a way under, to sate the seemingly nameless need—maybe the same need I came to punk rock with. I came to punk at fifteen with a

hunger for music that spoke a language I was just starting to decipher, desperate for music that affirmed my
ninth-grade fuck-you values. I was lucky I found music
that encouraged me to protect my budding feminist ways
from being bludgeoned by the weight of mainstream, patriarchal culture. I was lucky I was met at the door with
things like the Bikini Kill demo, Fugazi, and the first *Kill
Rock Stars* comp. I was met with polemics and respectful
address; I heard my life and concerns in those songs. I
was met with girl heroes deep in guitar squall, kicking
out the jams under the stage lights. I was being hurtled
toward deeper rewards. Records and bands were triggering ideas and inspiration. I acknowledge the importance
of all of that because I know I would not be who I am
now, doing what I do, twelve years down the line, if I had
not received such fundamental ideas about what music
and life can be about.

Now I watch these girls at emo shows more than I
ever do the band. I watch them sing along, to see what
parts make them freak out. I wonder if seeing these
bands, these dudes onstage, resonates and inspires them
to pick up a guitar or drumsticks. Or if they just see this
as something dudes do, since there are no girls, there is
no *them* up there. I wonder if they see themselves as participants, or only as consumers, or, to reference the songs
directly, the consumed. I wonder if this is where music
will begin and end for them. If they can be radicalized
in spite of this. If being denied keys to the clubhouse is
enough to spur them into action.

I know that, for me, even as a teenage autodidact who

thought her every idea was worthy of expression and an audience, it did not occur to me to start a band until I saw other women in one. It took seeing Babes in Toyland and Bikini Kill to truly throw on the lights, to show me that there was more than one place, one role, for women to occupy, and that our participation was important and vital—it was YOU MATTER writ large.

I don't want these front-row girls to miss that. I don't want girls leaving shows denied encouragement and potential. As lame as punk rock can be, and though our claims that its culture is somehow distinct from median society may ring hollow, at punk's gnarled foundation the possibilities for connection still exist. There is still the possibility for exposure to radical notions, for punk rock to match up to what many kids dream, or hope, for punk DIY to mean. But much of that hinges on the continual presence of radicalized women within the leagues, and those women being encouraged and given reasons to stay, rather than diminished by the music which glues the community together.

We girls deserve more than one song. We deserve more than one pledge of solidarity. We deserve better songs than any boy will ever write about us.

TV ON THE RADIO, *RETURN TO COOKIE MOUNTAIN*

CITY PAGES, AUGUST 2006

My friend Chad insists that the hottest thing you can say to someone is "Don't stop," but clearly, he's never heard TV on the Radio's Tunde Adebimpe croon, "I meant every word." This sung assurance is one of the hottest punk prostrations since the zipless fuck of Sonic Youth's "Shadow of a Doubt." Right now, passionate pledges of sincerity hardly have a place in popular music outside the pejorative turf of emo, but TV on the Radio isn't jinxed by these things; here on *Return to Cookie Mountain* they are merely matters for the grown and sexy.

The quintet of TV on the Radio comes via the Brooklyn dance-punk explosion of 2003, though speaking of "dance-punk" these days is a bit of mortuary science as most of those bright lights are now burgeoning alt-pop also-rans or jam bands of the coke-set. Yet the few acts that made that scene feel invigorating and new—namely TV on the Radio, Ted Leo, the Yeah Yeah Yeahs—have since superseded that scene. While their ostensible peers put out low-stakes dance-floor anthems, they were spitting ennui back in your face and stealing your breath with a sigh and a lick. Still, having a band save your life is an awfully bourgeois fortune in the face of the tragedies of the current Bush-begotten apocalypse, but if the suggestion exists, it exists within TV on the Radio's *Cookie Mountain*. It's an album of an eyes-open cynicism and prurience ripened amid wartime, ribald joy and grief-tempering hope, living and dying, living in the streets and between the sheets.

While every band member's talent is put to exhaustive use on *Cookie Mountain*, front man Adebimpe is the core, the molten heat of his voice radiating through the album's dense collage of samples, horns, and guitar detritus. The sound is a gorgeous, multitrack, multi-voice dichotomy of femme aggression and masculine vulnerability copped directly from Prince's *1999*. Adebimpe's angelic falsettos layer over grosgrain tenor and vocalist/guitarist Kyp Malone's baritone oohs. Adebimpe learned to sing by joining a barbershop quartet, and the space he leaves around his voice amid harmonies bears the mark. Often, he's accompanied by Malone or the witchy voice of Celebration's Katrina Ford, her voice cutting through these richly toned sensual doxologies.

Cookie Mountain is a love record, which, by its nature, makes it an anti-war record. Hearts and love are its main currency: "your hands reach 'round my heart in love," "my heart's aflame," "hearts courageous," "under the stars, talkin' 'bout love," "hearts that blaze," "rusty hearts," "open my heart, let it bleed onto yours," "diamond-encrusted love," "unbridled love." The album's manifesto lies within "Province," wherein they instruct that "Love is the province of the brave." For all this romance, *Cookie Mountain* forgoes the mushy or mystical shit for a pragmatic ecstasy that is rooted in survival and connection. Its ardor is of the here-and-now, spring-green, and corporeal; its terra firma is liquored tongues and sexual entropy playing out on the platform of the F-train stop.

The record has another side that is less sweet. The solemn album opener, "I Was a Lover," is forged in disgust, with martial beats and looped samples that come on like cheap drugs. The song details a divide; as Adebimpe's voice stretches sinuously, he snaps, "We don't make eye contact," each syllable getting its full weight in venom. The accusation is directed inward, not outward. But it's "Tonight," a please-live lament near the end of the album, that is the locus of *Return to Cookie Mountain*, born of both its darkness and its light. It's a desperate lullaby, an echo of Neil Young's junkie elegy, "Needle and the Damage Done": "The needle, the dirty spoon, the flames and the fumes / Just throw them out tonight / The time that you've been afforded / May go unsolved, unrewarded," sings Adebimpe, over the tidal beat of a tambourine.

Cookie Mountain is a cool come-on, an album-length exploration of love and brokenness in a half-wrecked world, one which arrives humbly amid lucid dub, double-Dutch beats, and the most intoxicating guitar bombast to come down the pike since Talk Talk's *Spirit of Eden*. It's an enrapturing gift from a band that continually promises greatness. TVOTR have come down from *Cookie Mountain* with a stoned tableau, a commanding work etched with a lust for life.

SWF, 45

Mecca Normal's *The Observer*

CHICAGO READER, APRIL 2006

The Observer is hard to listen to. Not for the usual reasons; it doesn't suck. What makes it tough going is the same thing that makes it great: unofficially subtitled "A Portrait of the Artist Online Dating," it's so mercilessly personal it's hard to believe it can exist in the pop-music marketplace, let alone anywhere outside of a diary. A concept album about Jean Smith's romantic life as a single woman of forty-five, it develops a grim, intimate picture of her solitary struggle for connection that doesn't go easy on anyone—not Smith, not the men she dates, and certainly not the listener.

The pop canon is so full of songs about romantic longings and failures that we've been conditioned to expect certain story arcs, delivered in each genre's codified language: blues and its backdoor men, contemporary R & B and its baby boos, classic rock and its lonely motel rooms. There's pleasure in having one's sufferings and hopes reaffirmed, however approximately, by such archetypes. But Mecca Normal, the Vancouver duo of Smith and guitarist David Lester, have spent two decades hammering away at musical and social convention. They're overtly political artists; anarchist-feminists both, they've developed a traveling workshop called "How Art and Music Can Change the World," and their loose, abrasive, drumless songs don't rest easily in any genre. And even coming from them, *The Observer* is startling.

It's natural to try to relate to a singer's experience and to inhabit a song as one's own, but getting invited along on Smith's blind dates and hookups is discomfiting; as a storyteller, she skips the niceties and just plunks everything down on the table. "He tries to put the condom on / He curses / I try to see what he is doing," she sings in her low, acidic croon. "But I'm pinned beneath him / I hear him stretching the condom like he's making a balloon animal."

All but a few of the album's twelve songs are connected to its basic theme of heterosexual relationships between men and women, and half are diaristic synopses of actual dates Smith went on with men she met on Lavalife.com. She's a sharp, literate lyricist, driven more by prosaic interests than melodic ones; Smith's attention to detail and detached, acerbic tone make *The Observer* a particularly apt title. Each diary song is a separate scene unified by Smith's blunt portrayal of herself; you learn about her as a date, not just an artist, and she makes a messy, inconsistent impression, veering from cynical and judgmental to petulant and needy.

On the album's centerpiece, the twelve-minute "Fallen Skier," she skips between snippets of dinner conversation and an internal monologue about her date, a forty-seven-year-old student and recovering addict who describes himself as a "fallen waiter/ski bum/party guy." From the moment she says "guy," drawing it out and accenting the word, you can tell she's mocking him. She repeats his story without sympathy, sounding frustrated, almost disgusted: "I feel I'm with a boy, a very young boy / He's only been away from home for twenty-seven years / Only twenty-seven summers, twenty-seven winters / Partying and skiing / I guess that's why he hasn't gotten anything together yet / I don't think he realizes it, but his life has gotten away from him." When he seems concerned that her band might play hardcore punk, she makes a half-indignant aside that lightens the mood: "I stand, a middle-aged woman in a fantastically subtle silk jacket / Hush Puppies / Curly hair blowing in the wind / And this guy's fretting over the possibility / That I'm actually Henry Rollins." But almost immediately her complaints begin to boomerang, telling us as much about her as they do about him. "He never asked the name of my band," she says, "never tried to touch me." Suddenly she sounds vulnerable, even wounded; though her date's clearly wrong for her, she can't keep herself from wanting to be interesting and desirable to him. When she hugs him goodbye at the end of their chemistry-free evening, it's unclear which one of them she's trying to console.

The Observer is a harsh toke, but it's compelling on all fronts; Smith's lyrics force you to think about loneliness, need, and bad dates; the songs are as engrossing as they are exhausting. Her voice flits and dips like a plastic bag in the wind, moving from a moany sort of sung-speech to a deep, silky quaver to a thick, shrill trilling, and she often drawls out her words like she's trying to fill the room with distended consonant sounds. The self-explanatory album opener, "I'm Not into Being the Woman You're With While You're Looking for the Woman You Want," is a glowing example of the interplay between her vocals and Lester's guitar, which is equally distinctive and powerful. On "To Avoid Pain," the duo toys with early-sixties pop country as Smith hee-haws like a half-drunk Brenda Lee, trying to talk herself down on the way to a first-time hookup: "Take a city bus / To a downtown hotel / I don't feel weird / I don't feel weird / Ask me / Ask me / Ask me if I do." Then, as a dark, discordant synth tone rises out of the music, she eagerly proclaims a dubious victory over her own unease: "Soon enough it's true-ooo!"

On "I'll Call You," Lester's buzz-saw guitar gallops around Smith as she reads a fake personal ad—her version of what a truthful guy would say—that sounds like it was placed by a sketchy frat boy. "Attraction Is Ephemeral," which provides the most complete picture of Smith and what she's about, the way she begins to doubt her own doubts, wondering if she'd be able to spot genuineness in a man even if it were there, is also the most musically moving track on the album. It's the most romantic, too, or rather, it's most explicitly about romance and the yearning for it, though in typical Mecca Normal fashion, it does so while addressing gender and class inequality, patriarchy, and how they can really ruin a date.

In press releases and online materials, Smith provides links to photos she's used in her dating profile, including shots where she's posing in her underwear and others where she's wearing nothing but the ribbon in her hair. But given how unpleasant *The Observer* makes her dating life out to be, it's hard to argue that the pictures are just convenient exhibitionism; if you're gonna use sex to sell records, you don't usually linger on the vulnerability that intimacy requires.

In the band bio, Smith notes her reluctance to make an album about dating; as evidenced by the fallout late last year over the book *Are Men Necessary?* by *New York Times* columnist Maureen Dowd, romance is a loaded topic among the feminist cognoscenti. Dowd claims that successful men don't want competition from their partners and thus tend to date or marry down, choosing women who are younger, less educated, and less accomplished. Though she makes her argument largely with generalizations, as opposed to Smith's nuanced particulars, both writers are suggesting the same thing: independent women wind up alone.

Smith is forthcoming about the concessions she makes for intimacy. While she holds to her standards with men who aren't good enough, she swallows her pride and sells herself out to others who don't have much idea who she is or much interest in finding out. Throughout the album, her artistic integrity never wavers, and throughout it's clear she knows herself and understands the choices she's making. It's brave for her to admit that she quietly shushes the "difficult" parts of herself in order to connect with men; in doing so, she is airing a common secret of women's lives.

AN INTERVIEW WITH
LIDO PIMIENTA

THE BELIEVER, OCTOBER 2018

In an era when musical icons are being held more accountable to their politics, Lido Pimienta positions hers front and center. To her, the art, the artist, the political, and the personal are inextricably entangled. Her work is of her life, and is fused and suffused with it.

Since she began making music in punk and metal bands, when she was still, as she insists, "a child," her lyrics have been about confronting injustice in her native Colombia. After immigrating to Canada in 2006, Pimienta continued making her own music, which connected to her Colombian roots. She became immersed in the Toronto art scene, pursuing a degree in art criticism while raising her young son. Her second album, 2016's *La Papessa*, catapulted Pimienta to international renown and won that year's Polaris Music Prize, Canada's top music honor. While accepting the award, Pimienta spoke of her experiences with racism in Canada and reminded her audience that they were standing on colonized First Nations land. She also expressed

her frustration with the sound person, who conde-
scended to her before the performance. *Billboard*'s reporting characterized this powerful moment as "an
unexpected, obscenity-spiked outburst." Since then,
it's become evident that the music industry wants credit
for putting Pimienta—an outspoken, indigenous queer
woman—on the stage, but doesn't have much interest in
hearing what she's saying or addressing the racism and
colonization she's asking the industry and her listeners
to account for.

When I saw Pimienta perform in Chicago in January
2018, she was several months pregnant, and her energy,
joy, and humor were unyielding. Pimienta courted the
audience with jokes and pointed invitations; she constantly asked them to engage, to connect, to bridge the
chasm between audience and artist, to move beyond their
role as consumers. She beckoned them to see themselves
in her. Between her danceable incantations, she riffed on
border crossing, lovingly mocked her own bandmates'
privileged upbringings, addressed the audience in Spanish, and invited marginalized folks in the room to come
to the lip of the stage. Pimienta was the personification
of the message within her songs and of the work she has
released during the last half decade.

A few weeks after that Chicago show, I spoke to Pimienta by phone, while she was still on tour, maximizing
her time on the road before giving birth. She reflected
on the ways motherhood has shaped her disciplined
approach to her music, her forthcoming album, *Miss*

Colombia, and the porousness between her art and her politics.

1. "I Envy People Who Take *Friends* Seriously"

THE BELIEVER: I imagine you've experienced people insisting that your lived experience and identity are supposed to exist outside of your music and art criticism. Your work really resists that.

LIDO PIMIENTA: I don't want to be a white man. Right? It's not what I want. Like, the aspiration is [in the voice of a protester] "We want equality!" It's just like, actually, I don't want equality. In fact, we should have four bathrooms for women, as far as I'm concerned, because the period is a real thing, okay? You go to an airport, there's never a lineup for men. The lineup for the women's bathroom is so long! And there's, like, moms with strollers waiting in line with a baby in a shitty diaper. I don't want equality! In fact, I should be paid more than men, okay?! Because you gotta add emotional labor to this shit. That's just the world I live in, and I just won't conform. I can't conform. I just don't know how else to be. I just can't. I do have friends who are like, "Lido, you are crazy. You have to chill out. Why do you have to say the things you say?" And I'm just like, "Because I can!"

Even in my own oppression, I'm still far more free than a lot of people that can't say shit because they'll literally get killed. It would be easier; I think about it, right? Like, it would be nice if I would enjoy radio music. It would be so nice! It would be so nice if I turned on the radio and turned on the TV and [was] content. I envy people who take *Friends* seriously. You know, those shows. What's that one with the nerds—that one show that's, like, the three nerds and then the hot neighbor and—

BELIEVER: I don't know! [*Laughs.*]

LP: I envy those people. That you're content with that level of mediocrity—I admire that. I would have less cellulite, probably, if I wasn't thinking about all of these things. I wouldn't have any heart issues! But that's not who I am. I am someone who's just like, "That is garbage." And I will look at it always with a critical eye, and that's just who I am.

BELIEVER: That applies to music-making as well. Just the process of you trying to make a living, you're touring colonized land most of the time. For other musicians, it's "Oh, cool, I get to be in a van away from home and drink free beer." They don't have to think twice about crossing borders.

LP: Crossing that border is nerve-wracking. Nerve-wracking. Like I said at the show in Chicago, "If your white tour manager is afraid, I'm petrified!" I know that they're all afraid, because they're just like, "Please don't do a Google search of Lido." [Homeland Security] can just decide that I am a terrorist, and there goes the seven-thousand-dollar visa. To me, the creative process is the only relaxed part about this entire experience of having the need to perform in front of an audience. If I could create music that I would be happy with just posting online, I would get a job at a cafe and just "keep calm and carry on!" But that's not what it is. It's like this itch that you get as an artist.

I started, in 2010, performing in Colombia. I look back at the people that I started with and how most of those people went on to get Grammys. I was like, What happened? Then I realized, Oh yeah, their songs are about romantic love; my songs are about dismantling white supremacy. [*Laughs.*] They did an English album and they are blond. Oh, I am not; I am actually onstage, pregnant, with pigtails. Okay, all right. I just know one way to be. The more comfortable I am with this way of being, the more I see that people are comfortable in their own skin as well.

When all the bad things in the music industry happened to me, when labels were abusing me, stealing money from me, or managers were . . . all that bad stuff that happens when you're really young and eager and you don't really understand what's going on around you, that had to happen. That had to happen for me to take a break from the music industry. And during that break I learned about the music industry, and now I use my voice to empower mainly women in the music and arts industries, because that's just what I know. I stay in my lane. I don't mess with other stuff that I don't really have to talk about. I am a testament [to] that. There's different ways to be an artist. The way that I am is working out just fine.

Hopefully with the album I'm working on now,

I feel like sonically I've cracked the code of entering a bigger audience realm, but I'm still being me. 'Cause that is the most important thing. I cannot have those same pressures that I had before, almost allowing myself to be convinced that if I lose ten pounds [*laughs*], then people will listen. That's not how it works! [*Laughs*.] Even if I lose twenty pounds and get breast implants, even if I do that, because of the stuff that I'm saying, it doesn't really matter how I look.

2. "Even When I'm Joking, My Shows Get Shut Down"

BELIEVER: I was talking to [Chilean American pop artist and feminist organizer] Francisca Valenzuela last year about the new music that she's working on, and she was saying, "Until I sing in English, people are just going to keep writing off what I'm doing as 'world music.'" And even though she's making electronic indie pop, she's not going to get booked on certain festivals until she sings in English. In terms of attracting an audience, was language something that people tried to get you to consider?

LP: Absolutely. "Why don't you make English versions?" Well, the thing with English is that, you know, it's not about a translation, and even the interpretation wouldn't be right. That's not how it works. I'm pretty good at speaking English. I'm pretty good at communicating in English, but writing a song in English is a whole other . . . I just can't do it. If I wrote in English, the whole vibe would change.

The stuff that I say is so obscure but the rhythm is way accessible. People are like, "Oh, I can dance to this!" But I'm actually talking about death; I'm talking about polyamory; I'm talking about possessive partners, and violence against women. But I'm not saying, He beat me. I'm not saying, He raped me. I'm not using those words; I use poetry. I cannot write in the same poetic fashion in English, because my musical ear . . . The songs in English are, like, way more simple. I try to explain it to those people that wanted me to do the songs in English. What Francisca is saying is very true.

I hope that if I do crack the code, and I do write in a different language, if I do write in English, it's not because of the pressure of writing in English, but because that's just how the song came to be. In the new album, there's this one song [where] I say one thing in English. That was because I was forcing myself: No, Lido, you can do it! Challenge yourself! And then, like, one phrase came in. Empress Of is really good at that. She's really good at writing things in both languages in the same song. Helado Negro as well. Maybe it's because they lived in the U.S. for longer [than I did]. I grew up in South America. I came here when I was nineteen. I was formed into an adult knowing what I wanted. It's the whole thing—sing in English but also [be] married to an aesthetic that is very U.S.

I'm more worried about the sound. There's times when I have on a full-on outfit . . . and my friends do their hair and they're like, "We're going to go to a show, and we're going to do you up, girl!" I'm like, "Yeah, yeah, yeah. Great. Come." Nothing gets done, because I had a fight with the stupid sound person. One time, we're at South by Southwest, which is, you know, classically white, rock 'n' roll, whatever. Then you have this plethora of diasporic sounds. We're having such a good time, and then he comes onstage and says, "No, no, no! You can play for longer!" And I'm like, "Guys . . . the white man just said that we can play for longer. We're free!" It was hilarious! It was so funny. It was like one of my funniest moments. And he just stopped the show.

At this other particular event, we were doing our sound check. When I layer myself—'cause I have my looper thing—I notice that whenever I would layer myself or have, like, four voices going, he would turn me down, and he wouldn't turn me up again. I'm like, "I know my limits. Don't worry; I've been doing this a long time."

BELIEVER: You're a professional!

LP: I'm being super cool about it. Then he goes, "You know what, I think you really should use my microphone because it sounds really good on female voices. I think that's what's happening."

BELIEVER: What?!

LP: He said that shit to me, and at that show—it was a show in L.A.—my managers are like, "Ooh, this per-

son's gonna come, and this person's gonna come!"
And I'm like, "I don't care." [*Laughs.*] They don't
give me money; they don't pay my rent. I just want
to have a really good show for the people that are
paying to see me. So the sound guy is like, "Yeah,
this microphone works so well for female voices."
Because of the traumatic experiences I've had before
with soundmen, I'm like, "Oh! Oh, well, you know
what? I feel like I'm getting a cold. I don't want to get
anyone else sick if I use that microphone. Let's just
keep trying." But it was, like, a two-hour ordeal. If I
knew that everything was going to be perfect, sound-
wise, maybe I could relax and put a little more care
into, you know, my sexy side or whatever. I want to
sound good and I want to inspire people with what
I'm saying, not with what I look like.

BELIEVER: What are some of the nonmusical things that
have really inspired you, especially in the face of you
catching enormous shit for being yourself and sticking up for the people who are in your audiences?

LP: I just see myself in the audience. If I see myself in
the audience, it means that they see themselves in me.
That's very powerful. [As] the caregiver that I know
I am, I have this need to create a safe place. I have
this need to connect with people because I don't want
people to see me as this unattainable, unrealistic . . . I
don't want to be a fabrication. Even in activist circles,
the moment that you say that you have any kind of
political engagement, or the moment you have a feminist viewpoint, you get these stupid little requests, or

stupid questions. I feel so often that I can't really be free. I love shoes. I have a huge shoe collection. And that part of me . . . like, I don't feel like I should be talking about that, because I feel like I would disappoint the vegans that listen to my music or whatever. [*Laughs.*]

BELIEVER: Or the people who fantasize that you have only one pair of shoes and you made them yourself.

LP: Exactly! When I went to South by Southwest, [I got] so many messages about "This venue that you're playing at, well, they're neighbors . . . A woman got harassed there. So you shouldn't play." And I'm like, "Excuse me?" [*Laughs.*] And then I get a message like, "I'm so disappointed that you went and you played at this venue that's next to the venue [where] one woman got assaulted. And you didn't even talk about it!" That's really hard, because as much as I'm there and I will talk about it, I also don't know who the managers are. I am still a minority. I am still a vulnerable member of society. I am not gonna go and confront any manager in any of the venues that I go to, because even when I'm joking, my shows get shut down. And the people that play with me are counting on this money because they have to pay rent. You know, there's just this whole circle of things that happen behind a performance, that happen behind a person, and I cannot be expected to be this perfect being. I can just say, "I'll try to do better!"

3. "A No-Bullshit Policy"

BELIEVER: How has motherhood stoked or worked with your creative impulse?

LP: I always wanted to be a mom, and I always wanted to be an artist. I always loved kids, and I wanted to be a teacher. I just never really thought that I would have to wait until I accomplish this until I can be that. When I turned twenty years old and I still didn't have a kid, I was worried—the idea is that when I'm forty, my kid's gonna be twenty, and we're gonna be playing in a band together. That's what I thought about while all my friends were thinking about what school they were going to go to. To me, going to school or getting a job is so easy, but raising kids and having the energy for it is so hard.

The motivation that I get, and the creative impulse, or the encouragement—the way that I see it as a mom is that it really helps me prioritize and understand my value as a person, and as an artist. If I wasn't a mom, if I didn't really need to organize my time really well, I wouldn't be as disciplined as I am in what I do. For me, in my environment, and growing up in an extremely matriarchal family, having kids was just like, it's what I have to do.

My son is ten years old, and I'm pregnant with my second one. [*Laughs.*] And I'm so happy! Managing my schedule around my son's schedule helps me live under a no-bullshit policy, you know? My peers and people my age don't have the same pressures that I have to be excellent.

BELIEVER: Did becoming a mother change your worldview in a way that also impacted your art-making?

LP: I feel like I'm a mom to a lot of people. I am a caregiver, and my relationship with my son and my relationship with my partner and my family home life is just one thing that I have. But my activism, my social awareness, and my political engagement [are due to my being] a person of color, and [to the fact that] my family is indigenous. My family is being persecuted and has been persecuted by the government since I was born. So then you have to learn how to cope and how to communicate and how to express yourself and how to fight for what you believe is right. And then you have to do it in a different language, and then you have to do it in a different country, and then you have to do it within the limitations of whatever industry or whatever job that you think that you're able to do. I didn't know what else I'd be doing with my life. I just know how to be an artist.

With my art, I try to accomplish this level of greatness, or financial stability, or notoriety, so that I can put the attention back into my community and my people. And sometimes I feel like, Man, Lido, do you really want another baby? Do you want another baby in this disaster-ass of a world? And then I'm like, I want another baby and I want to adopt two more! [*Laughs.*]

I just have this need to nurture that is fueled by this need to see things work properly and to see things in harmony, because I don't know what that is like. I don't know what it's like to live in a country that is peaceful. I don't know what that is. I live in Canada, and it's relatively peaceful compared to Colombia, but even though I live here, I'm so connected to my indigenous land. When I see that land in peace, then I can have peace! And in the meantime, I'm going to be writing about all the things that I see.

4. *Miss Colombia*

BELIEVER: Can you talk to me about *Miss Colombia*, and what is at the center of it?

LP: I don't know if you remember when Steve Harvey first guest-appeared on *Miss Universe*, and he made the horrific mistake of giving the Miss Universe crown to the wrong queen. [*Laughs.*] And the queen [he took the crown from] was Miss Colombia. He was like, "Oh, sorry, I made a mistake!" He didn't really understand the whole runner-up part. So he gave the crown to Miss Colombia and took it away and gave it to Miss Philippines. What baseball means to the U.S., beauty pageants are to Colombians, okay? This is our national sport. Women are this thing that we export to the world.

Beautiful women is what Colombians are about. We're right up there with cotton, and pearls, and sugar, or oil, or whatever. We're currency; that's what we are as women in Colombia. [*Laughs.*] No one goes to school if *Miss Universe* is on and Colombia is runner-up. People will leave their job early and your boss will be like, "Yes, we have to root for Miss Colombia." So just to give you an idea of how big of a deal it was that they took the crown from her.

I have my English Facebook and my Spanish Facebook. I'm scrolling, scrolling, and the comments made by the Colombian diaspora I follow are horrible; they're disgusting. For weeks, months, people were so sour about this. There's three-year-olds that are going blind because of malnourishment. But this is what, collectively, Colombians have decided to be united about?

I've been so invested in indigenous rights on colonized land in North America, I forget that we're also on colonized land in South America, right? Instead of looking at these issues from a visitor's perspective, or as an immigrant, I thought about what makes me Colombian, and what makes me South American, and do I still even consider myself a Colombian, a South American? Do people even see me [that way]? What happens when I go back to Colombia and I feel like I can't breathe, too many people. Too loud! And then I'm in Canada; it's so quiet in Canada. It's so depressing. Where is the balance?

I started writing these songs as a response to colorism, shadeism, xenophobia. How South Americans living in Europe or living in the States [are] ashamed to show you pictures of their Black relatives. How embedded racism still is in South American culture.

How the idea of a Latin person is a picture of a white or light-skinned South American—Eva Longoria, Sofía Vergara. The closest thing I feel like we have is, like, Cardi B, like the people that she's putting on. We don't really think about indigenous South American entertainers. We can't name one! Who are the Black ones?

This is why I'm expected to "Okay, Lido . . . Just do something more exotic. More Latina! Just throw in some Latina stuff." And I'm like, "You want me to wear a traditional hat? You want me to drape the flag around me? Just look at me! What else you want?" [*Laughs.*]

And that's what *Miss Colombia* is all about. The album was recorded in three different countries. Every time I travel, I try to add something to it. So far it sounds like industrial reggaeton with some accordion and some brass. [*Laughs.*] And I'm trying to decipher it, still sonically, but I do know that that album is the *Seat at the Table* of South America. It's for us, for me, for us.

ROBYN KNOWS WHAT IT'S LIKE TO FEEL BAD

THE CUT, NOVEMBER 2018

It's a Saturday morning in early October, and electro-pop artist Robyn is at home in her native Sweden, gearing up for a long day of press to promote *Honey*, her first album in eight years. The year 2010 is a lifetime ago in pop. While we talk over Skype, her phone and computer bing and buzz with a stream of alerts and demands for her attention. The world is hungry for her return to music. Robyn has been off the grid for years, grieving from a lot of loss: a decimating breakup with her on-again/off-again fiancé (with whom she's said to have reconciled this past year), followed by the 2014 death of her longtime friend, collaborator, and producer Christian Falk. And with that grief came a deep depression. But she managed in that time to learn to produce her own music, painstakingly tracking and revising her new album. When she needed relief from her heartache, she sought it in Paris and in L.A., where she'd dance off her blues in the disco.

Honey evokes that time, and all the feelings and observations and growth that come with mourning, and getting to know a new side of herself, arriving at an expansive, pulsing, liminal space of pleasure and aliveness. To say *Honey* is rich is an understatement—it's masterful, and fruitfully bears out the lust as well as all the joyous fuck-yous of Robyn during the *Body Talk* era, but now that she's older and has emerged from these life-and-death-changing experiences, she brings to it her brand of maturity.

Throughout our chat, Robyn shifts between being forthcoming and self-protective, politely circumventing certain conversational territory as "too private to speak about." She's open about her sadness but then offers guarded platitudes borrowed word for word from her album's press release. She is an artist who knows precisely how much of herself she is willing to reveal.

The thirty-nine-year-old singer spent six years, starting in 2010, in intensive psychotherapy, devoting several sessions a week trying to understand how fame had warped her sense of self, and the impact of her parents' divorce, and to get at who she really was. She says the album was preempted by a level of despair that she coped with, in part, by withdrawing from the world and its constant flow of information. "I was in a period of deep self-reflection, trying to get rid of a lot of things that I didn't like about the way I was thinking or feeling," she explains. "One of the greatest things about feeling like shit is that you can empathize with other people that feel like shit."

Robyn's depression eventually began to lift amid the recording process; in its wake came a sense of clarity that would eventually inform the songs and process of recording *Honey*. "When you're sad or really depressed, it really strips you. There's something really cool about getting down to the minimal amount of security that you need," she says. "That's what happens when you're really sad, you become really unstable, and you don't put yourself there unless you have to because it's really uncomfortable. But once you've gotten used to that and you don't—" She haltingly reframes her explanation of this life-shifting perspective: "In the beginning, I was really, really scared, and then after a while, I felt like I didn't need a lot of safety that I thought I needed. I was disabled in a way by my sadness. I couldn't push through, which would be my natural go-to reaction. Then you decide to do things really, really, really softly, and you realize that's more effective."

The process—and the vulnerability, connections, friendship, and music that kept her afloat—fortified and liberated her not only as a person but as an artist. "You just become way lighter and, in a way, stronger. I would say that's the other way of saying strong, maybe—it makes you free. 'Strong' is the word. It's nice to use the word 'strong,'" she says. "The feeling that actually stayed with me and that kept coming into my life after I started feeling better is this pleasure kind of feeling that was really not to do with anyone else but myself. A self-generated energy that I could tap into on my own terms and whenever I wanted, which was a totally new thing for me."

While Robyn has a solid dozen songs that could be categorized as flawless, it's *Honey*'s title track that most readily joins the canon. When I ask her how long she worked to finesse "Honey," she pauses to do the math. But it's beyond measure in hours—she guesstimates: "Six months, working full-time? A lot of it is things that don't end up on the record but things that you have to do to get there." The thought that allowed her to dive so deeply into her own creative vision, into a single song for months on end? "Realizing that everyone's just winging it."

In the wake of Falk's death, she says, there was a shift of perspective, and she realized "all the things you thought mattered might not matter so much." During this time she stayed off the road, became reclusive, traveled extensively, and spent a lot of time dancing (turns out her "Dancing on My Own" was a prophecy). Robyn was very much having the relationship with other people's music that many have with hers—attempting to use it to summit her heartbreak, to transmogrify longing into something, anything else, one track at a time—not so much to blot out pain but to move through it with the aid of pulsing 808s. "I danced quite a bit. I started moving my body and that really helped me, but like in a way that wasn't about what it looked like or whatever. Just trying to find a way to move that felt good and restored [my body] to me.

"I think, though, that music doesn't change you. I don't think music changes anyone. I don't think music changes the world," Robyn says, quick to qualify she's not naive or insisting dance music can save the world. "I think people change the world, and you have to want to change. But, for it to happen, music can be this space where people get their energy back or kind of recharge."

"Missing U" is *Honey*'s lead track and first single, and it is an electro-disco epic; nearly five minutes of cascading, arpeggiated synth that draws its matrilineal inheritance from Donna Summer's disco classic "I Feel Love." Robyn breathlessly declares a state of disunion, tries to reconcile a happily never after. She sings, "Can't make sense of all the pieces / Of my own delusions / Can't take all these memories / Don't know how to use 'em." The unease and desperation of "Missing U" (and the pointed sass of her canonical hits like "Don't Fucking Tell Me What to Do") is an especially appropriate soundtrack to, say, America's high-speed skid down the shit-glazed Slip 'N Slide™ of the Trump era. On *Honey* she sings: "There's no control," "I'm right back in that moment / And it makes me want to cry," "If you got something to say / You've got nothing to lose." The dumb, numb, forgetting, relaxing mode of dance pop doesn't quite hold when so much of the last year has been about reconciling lingering memories—be they historical, personal, or indelible on the hippocampus. *Honey* splits the difference between propulsion and plaintive darkness, duking it out with nostalgia that is more bitter than sweet under the thrown light of the disco's mirror ball—and it all affirms, as if anyone ever doubted, that Robyn's return is right on time.

M.I.A.

Portrait of the Artist as a Young Artist

SPIN, NOVEMBER 2013

"I was the only one who was able to draw in the whole class," says Maya Arulpragasam, aka pop icon M.I.A., of her earliest school years in Sri Lanka. "So, when we were doing our alphabet and we had to do little illustrations, I would draw in everybody's books . . . I was the go-to person in the class."

The M.I.A. origin story—unchanged since the earliest articles about her appeared a decade ago—is not the definitive story. That tale is just a history of her career and its obstacles: her "terrorist" dad, her Brit-pop benefactors, Peaches' gifted drum machine, Diplo's affection and production on those early bamboo bangers, Madonna taking her along to the Super Bowl halftime show. But this myth of M.I.A.'s pop ascent should rightfully be viewed against the dazzling backdrop of an underdog artist who started as a child in Sri Lanka, when she discovered that fastidiously sketching images gave her the ability to transcend her circumstances.

"It's a really difficult story," says Arulpragasam. "Basically, when I went to school in Sri Lanka from age five onward, the classes there were sometimes sorted into a hierarchy of your skin tone. So the fairer-skinned kids sat at the front row, and the darker-skinned kids sat at the back by the poor ones who played out in the street all day long. They would turn up to school with no clothes on and they sat in the back row. I'm a Tamil, so I had darker skin, so I was sat in the back row . . . I was very useful to all the kids because I was good at drawing, and then I could sit anywhere that I wanted. So I kind of earned my way up the seating rank." This is how art became her passport, the origin story of Maya the Artist.

She had no formal exposure to art as a child—just what she encountered in cinema posters, and the vibrant colors and prints of clothing worn by the women around her. She grew up next door to a textile factory that made and printed saris. "I used to hang out in the yard all the time, and they chucked all the paints out in the corner of the garden. I remember the smell of it, paint of all different colors." These color combinations and print patterns became a part of her visual vocabulary, showing up in her earliest work after she attended the public Central Saint Martins College of Art and Design in London, and continuing up to the clashing hues of M.I.A.'s 2005 breakthrough, *Arular*. That aesthetic still mirrors the sound of her latest album, *Matangi*: bright, tight, repetitive, and as busy as the Tamil Eelam's tiger-print camouflage.

"The thing that's always very consistent [for me] is the colors," Arulpragasam explains. "In India, you see the way they embrace color in the culture—it's very celebratory of the existence of color. There's no rule of what color belongs together or doesn't belong together. They're not precious about it. It's very full-on." Once she immigrated to London in 1986, when her mother fled Sri Lanka's civil war, she didn't see those sort of colorful combinations on clothes or houses. For her, the use of these electric pairings and patterns is nostalgic, memetic. It's also a matter of like-recognizing-like: her entire aesthetic as M.I.A. is an endless neon riot born of the so-called Third World. Arulpragasam is quick to clarify: the throughline is *celebration*, not chaos. "It's not any more chaotic than life on a normal day. Other people see it as chaotic, but it's just *not precious*. It's trying not to waste information and also not being afraid to build a narrative out of it."

As a young refugee in London, her visual expression became a way to maintain her identity amid a new culture. Her skill as an artist kept her afloat in school: "I didn't know how to speak English. When I was in English or science classes—when it took speaking English—they would get me out of the classes, and have me paint the drama sets or draw, make art, stuff for the play."

When she gained admission to Central Saint Martins College, she found herself at the very center of London's artistic life in the late '90s. After graduating in 1999, Arulpragasam first tried film—shopping a screenplay titled *Gratis* about her brother Sugu's life in juvenile detention, even going to Hollywood, and fruitlessly pursuing a documentary on her missing cousin Janna, who'd gotten caught up in the Sri Lankan civil war. She then returned to London in 2001, and became friends with Elastica frontwoman Justine Frischmann, also a painter.

Arulpragasam began flirting with more accessible media (the digital revolution had just barely begun for film) and directed Elastica's video for "Mad Dog God Dam," piecing together tour footage filmed off TV with the tandem footwork of two London girls on a basketball court. She revisited the same scuzzily pixelated, street-style choreography six years later for her own "Boyz" video.

The thwarted documentary actually intensified her interest in the Tamil plight. At Tamil shops in London, she picked up VHS tapes, something akin to war newsreels, degraded by generations of dubbing. One of the groups featured was Freedom Birds, the Tamil Tigers' women's combat regiment. Arulpragasam took the image of one of these women, using a video still from a 2002 animated short, and stenciled it over a hot orange tiger and a blast of electric red. It became one of Arulpragasam's most perdurable visual works: in addition to appearing in her first public art show and subsequent 2002 book, *M.I.A. No. 10*, it served as an animated backdrop for her "Galang" video. Arulpragasam's fascination with Freedom Birds would show up again in her decision to cast Tamil girls for her "Sunshowers" video, and then style them to recall the combat unit. The iconography imagined a parallel life of another pretty Tamil girl caught up in a different fate, a different fight.

The disappearance of Arulpragasam's cousin Janna was a turning point for her work, reconnecting her with Sri Lanka, her family, the war—though it was something shy of a full-tilt radicalization. Longtime collaborator and Saint Martins classmate Steve Loveridge suggested, in his introduction to *M.I.A.*, the 2012 monograph of her work published by Rizzoli, that the easy success and white privilege of the Britpop set she was hanging with—including Loveridge himself (they've since become estranged)—riled the young artist deeply. He says she suddenly started talking about the effects of growing up amid the terrorism and strife of the Sri Lankan civil war and the systemic oppression of Tamils. She was surrounded by work that Loveridge suggests was "puffy, trivial." The artists around her were "exploring apathy," she writes in *M.I.A.*, "missing the whole point of art representing society." Arulpragasam was interested in confronting it all with harsh realism, making work filled with Molotov cocktails, guns, flaming palm trees, and prints of execution-style killings streaked with red. It was all reflective of the life that she'd lived before joining the rarefied world of "Cool Britannia."

After her inaugural, wildly successful art show, she was short-listed for the 2001 Alternative Turner Prize. But instead of pursuing that path, Arulpragasam reflexively shifted into making music. In some of her early press, the music was simply seen as an extension of her visual art—though in hindsight, one clearly sees the fomenting of M.I.A. the pop star, the savvy, aspirational culture worker anxious to illuminate her ideas with a brighter light. She has never wavered from that vision, her aesthetic, her brand, her way of synthesizing sources into a larger narrative or pattern. "The medium is secondary," she says. "You always have to have an essence, an idea. You do it in a song or a painting, or you make a signpost, or you make a T-shirt, and it's not enough. It can be even more than that."

Now that she is functionally inside the pop-culture machine, does that negate her ability to criticize it? Does her achievement and her visibility undermine her art's effectiveness as an act of resistance? On this point, she's emphatic: "That's bullshit."

Yet, as Arulpragasm has evolved as an artist and found real market success more and more, her art is no longer the product or expression—*she* is. As a result, she doesn't want to ease up.

"You have to constantly redefine who you are," she says. "The fact that I bombard myself against many industries, many cultures, many people, shows me putting content into my head and putting that dimension into my life . . . Politics has become a big mash of nothing, and to give it time would be a waste, because now with the internet, it's obvious what's going on. It doesn't take an artist making a huge album about it to understand. It's right there, on the front page of everything. We already know and we're already past it. It's more about what is keeping the people down from reacting to it."

JANELLE MONÁE IS BREAKING RULES AND CREATING SPACE FOR OTHERS TO DO THE SAME

BUSTLE, AUGUST 2018

Janelle Monáe is utterly composed as she tromps to set through mud puddles in lengths of banana-hued silk organza and a pair of rain boots from Lowe's. Handlers and helpers hold her hem high, their umbrellas lofted to protect the Mongolian lamb fluff on the David Ferreira overcoat dress and Monáe's flawlessly made-up face. Amid the downpour soaking the set on the historic Pullman Yard, a former munitions factory on Atlanta's east side, Monáe approaches the camera poised, focused. She kicks off the boots and climbs atop a small tower of crates; she summits and smiles. She knows her angles.

Janelle Monáe carries herself like a person living by a stringent code. She clearly holds professionalism as a virtue. Historically, this has played as Monáe being in tight control of her image. Her early career was built on a persona, with the young singer identifying herself as the android Cindi Mayweather, here from the year 2719 on a mission. The conceit contextualized her as androgyne, but in other ways was distancing and thwarted reading Monáe's robot-love material as biographical. Her latest album, *Dirty Computer*, is still as conceptual as ever, but the crucial difference being that Monáe is beckoning her listeners in, eager to make clear her motivations, fleshing out the meta-text with videos ripe with can't-miss references and AfroFuturistic imagery. The ideologies she refutes implicitly and explicitly in songs like "Django Jane" and the album's closer, "Americans" ("Try my luck, stand my ground / Die in church, live in jail / Say her name, twice in hell"), underscore that *Dirty Computer* is being issued from the grimpossible American now.

In the back seat of a black Suburban, Monáe is en route to a pop-up screening of *Dirty Computer* at a local arthouse movieplex, here in her chosen community of Atlanta. She has ditched the day's couture for her traditional uniform: an immaculately tailored slate gray pinstripe suit, her face framed by white-tipped, waist-length Dutch braids. She's starving after a long day slipping in and out of statement gowns but makes do for now with a small bag of chips. Monáe is reserved but warm, honoring any minor accommodation with an emphatic "Thank you so much." Her assistant sits up front, mutely typing away on her phone. The rain has not let up.

Monáe says that ultimately the message of the album isn't anything new to her work at all, it's always been there: "It remixed itself. Some of the things I talk about in the music I have always spoken about. It was just packaged in a different way—same person, just in a different time." All the distance that being Cindi from

2719 afforded her maybe muddled what she was getting at all along, making the material of *Dirty Computer* seem sudden to some, or at least as big of a surprise as when Tessa Thompson popped out from between Monáe's ruffled pussy-pant legs in the "Pynk" video. But Monáe insists she's the same artist, same message, but a more explicit articulation of what you stand for (and who you ally yourself with) is called for in the Trump era. Monáe admits that without the buffer of fame and success, the fact of who she is makes her a target: "I've been very fortunate to be able to have a career and to perform. When I walk off the stage, I'm still a young Black queer woman, born to working-class parents."

Dirty Computer posits a galactic shift for Monáe as an artist, both metaphorically and narratively, broaching something more earthbound and decidedly more human. "It was really about just creating more space for me and other artists, Black women in particular, to create new rules. If I can't be all of me, whatever that may mean to me during that time where I am spiritually, mentally, whatever person I identify as when I'm releasing music, then I don't want to do it." The album is given deeper context through the forty-two-minute "emotion picture" of the same name, each song's video lending itself to a loose story arc. Somewhere in a dystopian near-future an authoritarian power is rounding up and cleansing "dirty computers" of their memories and personhood under the guide of turning them into pure vessels, willing tools of the regime. In the videos, Monáe runs with a joyous and highly styled cabal of Black and brown women; their vibrance is put into dazzling neon relief against bland institutional spaces and decimated landscapes. They party and seek pleasure while attempting to elude drones and a militarized police force that behaves as aggressively as America's own. In the world of *Dirty Computer*, connection in all its forms is seemingly criminalized. In this world, connection is most often portrayed as fundamentally queer, Black, feminine, vibrant, powerful, and freakily free.

At the packed Atlanta screening later that night, the boldest portrayals get the audience—young, almost exclusively Black, in a wide array of gender expressions— extremely hyped. Hands went up for "Django Jane," the whole theater shouting along with the lines "Black girl magic / Y'all can't stand it," and moments of intimacy between Monáe's character and Tessa Thompson's "Zen," the film's heroine and love interest, elicit hoots of approval. When the lights went on, some folks were wiping away tears. Monáe spent the rest of the evening autographing film posters for her fans in the lobby.

"One of the things that I wanted to do was to be very clear in where I stood around women and us having to always defend natural desires. As I started to read more, I realized sex is a gift," says Monáe, who identifies as pansexual. She cites *The Great Cosmic Mother* by Monica Sjöö, the classic feminist tome on Goddess culture, as the source of particular revelation; the title shows up emblazoned on a pair of underwear one woman shows off amid a bedroom party in the "Pynk" video. "I wanted to make sure that in songs like 'Pynk,' we're celebrating women—

and not all women have vaginas or need to have a vagina to be a woman—but celebrating all of us. Celebrating all of the things that are beautiful about us in our sexuality," she says, adding, "I was taught at an early age never to be open about how I feel sexually."

At turns Monáe speaks obliquely, referencing herself within a "we" that alternately encompasses women, well-intentioned Americans, and, broadly, humanity. When discussion turns to the women in the last few years who have influenced her with their thinking, she becomes eager and animated. She shifts to first person and stays there, speaking definitively about where she's at and what she believes, as if immediately pinging off the inspiration of the Black women she admires: Yara Shahidi, Amandla Stenberg, Lena Waithe, Lupita Nyong'o, Issa Rae—all women, she says, who use their platforms in service of something greater. They encouraged her "to do more and to be better." And what does Monáe's *more* look like these days? Well, *Dirty Computer* is part of it.

Though she suggests her work is that of an ally and less an activist, the acceleration of the erasure of human rights under the Trump administration factors in both Monáe's art and her acts, as she has publicly aligned herself with the Women's March, Time's Up, as well as Black Lives Matter protests around the country. "There are some of us who are told that we had to pull ourselves up from the bootstraps and some of us don't even have boots to even pull straps, and that's a metaphor for a lot of things. That is what I was trying to do with *Dirty*

Computer," says Monáe. Her abiding belief is in the radical power and possibility of music; she says her mantras are "choose freedom over fear" and "I come in peace, but I mean business." For Monáe, *Dirty Computer*'s celebration, truth-telling, and joy are acts of resistance, but she also offers it as a safe space: "Things could absolutely get worse and so what I'm choosing to do, instead of wake up every day with hate in my heart for the abusers of power in the White House, is focus on celebrating the folks that need it most. Focus on the marginalized. Focus on the people that I can directly impact through my music, through my art. I think that my time is better served there with making them feel like they have community."

The singer offers up an explanation, lest there be any misunderstanding or willful complication around her album's deeply funky orientation point: "We have a vice president who believes in conversion therapy. That is a form of trying to cleanse somebody. That is a form of saying you have bugs and viruses, you need to be cleaned. That is what it means to have to live in the world as a 'dirty computer.'" A dirty computer in this specific instance is a stand-in for queer identity, but a dirty computer is anyone who is persecuted, marginalized, left unsupported. A dirty computer is anyone whose mere existence in America is criminalized. Monáe knows where she stands amid this, and she refuses such illogic on "Crazy, Classic, Life," singing: "I'm not the American nightmare / I'm the American dream." Monáe, cool as anything, grows emphatic: "This is a very American album, through the lens of a Black woman, and it's saying that this country may not be working in my favor now, but it will be before it's all over. That is the hope that I want to leave, because that's the hope that I mean."

THE SILVER LINING MYTH

MTV NEWS, NOVEMBER 11, 2016

In the months leading up to the presidential election, some journalists, musicians, and fans defaulted to the same glib joke: the silver lining to four years of increased oppression during the Trump administration is that music will be better. Punk will rise up and "be good again," pop will get "real," gain meaning, become explicitly political. Since Tuesday night's election results, this lame sentiment has been making the rounds on social media, but it's no joking matter; it's indifference to the plight of others and to the many possible ways by which Trump's presidency threatens to ruin lives. And indifference is how America got into this fucking mess in the first place.

Rather than fostering the fantasy that struggle makes anything more pure, more authentic, or better, let's consider how this hateful prick's presidency will impact art and artists. Let's consider how self-employed musicians, artists, and folks on the lower rungs of the music industry, many of whom have only just gained health insurance in recent years because of the Affordable Care Act, might be impacted by having that safety net taken away. Consider how access to mental health care, affordable medication for anxiety and depression, and access to birth control shapes their lives and their ability to write music, record, and tour. What about the musicians and producers who will have to give up pursuing their artistic careers because they have to support a chronically ill family member who has lost their health insurance?

To suggest that music is going to be "better" under this oppressive batshittery erases music from the past few years that explicitly confronts injustice. From Beyoncé's *Lemonade* to Vince Staples's *Summertime '06* to Helado Negro's *Private Energy* to Solange's *A Seat at the Table*, Kendrick Lamar's *To Pimp a Butterfly*, Frank Ocean's *Blonde*, and many others, there are countless examples of artists already making deep, passionate, personal-political art *right now*. Failing to recognize their music and the discourse around it as valuable, visceral, intellectual, and inherently political work furthers a hierarchy where some people's pain and experience counts and others' does not. The racist violence, police brutality, misogyny, transphobia, and marginalization that so many artists are responding to is *already bad enough*. Artists have been singing about facing those struggles since the dawn of recorded music in America; some just chose not to hear, or perhaps just got tangled up in some bullshit hand-wringing over whose music was "real," whose experiences they were willing to take in, whose disquieting reality they were willing to listen to. Suggesting that punk, or rock, in particular, will finally "start reacting" really means things will be so bad that cis white people will finally start doing something because the floodwaters have reached their door.

It also brushes aside the recent swell of a musical constituency in Obama's hometown, the second-term wave of Chicago artists finding a national audience for work that is very much *of the city*. These artists have released albums and mixtapes that are engaged, clear-eyed, and progressive, songs that offer complexity, beauty, wit, incision, mourning—all richly centered in Blackness and independence: Noname's *Telefone*, Mick Jenkins's *The Water[s]*, Chance's *Coloring Book*, Jamila Woods's *Heavn*, Saba's *Bucket List Project*. Add to that Vic Mensa, CupcakKe, Tink, Ric Wilson, Sol Patches, and DJ Rashad's opus *Double Cup*.

The notion that great art is best born in a hothouse of desperation is a false one. Music fans would be wise to interrogate the bootstrapping ethic that underlies that idea. It's not a challenge to Trump, or thoughtful resistance—it's a dare for artists to come out on the other side of trauma dancing. Survive, and entertain us, too. It is freighted by the expectation that *real* artists make the most of their pain. The insistence that music will "be better" makes clear you are watching from the security of your seat. It suggests that listeners are owed something by the artists they love. It abandons the work of bearing witness, of solidarity, and transacts on someone else's suffering.

To imagine that low times in America will inspire a

stream of remarkable and bold art is to misremember the past. Don't let the movements and sounds that bloomed in Reagan's America mislead you into romancing the trickle-down horror show of the 1980s, when a president's racist and homophobic public policies made it all too clear whose lives and deaths mattered to his administration. Don't forget what happened when Bush's war was imminent in the early 2000s. Most folks who were actively involved in the American rock and punk scenes didn't retreat to their practice spaces to jam out resistance anthems. Instead, many spent those years treating their despair by liberally dousing themselves in "recreational" cocaine and dancing to electroclash. If anything, it was an era of music that was defined by a lack of meaning, an ironic lilt, and willful obtuseness. Popular music rarely turned its attention to all that had come in the wake of 9/11. By and large, sentiment was vague and ironic distance was king. The most pointed and reactive works indie rock delivered in the Bush era were Pedro the Lion's glorious "Backwoods Nation" and Bright Eyes' "When the President Talks to God," which are easily remembered because they were among the *only* noteworthy rock 'n' roll reactions to the invasion of Iraq.

America is staring down the barrel of four years that are certain to be frightening and have an unfathomable impact on the fabric of life both in and outside of this country. For many music fans, music is not just for entertainment or distraction: it is for healing, comfort, where you go to find community, to find your people. Some of us joke that a particular song or band has saved our lives, others really mean it. Yet, this is a time when music can only provide so much cover. We're going to need to work closely together, and we're going to need to get real.

PART IX
SHE SAID

YOU WILL ACHE LIKE I ACHE

The Oral History of Hole's *Live Through This*

SPIN, APRIL 2014

What if *Live Through This* had gotten a proper introduction? What if the image of Courtney Love etched in collective memory was of Courtney-as-rock-star and not Courtney, grieving widow, giving away her dead husband's T-shirts to mourning teens? How would such an iconic album be understood now if it had not been bracketed by Kurt Cobain's suicide? And what would Hole have become if bassist Kristen Pfaff had lived?

That *Live Through This* made its way outside of the long shadow of death is testament to just how masterful it was, and is. It's an incontrovertible work that Love and her band fought to bring into the world to legitimize Hole as a band and as peers to Nirvana, Smashing Pumpkins, and the sensitive boy-geniuses of the alt-rock era. It is a ferocious album that ultimately broke through on the strength of "Doll Parts," a song so tender it crushes you, a song written years earlier but transmogrified later by collective grief. *Live Through This* was full of wrought anthems that married Love's lyrical genius and the absolute power of the band; the revelation of Love was that she was a contemporary feminist icon, one blessed with the cocksure strut and don't-give-a-fuck of rock's true greats. Love's surety of her band's rightful place in the hierarchy was fortifying, permission writ large for every weird girl with a guitar. She was compelling, terrifying, and incandescent. *Live Through This* was the portrait of a woman claiming her power.

Yet, for too long, the story of *Live Through This* and the true impact of the album have been overshadowed by sexist rumors and sick conspiracies. Here, for your edification and grunge nostalgia, is an accounting of what really happened and how *Live Through This* came into being, according to the people who made it.

COURTNEY LOVE, SINGER/GUITARIST: Our first record [1991's *Pretty on the Inside*] wasn't supposed to be melodic. It was supposed to be a really raw expression. It wasn't designed to sell any records. It was designed to be cool, really. And I don't mean that in a super-contrived way, but sort of contrived. We had a skeletal band, not very skilled. The next record was going to be more commercial.

ERIC ERLANDSON, GUITARIST: During the tour for *Pretty on the Inside*, we had been going more pop, less journal-entry noise stuff. The whole industry was going, like, "Look, you can be melodic and punky and be successful!" We never said "Let's do *this*, let's copy *this* formula." It was natural.

COURTNEY LOVE: I was very competitive with Kurt [Cobain] because I wanted more melody. But I already wanted that before *Live Through This*.

ERIC ERLANDSON: Courtney brought that pressure about competing with *Nevermind*. I thought that none of that's gonna matter. What matters is just that we make as good of a record as we can with *our* songs.

MARK KATES, A&R AT GEFFEN RECORDS: When Gary Gersh left DGC around May of 1993, I became Hole's A&R person. There was no question that there was skepticism within the company about Hole, to be honest. Anytime you sign an artist that has notoriety, some people are going to look at it differently. As far as looking forward to working on it, it's hard to say. You have to sort of go back in time, and yes, we knew Courtney as Kurt's wife but this wasn't about that. It was never—sadly, unfortunately—about that.

PATTY SCHEMEL, DRUMMER: That was *always* the thing looming, that her marriage and her life was bigger than our band. We always had that battle of having to prove ourselves as a legitimate band. All we had were those songs. That was it.

COURTNEY LOVE: Kurt got me Patty. I wanted to fire Jill [Emery, Hole's original bassist] but I still liked Caroline [Rue, Hole's first drummer]. Kurt made this whole lecture to me about that fundamental fact in rock 'n' roll that I really didn't know, which is that your drummer is the most important person in your band. Patty fit in perfectly.

ERIC ERLANDSON: Kurt was like, "We're moving to Seattle but we have to have the baby down here [in Los Angeles], so you go up to Seattle and start working with Patty and we'll meet you there later." I moved to Seattle in May or June of 1992. And of course, they didn't move up until 1993, so I was flying back and forth between L.A. and Seattle the whole time.

PATTY SCHEMEL: Eric and I were practicing *all* the time; we set up out in Carnation, Washington, at Kurt and Courtney's house out in the woods. We worked while Courtney was pregnant and having Frances and going through that whole drama with *Vanity Fair*. That was a tense time; I was drinking a lot. So there was party time and there was also the time that me and Eric spent relearning the back catalog.

COURTNEY LOVE: The songwriting process was really easy. We started at [defunct L.A. punk club] Jabberjaw. I wrote "Violet" there. Then we moved to Seattle in the middle of that. "Miss World" was written in Seattle, if I remember correctly. Look, I don't even remember who I don't like anymore. My brain is a little addled in terms of my long-term memory. It could be PTSD, which is everyone's excuse for everything. But anyway, Jabberjaw was the salad days of it all. I wrote "Doll Parts" in Cambridge, Massachusetts, in a woman named Joyce's bathroom. That one was easy.

PATTY SCHEMEL: Me and Courtney came up with "She Walks" in the laundry-room studio in their house and put it together when we went to Hollywood Rock Festival [with Nirvana]. [Nirvana was recording demos with their sound engineer Craig Montgomery] and when they were done working on ideas for *In*

Utero, Courtney and I went in and worked on stuff. We did the idea for "Miss World" and "She Walks." Big John from [U.K. punk band] the Exploited came up with the middle section of "She Walks." He was the guitar tech for Nirvana, and he was like, "Why don't we go at half time, at that part?" Me and Courtney went up to San Francisco when Kurt was working with the Melvins on *Lysol*. We went in and messed around, and came up with "Jennifer's Body."

COURTNEY LOVE: We had this great rehearsal space [in Seattle]: It was just perfect, up on Capitol Hill, near the Urban Outfitters. Everyone got really close. There was just a great flow. This all came about after the whole *Vanity Fair* thing and all the stuff with the baby. Those rehearsals were a really great escape from all that shit; the only way to escape it was drugs and music.

ERIC ERLANDSON: It was a refuge. It was an emotional time for Courtney and Kurt. I was involved in their drama and was trying to hold it together and replace members and get a record together. So how did I feel emotionally? I was a wreck.

PATTY SCHEMEL: Courtney would come in and add vocals and her guitar ideas—which were great—and Eric would fine-tune her ideas and make them amazing. But her initial guitar ideas were really, really cool. That's what Hole is: that sound of Eric's guitar and Courtney's vocals. Hole isn't Hole without those two together.

ERIC ERLANDSON: Even if it was just the three of us playing, you could tell something was happening that was bigger than all of us.

COURTNEY LOVE: The rehearsals just flowed. On this record, we didn't really need anyone to help us.

MARK KATES: It's one of my clearest memories ever from doing A&R, going up to see them rehearse in Seattle, and I thought, "There's an album here." I think it was always going to be great—it was just a question of how great.

COURTNEY LOVE: I put a lot of energy into the music because it was the place I could put my energy. And the title of the record is not a prediction of the future. It's, like, fucking live through what I already lived through, you motherfuckers! It wasn't meant to be about anybody dying. It was about going through fucking media humiliations like this. You try it—because it ain't fun.

PATTY SCHEMEL: Being a wife and being a mother, and all the drama that came with that; being a feminist, and then being known as Mrs. Kurt? I think a lot of all of that frustration and competitiveness went into lyrics, went into the force behind that record.

ERIC ERLANDSON: I found Kristen [Pfaff, bassist] in L.A. and said, "Come with me to meet Courtney and Patty when you get to Seattle." She joined the band, she moved to Seattle, and that's when all the songs came to life, literally. She was the star of her band and so she was bringing that to Hole and that created sparks in everybody; we all saw an even greater potential than before.

MARK KATES: I remember sitting in that very small rehearsal room, watching them and thinking, "No one knows how great this is. No one I work with has any idea how great an album this is going to be." That was really special. I knew it would blow people away.

PATTY SCHEMEL: She was in a band called Janitor Joe. We saw her play, and she was *amazing*. She was just cool. Her playing was heavy, and she was knowledgeable, and she had command of her instrument. When she played, that was it: we knew.

SEAN SLADE, ENGINEER AND PRODUCER: When we got the *Live Through This* demos, I realized very quickly that Hole had gotten a new rhythm section—it was much more musical.

COURTNEY LOVE: Kristen was just really, really, really good. She had studied music, studied cello. She couldn't do backup vocals. And that was okay because her playing was like, *you know*.

ERIC ERLANDSON: I kept on making her listen to the Beatles to expand out of that driving, aggressive boy-rock that was big in Minnesota at the time. Kristen was very into that. We got into fights over it. And I'd be like, "I like that, too, but you've gotta pretend you're Paul McCartney playing a country song right now."

PATTY SCHEMEL: There was such a confidence in her playing that it just all happened, as soon as she started to play. It was really natural for her. "Plump" was one of her ideas.

COURTNEY LOVE: I was really anti-heroin while we were working. And everyone did heroin anyway. If you recall.

PATTY SCHEMEL: Kristen became Eric's girlfriend, so they were tight. They had each other. Then there was me and my addiction with alcohol and drugs. Kristen and I would get together, and we were always trying to keep the amount of drugs we were doing secret. "Don't tell Eric." There were so many secrets. We were all frustrated, and we all had a lot of downtime. And so to deal with that, there was a lot of "hanging out." I was frustrated. I wanted to play. I wanted to record.

ERIC ERLANDSON: Kristen came on tour with us in Europe [in 1993] and we did a few festivals and a few shows, and there's people going nuts for a song that's not even on record yet.

PATTY SCHEMEL: At the Phoenix Festival, we were playing all these brand-new songs and there was just this sea of people moving up and down. It was amazing. Kristen was so great live. That was the one tour that we had Kristen on, but it was a glimpse of what was to come.

MARK KATES: I went to England with them in July of '93, and saw them at the Phoenix Festival and I remember walking backstage after this show and saying, "It really doesn't matter who's gonna produce your record because it's gonna be great."

COURTNEY LOVE: I wanted to be better than Kurt. I was really competing with Kurt. And that's why it always offends me when people would say, "Oh, he wrote *Live Through This*." I'd be proud as hell to say that he wrote something on it, but I wouldn't let him. It was too Yoko for me. It's like, "No fucking way, man! I've got a good band, I don't fucking need your help."

ERIC ERLANDSON: I knew there was that competitiveness inside Courtney. Because he's so talented, but at the same time, *not* wanting him involved. She had that conflict inside her. I had the same problem, I had the same desire. Wanting to work with him and also not wanting him to touch our art. It's so different than Nirvana: our energy, Courtney and my—our thing that we had been building. It's so different from Nirvana. I didn't want that inside; I didn't want the wrong influences to come in.

COURTNEY LOVE: I'm listening to the Breeders' *Pod* twenty-four-seven and I'm listening to the Pixies twenty-four-seven and I'm listening to Echo & the Bunnymen and Joy Division. I come from a different place [than Kurt]. It wasn't like I was just taking from Billy [Corgan, Smashing Pumpkins front man] and Kurt. I was taking from my own influences, hugely.

ERIC ERLANDSON: We never finished writing; we were writing the whole time, trying to come up with more and more songs because even though it looked like we had a good, solid album, we knew we were missing some pieces. We were still writing intensely and frantically putting songs together. It wasn't like, "Oh, we have these twelve songs, they're done, and we're going to go in and record now." It's never been like that with this band.

SEAN SLADE: There were only a handful of songs on the *Live Through This* demo—four, five at max. We liked to hear as many songs as we can before we say yes or no to an album. But, in this case, the four or the five songs we heard sounded good enough.

PAUL Q. KOLDERIE, PRODUCER AND ENGINEER: Early on in the process, we got a demo from Mark Kates and it completely blew my mind. A lot of times in my career, you hear something and you just know. When I heard the lyrics to "Doll Parts," I just thought, "This is going to be big."

COURTNEY LOVE: I don't know why we picked Paul and Sean. Because [Hole manager] Janet Billig told me to? Because they'd produced the Lemonheads? I didn't really think much about producers at the time.

ERIC ERLANDSON: We picked Paul and Sean because Kurt would just sit there and watch MTV all day, and he's like, "Get the guy that did the Green Day album." [*Laughs.*] Those were the videos that were on all the time then. It was Radiohead's "Creep," and then Green Day. I remember him saying, "Get the Green Day producer or get the Radiohead guy." I don't know what happened with the Green Day guy, but for some reason we got Sean and Paul.

PATTY SCHEMEL: I don't know why we picked them; I guess maybe because of that Radiohead record, I'm not sure.

MARK KATES: Courtney was kind of obsessed with getting either Brendan O'Brien [producer of Pearl Jam's *Vs.*] or Butch Vig to produce the album and neither was really responding. People who had done multiplatinum records.

COURTNEY LOVE: I didn't go to [Smart Studios, in Madison, Wisconsin] with Butch. I didn't want to go down that road and copy Kurt.

PAUL Q. KOLDERIE: I was at [Boston-area recording studio]

Fort Apache and I got a call from Butch Vig's manager, Shannon O'Shea, and she said, "You don't know me, but I did you a favor." I asked, "You wanna tell me any more about what it is?" And she says, "No, let's leave it at that and see what happens." Courtney and Kurt were meeting with Butch to see if he wanted to do it, since Butch did *Nevermind*, but Butch was tired after doing *Siamese Dream* and he wanted to work on what turned out later to be Garbage. He wasn't up for a Courtney record. Shannon said, "Why don't you get the guys that did 'Creep'?" And Mark Kates said, "I can get you those guys."

SEAN SLADE: Courtney was aware of us probably because of the Dinosaur Jr. connection, because Kurt was not only a fan of Dinosaur Jr., but at one point J Mascis was considering playing drums in Nirvana. I remember her referring to us as the "Boston guys."

PAUL Q. KOLDERIE: We had a phone conversation with Courtney that went pretty well. She didn't really ask us about anything, we just talked about the Lyres and bands from Boston that she was obsessed with. I remember, embarrassingly, she was talking about *Let It Be* and how she loved that record, and I said, "Oh, yeah, the Beatles are cool." And she was like, "No, I'm talking about the Replacements." I thought I had lost the gig right there.

MARK KATES: I remember it vividly. It was my idea. One day we were on a conference call: me, Courtney, and Janet Billig. Those guys were old friends of mine. I mentioned them tentatively, I didn't know if anyone knew who they were, but I knew that the first Radiohead record was popular in Kurt and Courtney's house. And I mentioned Sean and Paul, and Courtney goes, "Wow, Boston. The Lyres." I mean, it wasn't even a band they had worked with, but she was very aware of the lineage of the music she was part of. The next thing we did was put them on the phone. And then it happened.

COURTNEY LOVE: Went to [Triclops Sound Studios, in Marietta, Georgia] because Billy made *Siamese Dream* there. And I loved the way that it sounds.

PAUL Q. KOLDERIE: I went out to Seattle and did preproduction with just the band; Courtney wasn't around. They had already hired us at that point. Courtney told us that she felt like she was getting two guys for the same price and she liked that. We picked the studio because Butch had been there with the Pumpkins and Courtney was convinced that we had to have a Neve board and Studer tape recorders, which were top of the line. We were thinking about Muscle Shoals, but she called Billy or Butch and talked to them about it and that's how we wound up in Atlanta.

ERIC ERLANDSON: Kurt had just made *In Utero*, he got all these notes about mics and guitars and the studio setup and everything. He mapped out this whole diagram and it said, "This is what you should do in the studio." Of course, that all went out the window. The one thing that made it was this all-metal guitar that I borrowed from some guitar shop in Washington—Kurt suggested that one guitar.

COURTNEY LOVE: [Cobain biographer] Charlie Cross found this document—it's credited as Kurt's drum map, except it's not Kurt's handwriting, it's mine. It's Kurt's studio drum map, the mics to use and Billy's [studio drum map]; I combined the two of them.

SEAN SLADE: About when we started getting the drum sounds, Courtney called Butch Vig. She had been hanging out at Pachyderm, where Nirvana had just finished *In Utero* with Albini. And Albini is very opinionated about drum sounds. [*Laughs.*] I guess Courtney really wanted Butch for *Live Through This*, but he was unavailable, and the only time she ever really got involved with what we were doing was when she came in when we were setting up drums and said, "What mics are you using?" I explained that we were using this on this drum, this mic on this drum. "Well, what's on the snare?" "We're using a Shure 57." And she says, "Albini says Shure 57s suck." I had heard that, but everyone uses a goddamn Shure 57 on the snare drum, okay? But Albini had to say it was for hacks, as if it was an insult to art. And so I said to her, "No, that's not a regular 57, that's a Turbo 57." I made it up. So, she calls Butch and tells him the mics we're using "and a Turbo 57 on the snare." And [I] wasn't privy to his side of it, but he told her those were all great, that we knew what we were doing. There was never any technical issues beyond that. We thanked Butch later for covering for us.

ERIC ERLANDSON: It was the first time Hole had worked with real producers. I was really happy to have somebody outside the band helping [*laughs*] because I was having my ideas shot down.

SEAN SLADE: We never really talked about any kind of grand artistic vision of *Live Through This* with Courtney. The only memory I have of any kind of goal she had was when she walked into the control room almost crying and said, "This album *has* to go gold."

SEAN SLADE: That Hole hadn't become stars yet was much to the advantage of the project. They were very focused and very ambitious. The whole world was trying to figure out what Courtney and Hole were gonna come out with on their first major-label album. They knew that this had to be a maximum effort.

ERIC ERLANDSON: I was there the most out of everybody. After we recorded the basic track, I set up this wall of amps and would just go in and plug in different ones to different guitars. I remember feeling like a kid in a candy shop.

PATTY SCHEMEL: I got my own drum tech, Carl Plaster, who came out and tuned all my drums, perfectly, to notes on the scale, which was *huge* for me. Just different snare drum options was a big deal; just having the resources to have different drum sounds was cool. I remember getting "Jennifer's Body" on the second take because I loved playing that song so much.

SEAN SLADE: Kristen was just amazing. She's such a natural talent, knew exactly what to play, played totally tight with Patty. I have to give her credit—and this has never happened on an album that we've done in all these years—every single bass track on *Live Through*

This was from the basic tracks. There was no bass overdubs because there was no need to because they were perfect. It was an exceptional performance on her part. That's like a singer doing an album's worth of vocals in just one take. It just doesn't happen.

PAUL Q. KOLDERIE: Kristen is the secret ingredient; she made the whole thing gel and happen. It's criminal she didn't get to make any more records because it would have been great to see what came down the road.

COURTNEY LOVE: Half the fucking songs were written in the studio.

SEAN SLADE: We witnessed "Asking for It" from when it didn't exist to when it got finished. It was fascinating. There was a certain magic going on.

PAUL Q. KOLDERIE: I always bring that up whenever people say "Kurt wrote the songs"—I can say he didn't because *I watched it happen.*

SEAN SLADE: At one point, Courtney was working out lyrics and she came up with a line that I thought wasn't that good and I said, "Ah, that's not happening," and she goes, "Sean, you're not my English teacher." And I looked at her and said, "But, Courtney, I *am*," and she laughed. It's rare to ever get someone with that level of lyrical talent. I stand in awe of that. When you are able to work with someone who is on that level, that literary level, who stands as a writer—it's an honor.

COURTNEY LOVE: We collaborated really well. I just think we had really good chemistry, to be honest.

PAUL Q. KOLDERIE: You know those cartoon things where people are fighting and there is a dust cloud with sparks and stars flying out? That's how I think of it. There was always a fight about something. There were ashtrays flying. But they were never fighting with us. We would shut the control room door. We'd send them home and just work.

ERIC ERLANDSON: There was a lot of tension going on. There's tension in the room whenever we got together. *And* there's tension between Kristen and I because we had been living together and seeing each other and then she moved out. We were having this difficult, on-and-off relationship, and we go to Atlanta to record and we have to room together.

SEAN SLADE: Kristen and Eric had just broken up, so there was interpersonal weirdness there. But when they were in the studio, they were focused on getting the work done. Despite all of Courtney's idiosyncrasies, she's really, really smart and she was there to work hard.

PATTY SCHEMEL: During basic tracks, me and Courtney ended up leaving and going to New York to see Nirvana on *Saturday Night Live*. I was so drunk that I could not see straight. It was so fucked up. RuPaul was there. And I remember coming back and then having to do more recording and being completely wasted for that. When I got back, I was like, "I gotta pull it together." So that's when I did a bunch of crystal meth. We pretty much finished up our basic tracks and then we were kind of imbibing.

PAUL Q. KOLDERIE: The studio was in the middle of an office park in suburban Atlanta. The only place you could get anything to eat was a Fuddruckers or TGI Fridays. There was nothing else to do but work on the record.

MARK KATES: I remember Courtney staying at the Hotel Nikko, and I was driving her to the studio one day and we passed a billboard for Hooters, which I think was still a regional chain, and she goes, "Hooters? Is that like a strip club for the whole family?"

COURTNEY LOVE: We recorded all the time. We'd go to this one club called Heaven and Hell and I think we debuted some of the songs there, and people were screaming, "Shut up!" It's like, "Fuck you, you little fucking punk rats." But I came to this conclusion a long time ago: "selling out" means there are no more tickets at Madison Square Garden.

SEAN SLADE: The label put us up in a crappy corporate condo with rented furniture and no art on the walls next door to a coke dealer; it was almost deserted.

MARK KATES: The studio was in a strip mall next to an insurance place.

COURTNEY LOVE: Me and Patty shared a room and Kristen and Eric shared a room in this apartment complex. We went to work every day and had something to look forward to. We were making good music in a good studio. It was fun.

SEAN SLADE: We got the basic tracks in about four or five days, so from that point on our schedule revolved around accommodating Courtney's approach to the studio. We quickly discovered that if you ask her to be at any place at any given time she would always be two hours late. But two hours late *to the minute*. And she couldn't be fooled, either. Knowing she was going to be two hours late, if you wanted her to be there at four, if you told her to be there at two, she would show up at six.

PAUL Q. KOLDERIE: Nirvana was on tour and Kurt would call and ask us to hold the phone up so he could hear what was going on. There were a lot of crazy distractions. We kept our heads down and kept working.

PATTY SCHEMEL: Courtney ended up moving into a five-star hotel for the rest of the time we were there. I was like, "Uh, I'm cool where I'm at." But she's like, "Well, come over and have room service." One morning, I was with her and she got a phone call and was like, "Oh my god: River Phoenix died last night." So that was a full day of her talking to people on the phone.

SEAN SLADE: They rarely brought the weirdness into the control room. And occasionally I would wander out and hang out with them, I would experience it, but it never really bugged me—what we were coming up with had such emotional force.

ERIC ERLANDSON: Sean and Paul were good at pep-talking me, like, "You don't realize that if you just relaxed, and just accepted that you're good and not be insecure about it, then you'd be better." I felt like everything I was playing was pretty much horrible. I had never played acoustic guitar, but I knew I had to use it on "Doll Parts." So I'm playing this twelve-string acoustic and I can't even press down on my strings. "What is this? What am I supposed to do with it?"

SEAN SLADE: Eric was like Eeyore. I told him it wasn't very rock 'n' roll—the spirit of it is really about reckless confidence and going with your gut instinct, not about wringing your hands.

PAUL Q. KOLDERIE: It wasn't an easy band to be in if you weren't Courtney; she expected a lot from them. She sometimes expected them to know what she wanted even when she had not been real clear about it. She wouldn't say what to do; more what not to do. Eric took it personally.

SEAN SLADE: We set up every evening for Courtney to do vocals and she would sing two or three songs, multiple takes of each song. And she put in a lot of intensity and emotion. Then, at a certain point, maybe about ten or eleven, she was done. So the next day Paul and I would come in each morning and spend three or four hours editing and putting them together. We did that every day for about two and a half weeks until we had tracked the album that way, very methodically.

PAUL Q. KOLDERIE: She didn't talk about competing with Kurt. The Pumpkins were at their peak and Nirvana was the biggest band in the world, but she was feeling like she was as good as either of those guys.

COURTNEY LOVE: I think it's pretty flawless for what it is, for the time. For going from *Pretty on the Inside*, which is atonal and has really brilliant lyrics, to fucking songs you can sing along to? I just gave it my best. I gave it one hundred percent.

SEAN SLADE: Paul and I had different ideas about what was going on. He was very depressed; he thought the album was coming out awful. Whereas I thought that

334 THE FIRST COLLECTION OF CRITICISM BY A LIVING FEMALE ROCK CRITIC

it was coming out great. I came to terms with, or accepted, Courtney's idiosyncrasies a lot better than he did. I thought her craziness was somewhat of a put-on, a defense mechanism to keep the world at bay.

PAUL Q. KOLDERIE: Kurt showed up during a break from tour, got in late and then came to the studio the next morning. We chatted for a bit, he wanted to hear the record and we played him all the tracks. He was complimentary; he liked the drum sounds, thought the songs were great. Then Courtney said, "Let's go in," and they're both sitting in front of the vocal mic, and she said, "I want you to sing some harmonies." And he said, "I can't sing harmonies until I hear the songs; I don't even know the songs." We played the song through a few times; he may have been loaded, but I had just met him so I don't know what he was like. He put a few things on. If you listen carefully, maybe you can hear it.

COURTNEY LOVE: Kurt came to Triclops and he sang on one song, and I mixed it up and released it, so you can hear him sing on one song. But that's it.

ERIC ERLANDSON: Kurt showed up; he's not in any good condition at that point. He was not in a good place.

PATTY SCHEMEL: I remember he was on so much Klonopin, too, and it was like, "*What* is going on?" I remember he did some stuff on "Asking for It." They were just messing around.

ERIC ERLANDSON: He didn't know any of the songs, there were drugs involved, and Courtney's like, "Change something on this." Mainly just to get some harmonies, I guess. Not anything about the writing of the songs, not anything with even the vocal melodies. Everything was already done. He was going in there mumbling harmonies over a couple songs. Those things were not used on the album; they turned up in a mix later. You can hear him on top of whatever song that was—I think "Softer, Softest"—but he was never actually *involved*.

SEAN SLADE: I had one conversation with Kurt when we were mixing it. Courtney called and said, "Kurt wants to talk to you." And I remember looking at Paul and Paul giving me a look like, "You're gonna do this one." I got on the phone and Kurt starts going, "I got these mixes, and here's what you gotta do—you gotta make the snare sound huge, and you gotta double all of Courtney's vocals." And I said, "Sorry, Kurt, but we're not gonna do that. That's not the album we are making here, that's not the approach we're taking." What Kurt was saying, basically, was make it sound like my album, make it sound like *Nevermind*. And I told him, straight-up, no way, we're not going to do that. I probably pissed him off, but I didn't care.

PAUL Q. KOLDERIE: By the end, communication was at an incredible low point: forty-two days straight, working every day, the pressure cooker. We had the world's biggest rock star coming in and saying he didn't like this sound or he did. We wanted to just mix and get out of there. We felt like the writing was on the wall—we thought Kurt was going to take it and mix it with Scott Litt. It's what they'd done with *In Utero*. I didn't care who mixed it; I was just done.

PATTY SCHEMEL: I enjoyed playing all of those songs, and I felt comfortable, and I felt at ease, and I felt excited about all of the songs. I think I remember Sean or Paul saying, "Oh, this will be a great punk record"—you know, not giving it its full due. It was weird because I was so proud of the record, but it was hard to get any perspective being so close to Nirvana. Everything they did was huge, so it was hard to get any idea of what our record would do. I was so proud of it. And that was all that mattered to me at that time.

COURTNEY LOVE: I didn't feel like I nailed that, but I nailed my own version of it. I feel fine about it. I have a pretty healthy self-esteem. Sometimes. I didn't think it was as good as *Siamese Dream*, I didn't think it was as good as *Nevermind*, but I thought it was fucking damn good.

PAUL Q. KOLDERIE: We were up so close to it, we couldn't see what a great album it was. She wanted to make a record as good as *Siamese Dream* or *Nevermind*, and we were trying our hardest, but we didn't know how to do that. There is no secret formula. Sometimes it happens, and sometimes it doesn't. In this case, it did.

ERIC ERLANDSON: One thing: Wikipedia is so wrong. I just read the whole *Live Through This* Wikipedia thing, and it's so wrong.

PATTY SCHEMEL: Oh, so full of shit, that Wikipedia. France? We didn't go to France. That's a load of shit.

COURTNEY LOVE: I had a plan for the fourth record, and the fifth record, and the sixth record. I had a really grand design that got messed with because of my own problems. But I made it all the way to the third record, which absolutely, exactly was my vision. I'm not quite sure why *Live Through This* is so iconic. I think it's because girls don't make angry records as much. I've always thought [PJ Harvey's] *Rid of Me* was a far superior record than *Live Through This*, but that's good—it just keeps my ego in check.

"IT WAS US AGAINST THOSE GUYS"

The Women Who Transformed *Rolling Stone* in the Mid-1970s

VANITY FAIR, AUGUST 2018

In 1973, *Rolling Stone* was an epicenter of American youth culture. Still a fledgling publication run out of a ragtag office in San Francisco, the magazine's focus had widened beyond the stoned musings of rock stars and had begun to offer journalistic deep dives. In the mid-1970s, they'd break massive stories—on Patty Hearst's kidnapping and involvement with the SLA, on the unsolved murder of whistleblower Karen Silkwood—that created tectonic shifts in American culture and ennobled the magazine's legacy. This period was unquestionably *Rolling Stone*'s golden age—one that helped define New Journalism, breach birth "gonzo" journalism, and, quite crucially, establish rock journalism's language, context, and form. At the dawn of the 1970s, rock journalism was in its infancy—outside of youth culture no one took rock music seriously—so *Rolling Stone*'s dedication to chronicling rock 'n' roll's history (and getting it right) in their magazine and books radically shaped music and its culture.

Yet, for all of *Rolling Stone*'s revolutionary moves and culture-shifting mores, in early 1973 there were no women working as writers or editors at *Rolling Stone*; they were secretaries. (Robin Green, the first female writer for the magazine, as she chronicles in her memoir, had come and gone.) But forty-five years ago this summer, all of that would change forever. Over the course of 1973, a group of these sidelined young secretaries would quietly change the shape of *Rolling Stone*, from the inside, in a way that defined the magazine it would become, and change the course of music journalism.

The history that follows is the story of the first six women to join the *Rolling Stone* editorial ranks, and create the magazine's first Copy & Research Department, as led by the magazine's first copy chief, Marianne Partridge. A galvanizing feminist force, Partridge deputized these ambitious young women to turn *Rolling Stone* into a true journalistic endeavor: a credible music magazine. Though, first, they had to convince the men on staff that a group of young women possessed the authority and ability to do so. The women banded together in solidarity, gathered together in feminist consciousness-raising groups, and followed Partridge's lead as she ascended up the masthead.

The history that these women recount, which dawned forty-five years ago, is not the history that will be familiar to you from the recent documentary *Rolling Stone: Stories from the Edge* or even Joe Hagan's 2017 Jann Wenner bio, *Sticky Fingers*. This story is not about the totemic men of *Rolling Stone*, but the unheralded women whose steadfast and defining work has long been obscured by the long shadows of those men.

This history follows the accounts of Sarah Lazin, Christine Doudna, Barbara Downey Landau, Marianne Partridge, and Vicki Sufian's experience of what it was like to work in journalism in 1973, to shape *Rolling Stone*, and how they were shaped by their work. The sixth, Harriet Fier—who began by answering phones and left a decade later as managing editor—passed away the day before our interview for this piece. It does not account for the experience of the women who worked in art, production, or advertising, who, like their editorial peers, also had significant and uncredited roles in making *Rolling Stone* what it was. These women, collectively, helped establish what *Rolling Stone* was, and what New Journalism would become.

SARAH LAZIN: In June of '71, after getting my master's, traveling, and having lots of jobs—secretarial, at type centers, proofreading—there were only two places I really wanted to work: the San Francisco Comic Book Company and *Rolling Stone*. I had no journalism experience at all, but I had a lot of secretarial experience, and I got the job. I was thrilled. Editorial assistant was my title.

CHRISTINE DOUDNA: In 1969, 1970, I was living in Africa, teaching French at the University of Lagos in Nigeria. I had a subscription to *Rolling Stone* that arrived about three months late by boat wet and damaged, but [was] passed around with friends like it was the grail. It was unlike anything any of us had ever read before—it had our truth. I started there in the late summer of '73. I had a master's in comp lit and French and I just wanted to be in publishing. The job was to be Joe Eszterhas's assistant, which is a glorified secretary.

BARBARA DOWNEY LANDAU: The war really dominated my college experience, and after I graduated, I was a little bit lost or a lot lost. I had some pretty strong feelings about not wanting to be part of what was going on, so I ended up going out to California. I was working at an entertainment giveaway magazine and heard that *Rolling Stone* was looking for a proofreader. I said, well, I could do that.

MARIANNE PARTRIDGE: I was working for *The New York Times* in L.A. I went up to San Francisco, to interview at a TV station, the guy said, "Oh my god no, you can't be on TV, your glasses are terrible and your nose is too big." I heard there might be a job at *Rolling Stone*. I just cold-called and talked to John [Walsh]. I came over to interview for copy chief, but I didn't know [that] until I got there. I said, "Of course you need a copy department, of course I could form it." I knew nothing about copyediting aside from what I'd observed.

VICKI SUFIAN: Back then, ads were either "Help Wanted: Males" or "Help Wanted: Females." I'd interviewed with the editor at the *San Francisco Chronicle* and he said, "You want to be a reporter here? Look around this newsroom, *do you see any women here*? There is one woman here and she does the women's page. That's all we need." That was the atmosphere. I worked for three years as a reporter at the *San Francisco Bay Guardian*. Then, in 1975, I was hired as a researcher and fact-checker at *Rolling Stone*.

SARAH: I was the only editorial assistant at *Rolling Stone* and I really needed help. Christine shows up, she's beautiful, she's tall, thin, and blond—right out of Kansas—wearing a silk shirt with no bra. Joe Eszterhas hires her in a minute. I'm like, shit, that's all I need, but she's incredibly sweet, generous, a hard worker, and really smart. We were all in the same situation, so we became very good friends.

CHRISTINE: I don't know what I ever did for Joe other than flirt and answer the phones.

MARIANNE: They said, "Here's a typical manuscript, take it home and send it in, and then we'll get back to you." I had met the copy chief at *New York* magazine and I called her; [she] said, "Here's what you want to do." I didn't think I had a hope in hell. I was doing it because I was running out of cash. John Walsh called and said, "You can hire whoever you want but I'd like you to hire from inside, there's some women here who might qualify."

BARBARA: The editorial department was all men until Marianne came along. There was a sign over Jann's secretary's desk in huge letters: BOYS' CLUB. I'll never forget that.

CHRISTINE: Jann [Wenner] gave John the mandate to go

ahead and kind of professionalize the office because, at that point, people would write and just go right into print. Nobody would check it for anything. Facts, style, spelling, grammar—nothing.

SARAH: I was assistant to both David Felton and Paul Scanlon. I did a lot of transcriptions. The first thing I transcribed turned out to be Hunter [Thompson] and Oscar Acosta in Las Vegas. It was for the second part of *Fear and Loathing in Las Vegas*. I had done a lot of transcribing in several languages, but this was pretty intense. One of the tapes, they're in this restaurant and they're essentially torturing the waitress. Yelling and screaming and throwing things and I had no idea how to transcribe that. I remember asking Paul and he said, "Just put down what you're hearing." I did and a lot of it appeared in the piece. I felt very lucky to be in the Boys' Room. Really lucky.

MARIANNE: Sarah [Lazin] had called me and she was saying how much the women there were eager for me to be there. She didn't say anything bad about anybody but I realized that whatever was going on there had something to do with gender.

SARAH: I worked [there] for three years and Christine's hired as an editorial assistant. Then there's Harriet [Fier] at the front desk, as a receptionist, and Barbara, in production. There were other women, too— secretaries. I had a master's, Christine had a master's, Harriet was Phi Beta Kappa from Smith. We're all there serving these gods—but it got old. I went to

Jann and said, "I don't really want to leave but I don't see anything happening here," and Jann said, "Please don't go. Things are going to change."

BARBARA: I'd had summer jobs as a secretary where you had to wear dresses and get the boss coffee. Jann was sort of like that, too, and I just accepted it at first, but after being there for a little while, I started to push back.

MARIANNE: I interviewed Sarah, Christine, and Harriet, who were hoping to have the jobs—that was very obvious. Sarah and Christine had master's degrees in history and literature. It was crazy! I mean it didn't *feel crazy* to me because I, too, was working as a secretary. That was the way you entered if you were a woman and had any hope of moving up. It wasn't a question of quality; you had to be really well connected to move in journalism.

SARAH: At *Rolling Stone*, there were no women writers at all but Robin Green and certainly there were no women editors, so there was no model. In New York, the major magazines did have women writers. Not a lot, but there was Nora [Ephron] at *New York*, and Joan Didion. They were few and far between but they *were there*.

CHRISTINE: There was this group of ambitious women who were doing menial jobs. So Marianne just talked to each one of us and asked, "Do you want to train to be an editor or fact-checker or proofreader?" We all just leapt at the chance. She hired me to be a copy editor, Sarah to be a fact-checker, Harriet to be a copy editor, and Barbara to be a proofreader. She trained us all; none of us had had that kind of experience.

SARAH: Marianne came in January of '74 and she looked around, saw these really smart women sort of languishing, and she hired us all. She took us all under her wing and we became the Copy & Research desk.

MARIANNE: I thought, "I've got to do a good job here. We've got to make this work." I really was not qualified for this position, so the first time I got there [they were closing an issue] and one of the women working in production took me on a tour of the flats. I was walking up and down the aisles and she was saying, "This is how we do this, and this is how we do that, and what do you think we should do?" I could see how eager she was, and that there was this impression caused by John Walsh saying, "I brought in a real professional here." It was clear to me they were awaiting my arrival. I'd walk around and say, "The magazine is successful, we're not facing a crisis, so let's just keep everything precisely as it is and then let's go over each step and decide if it's the right one," so I could understand what the steps are. They said, "Great idea."

CHRISTINE: Marianne was a very demanding boss. We get to work between ten and eleven in the morning, right, and then work until at least seven. Then, on deadline every two weeks, we were there till midnight, 2:00 a.m., or sometimes all night. I realized well into my first several months of trying to stay in law school that I just couldn't do it, but I decided I would much rather stay at *Rolling Stone*, so I quit law school.

SARAH: I started the fact-checking department. I had no idea what that was, Marianne showed me how to do it. Harriet was with me at the beginning, and then Marianne took Christine and taught her how to copyedit, and we established a *Rolling Stone* style. None of that stuff had been applied there—it was just really catch-as-catch-can.

MARIANNE: There were serious writers who had never had a copy editor and definitely never had a researcher. It was a rough transition.

CHRISTINE: It was very intense, partly because there was so much resistance to us from the guys. Marianne was very aware of that and she wanted to make sure we were perfect. She really wanted us to know what we were doing. We were studying manuals of style. We were developing a house style. We were just thrashing all that out. We knew that these people that had never been edited were not going to take to it well.

BARBARA: There was no style book. There was no real editing process even. Marianne was willing to stand up to Jann, the editors and writers. She was a real role model of what was possible. I didn't have any role models like that up until that time, so it was pretty huge.

SARAH: *Rolling Stone* was starting to become a national publication—this stuff had better be accurate and libel free. We're starting to do big investigative pieces and work with professional writers who had been published a lot in other places, but the reaction was hysterical—and these were our friends! The guys would go over across the street to Jerry's and drink and talk about how stupid all of this was and in the meantime Marianne and Christine and Harriet and I were working on their pieces. Joe [Ezsterhas] would lay his buck knife down on the table, threaten in his macho way. I remember Ralph Gleason, who was my mentor, calling me up and he said to me, "Okay, Sarah, Dizzy and Coltrane are standing at the corner of Fifty-Second and Seventh, June third, 1952. Fact-check that!" I was like, "Come on, Ralph, that's not what we're doing here."

VICKI: Sarah was great, I learned about fact-checking from her. It was a great job, we would re-report the stories all over, call all the sources, research everything in it, so it *was* reporting. It was really interesting. I once had to call Warren Beatty to fact-check a story about Jerry Brown when he was running for president, and he said to me, "You must have the most boring job in the world," and I thought, *He is so wrong.*

CHRISTINE: They had every reason to be suspicious of us. We battled over stuff. We had to get every single change that we wanted to make approved by the writer. We were very professional from the go, that was Marianne's big demand—that we be able to defend what we were saying to them. I have to say, we did some idiotic stuff. I remember trying to get some rock critic to try to change the word "girl group" because we all wanted to be *women* at this point, we were so sensitive to language about women and feminists.

MARIANNE: At that time, Jon Landau was the records editor and I started editing his stuff because that was going through completely untouched. I was editing the Who review. We go through this little review. At the end of this, his last sentence mentions Keith Moon. I said to him, "I think this piece would end more strongly with the last sentence deleted because this next-to-the-last sentence is so strong—*is Keith Moon important*?" [*Laughs.*] There was a big learning curve for me.

SARAH: Little by little, especially the reporters, they understood. Marianne was and is still an amazing editor; she will make you completely rewrite it in a way that you feel that you *lived* for this rewrite.

MARIANNE: We had to try to find ways to be very kind, but strong. The very big names, yes, they were carefully read, but there was a lot of stuff in that paper. *A lot.* Nothing was being done—I mean *totally unedited.* When it could come to the copy desk, I began working with writers directly instead of going through the editor, and that was an incredible experience.

VICKI: It was the most interesting time to be working at *Rolling Stone,* all the great writers working there—working on a piece about Maurice Sendak by Jonathan Cott, and the Patty Hearst piece, the Karen Silkwood piece. Greil Marcus and Dave Marsh made music-writing political and artistic. Ellen Willis—the great feminist writer, and Gloria Emerson. It was *always interesting.*

CHRISTINE: We were over on one side of the building, where we'd be there late at night working, going through everything again and again and again. We had our own offices. That was a big deal. There was kind of an uneasy tension with all the guys that had been there from the beginning. If they complained to Jann, he must have supported us. He just trusted Marianne enough to think that she knew what she was doing.

MARIANNE: The first piece I edited was Ben Fong-Torres's piece on Dylan's 1974 tour. I had to kill forty inches to make it fit and I did, and then [Ben] comes in and somebody breaks the news and he comes storming over to where I'm standing making sure that all the sentences fit together. This was maybe my first or second week. I said, "Well, Ben, here it is and we have another two hours, we can reinstate what you need, but it has to fit." I step back and so he starts [to read] and you could feel him calming down. I mean, it was only excellence they wanted. Almost all of them, it was only excellence they were worried about. He goes, "This is very good." I'll never forget that. I thought, *Oh, thank god.*

BARBARA: It was very much "us against them." You're fighting for your legitimacy. You really have to fight about cuts and word changes. The guys on the staff didn't like the authority that we felt we had.

CHRISTINE: We were realizing that we were going to have to fight these battles with these guys who we also really liked and admired. We needed each other for support and we got it.

VICKI: There was a camaraderie. There wasn't a feeling of competition, we all did things together. Harriet taught me to drive.

CHRISTINE: It's sort of amazing that we were able to do what we did and that Jann supported us. Marianne was one of the first women who really gained his trust because he was so dependent on her.

SARAH: We won everybody over, but there was a period of time, maybe even a year, where we were sort of huddled all together, in these two cubicles next to each other, working day and night, twenty-four-seven. And then there was Hunter filing on the mojo machine at three in the morning, and he would just file gibberish, and we'd have to put it together along with David Felton or Paul Scanlon. It was just us against the world, and us against those guys.

CHRISTINE: We'd be lying on the floor, kind of napping, and then another page would come in over the mojo and somebody'd get up, copyedit it, and send it to the printer or the art department. It took a village to get a piece of Hunter's in the paper.

MARIANNE: You worked thirty-two hours. And sometimes Cindy [Ehrlich] and I would fly to take the paper to [the printer in] St. Louis and then we were really up for hours.

BARBARA: [Working on the copy desk] I felt elevated. I felt like I had more value. I felt—I had more agency than I felt like I had before, and with that feeling, you are less likely to accept things the way they are.

CHRISTINE: The goal was to make it more not-mainstream in terms of the message, but in terms that you can rely on: This is the truth. It's been fact-checked and the names are spelled right and the language is fluid.

We felt we were helping to craft a better presentation. There was a kind of journalism that was being done that was not being done anywhere else. *Rolling Stone* was a different world. It felt like the one that really mattered.

SARAH: We were fact-checking things like spellings of Keith Richards's name and there was no authoritative source to tell us if there was an *s* at the end of his name or not and his record company had been changing the spelling. There were a couple of really good sources, there was Lillian Roxon, there was Irwin Stambler. These were books I just used over and over again, but one was good on spelling and not for fact-checking, one was good on history and context but not anything else. I loved fact-checking. I was really good at it. Correcting spellings and being on the phone in the middle of the night tracking stuff down—I just *loved* it.

MARIANNE: It was only maybe once or twice that I really flipped. This one particular writer that just kept coming to our desk and it was just a fucking nightmare, it was outrageous. And so I just said, "Okay, put this through. Sarah, be sure that we don't libel anyone and put this through," and so Jann read everything. Jann was a wonderful editor. His secretary comes running over. "Marianne, can you please come in the office?" I said sure. I go in Jann's office and he's got the galleys— "What is this?!" And I go, "This is what your copy desk has been struggling with for a year. This is the shit we have to deal with," and he looked up. I was scared a lot in the early days, but once I stopped being so scared, I was happy there. I personally found Jann to be a great editor. We were all there because Jann took the risk.

CHRISTINE: It was a guy's magazine. It was very *male sensibility*, always. That never really changed, even with whatever we were doing.

VICKI: Cameron Crowe did an interview with Jack Ford when Ford was president. I had to fact-check it, but [Crowe] had left on vacation and left his notes. One of the things [Jack Ford] said in the piece is, "I don't like being in the White House, I don't get laid as much as I used to." This is the great quote, and so I have to call the White House and ask Jack Ford if he said this, because I can't find it in the notes. Ford says, "Oh, no no no, I didn't say it. Please don't print that, I didn't say it." I couldn't find it in the notes and couldn't find Cameron, and so we had to take it out. Cameron comes back and says, "I'm really sorry, he did say it." A few years later, Jack Ford, in Page Six, talks about the time he lied to a *Rolling Stone* fact-checker—*me*. A few years after that, at the twenty-fifth anniversary for *Rolling Stone*, I mentioned this to Cameron, that [Ford] admitted it. In *Almost Famous*, which Cameron wrote, there's a journalist following a rock group, and someone from the group lies to the fact-checker about something he had actually said.

MARIANNE: Less than a year in, I became a senior editor. I was at my first story idea meeting in a big conference room, the only woman in that room. All the writers had been brought in for this big story idea meeting. I had worked on an idea with Ellen Willis. I'd called her and I had said, "Look, there's never really been any writing on rape that's been direct." She really did research and she found a case in Boston [to cover]. I presented this at the story idea meeting. I was sitting right next to Jann and I started to talk and I realized my hands were shaking so bad, I put them in my lap. At the far end of the table, someone says, "Why don't you just lie back and enjoy it?!" and everybody laughed. I was looking at Jann and he was the only person at the table that didn't laugh. He was nodding his head, like, "Please continue." I got through and he said, "That sounds great, how long do you think that's going to take? Okay, four months, it's going to run then." Who knows why Jann did that, but he didn't laugh, and I don't care why. Ellen won a big legal award for "The Trial of Arline Hunt" that year.

SARAH: She had a lot of courage. She would go into those meetings with those guys. I didn't—*we* didn't. She brought Ellen Willis to the magazine for a rape piece, and Joe Eszterhas is saying things like, "Just lay back and enjoy it." She had a lot of gumption, and was a big force.

CHRISTINE: Marianne was the only woman that got into editorial meetings until we were eventually all promoted. I became the news and opinion editor, and then senior editor. I specialized in politics. Harriet did a lot more of the music stuff. Initially, we didn't get into those story meetings, but eventually we were invited in.

VICKI: By the time I arrived, all the women there had been promoted: Barbara, Sarah, Harriet. We were all the same age. The fight had been won by the time I got there, the fight to have jobs other than secretaries and assistants. They were all promoted thanks to Marianne.

SARAH: Marianne started [a feminist consciousness-raising group], as she does everywhere she goes, and included all the women. The art department and production department always had a lot of women in it and they were part of it, and some of the other designers and production people, and women from the advertising department.

MARIANNE: It was just women from *Rolling Stone*. I said, "Do you want to meet at my house?" The same way you always form a group. You ask three or four people and then you ask them to ask a number of people. We did and it kept on after I went to New York.

CHRISTINE: The consciousness-raising group grew out of the magazine. It was this core group of editorial women feeling this cohesion, and inevitably, with what was going on in the outside world, it felt like it was changing really fast—the feminist revolution. Everybody was talking about consciousness-raising and so we started having these meetings every so often in people's apartments. It just felt quite organic that it came out of this time and place and because we were all kind of in this project together that we cared deeply about. I didn't know what I wanted with my life and that was sort of the environment where I started to find out. Out of that period came this incredible group of friendships that were really unlike anything I'd known before. A lot of us felt that way. Marianne left to go to *The Village Voice*, and when she did that I became the copy chief in San Francisco, and Sarah was by then head of the fact-checking department.

BARBARA: Eventually I became copy chief after that.

SARAH: Around '75, Jann had shut down Straight Arrow books, which was the book publishing division of the magazine. He came back from a trip to New York with five or six book deals with Random House. One was *Rolling Stone*'s illustrated history of rock 'n' roll, and he signed Jim Miller and Greil Marcus to be the editors of it, and the *Rolling Stone* album guide. Growing up in the '50s and '60s and having no one take music seriously at all—it's just something for the kids, right?—meant *there was no history*. Plus, putting this stuff in context, I mean, you can't imagine how revolutionary the *Rolling Stone* illustrated history of rock 'n' roll was. The idea of having a chapter on New Orleans music, and then a chapter on Stax Records, and then a chapter on Chuck Berry—just starting to pinpoint who was important by creating a history, creating a record. Now everybody looks and says, "Oh, it's so old-fashioned, it's boy-centered, it doesn't include much about race." That's all true, but at the time, nobody was doing that. So I said, "If we're going to do this, it should be fact-checked. We're going to be the source, it has to be accurate." I volunteered to work on it, and pretty soon,

I was managing it. I had no idea what I was doing, and I just learned on the job.

CHRISTINE: I realized how much I loved doing the work and was starting to feel like I was gaining confidence in it and was good at it. It was just a brand-new world and I think we all felt that way. Dreams might have been just nascent out there but they really started to become reality.

SARAH: It was a very intense period of time for everybody. Some of it was about drugs and some of it was about sex, but in the end, it was really about doing challenging work and being on the cutting edge of journalism and history.

VICKI: Working there made me a better journalist. There was such an emphasis on accuracy and factual integrity, and seeing amazing reporting and persistence with investigative pieces we did there, the level of writing and the originality and imagination, it was very inspiring. I spent a year at *Rolling Stone* in New York and left and got a job in television. It helped me to begin my career in television for the next forty years.

BARBARA: I was ambitious. I wanted to be important at the magazine and I didn't think about leaving until after I got to New York and things changed. The idealism wasn't part of the magazine anymore. I was disillusioned and confused about what I was going to do next. My life took a different turn when I met my husband. He was managing Bruce Springsteen and I had a chance to go to Europe with the tour, so I went and that was the end of my focus on *Rolling Stone*.

CHRISTINE: I left in 1978 and started freelancing and editing, especially for *Savvy: The Magazine for Executive Women. Savvy* doesn't exist any longer but it was early on the scene for reporting about professional women's lives and work.

SARAH: By '77, I was less engaged with the magazine and asked Jann if I could set Rolling Stone Press up as a division of the magazine, and sell things not just to Random House but to Simon & Schuster and Little, Brown and everybody else. He said, "Go ahead, just don't lose me any money." So then I really started running it on my own. In 1983, I set up my own packaging company, Sarah Lazin Books, and continued to represent the magazine's packaged books until they stopped the program in 2017. I also became a literary agent to writers and photographers, many of whom I had worked with at *Rolling Stone.*

MARIANNE: [In 1983,] I started a paper in Santa Barbara. I'm one of the owners and the editor of the *Independent*, which is a weekly paper in Santa Barbara and an online daily.

CHRISTINE: Marianne and I are still very good friends. We're still actually partners in a newspaper out in Santa Barbara.

VICKI: Sarah and I have lived in the same building for the last thirty-five years, and Christine is moving in here in June.

JONI MITCHELL, *THE STUDIO ALBUMS 1968–1979*

PITCHFORK, NOVEMBER 2012

Joni Mitchell once called fame "a glamorous misunderstanding." As America's finest living Canadian songwriter (sorry, Neil Young), few musicians have understood fame's fickle nature so well. In the 1960s and '70s, Mitchell was Mary Magdalene to Dylan's folk-rock messiah, making music that was bittersweet and relatable, carrying what Dylan begat even further. Her work helped birth a new idiom that was personal and poetic, creating a new space for songs that made artistic statements unbound by cliché and tradition. Such was the strength of her music that Mitchell's lyrics didn't have to make sense. But they did, particularly to women.

Mitchell's first ten studio albums, cut during an eleven-year span, have been gathered in this import box set. During this run, Mitchell charted one of the most solid career arcs in contemporary music that then detoured into one of the strangest, following her muse into places that very nearly cost her her career and exhausted her fan base's patience. Throughout, she was confident and unrepentant in her vision, in an era where any ego at all was considered unbefitting a woman, even if she did have the gold albums and Grammys to back it up.

This is a basic box set—no frills, just all the albums' original layouts reproduced in envelope sleeves, the fonts so tiny only mice could read them. There are no extras, outtakes, or re-anythinged. But taking these ten records in a row, chronologically, it is a striking reminder that few artists have had a run like Joni (even her acolyte Prince only got to seven perfect albums before he started to fall off). Mitchell was pop's first female auteur, an innovator of singular talent, whose influence on music and songwriting was vast, immediate (see: Led Zeppelin's "Going to California"), and continual.

Mitchell was "discovered" circa 1968 when ex-Byrd David Crosby came through the Florida club she was playing and brought her to L.A. At the time, folk was out of fashion, yet Mitchell managed to pull down an unprecedented major-label deal for a girl and her guitar: total and complete artistic freedom, with the caveat that Crosby would produce her first album. It was rare for a woman to be writing and recording her own material at the time, let alone to be an unaccompanied solo act. Though Mitchell's debut, *Song to a Seagull*, was a heavy precedent for the era, it's a harder listen now, the fin de siècle earth-mama lyrics playing strange against the stilted, formal musical settings. The delicate album suffers under Crosby's occasionally overbearing production; Mitchell would self-produce from then on.

Clouds (1969) is the introduction to Mitchell's real deal, where she begins shaking folk tradition and giving off a little humor and spirit. The album sounds casual. Lyrically, she was transitioning from the era's de facto hippie sensualism (colors! the weather! vibes!) to the classically prosodic style she'd become known for. The album's biggest signs of life are two of her most famous songs: the kicky "Chelsea Morning," which is about as straightforward as Mitchell ever got, and "Both Sides, Now." Though she'd known burden and heartache plenty by her still-tender age (she'd borne a child alone and in secret after dropping out of art school and married singer Chuck Mitchell in order to make a family; according to Joni, he changed his mind a month later and she put the baby up for adoption), she sounds a bit too young and chipper to be singing about such grand disillusionment. Still, *Clouds* was a landmark, and she landed a Grammy for Best Folk Performance.

Ladies of the Canyon, from 1970, is Mitchell's most accessible album and it introduces her earnest folk-pop style. Her voice is newly elastic and expressive, and it's the first record where she sounds like she might actually be fun to hang out with. *Ladies* also features her generation-defining work "Woodstock," "The Circle Game" (Mitchell's answer-back to Neil Young's nostalgic "Sugar Mountain"), and her blustery gentrification sing-along "Big Yellow Taxi." All were hippie-era sing-along staples; it hardly bears remarking that these songs are some of Mitchell's most obvious.

The genius of *Ladies* is often circumscribed by Mitchell's proximity to supergroup Crosby, Stills, Nash & Young, the vocal arrangement and production invariably propped to Crosby's influence, "Woodstock" supposedly inspired by Nash's recounting of the event (she wrote it before he'd even returned from the festival). If *Ladies* does bear the mark of CSNY, it's to the album's detriment. The fruits of the Nash/Mitchell romance— his gee-whiz domestic ode "Our House" and *Ladies'* "Willy"—are saccharine. Their subsequent breakup would inspire much more potent work: Neil Young's "Only Love Can Break Your Heart" and some of Mitchell's follow-up album.

About that follow-up: 1971's *Blue* is rightfully revered as one of the most gutting break-up albums ever made. After Mitchell's relationship with Nash dissolved, she headed to Europe to loose the tether of her fame, eventually taking exile in a cave on the Greek island Crete. The trip would inspire the how-Joni-got-her-groove-back ditties "Carey" and "California." The album is suffused with melancholy for all that is missing: her daughter ("Little Green"), innocence ("The Last Time I Saw Richard"), and connection ("All I Want"). Mitchell bleeds diffidence and highlights it with spare notes plucked out on her Appalachian dulcimer. While her pals Neil Young, Leonard Cohen, and Laura Nyro were also pushing the singer/songwriter genre forward, none of them managed to stride the distance that Mitchell did here in a single album.

"Will you take me as I am / Strung out on another man?" Mitchell pleads on "California." She was famously strung out on other talents that were as mercurial as hers, fueling constant speculation as to whether this song was about Leonard Cohen, or that one about James Taylor or Graham Nash or that puerile heartbreaker Jackson Browne. The year Mitchell issued *Blue*, an album that would be a landmark in any artist's career, *Rolling Stone* named her "Old Lady of the Year," a dismissal effectively saying her import was as a girlfriend or muse to the men around her more than as an artist in her own right. Worse still, they'd called her "Queen of El Lay" and offered a diagram of her supposed affairs and conquests. She'd made the best album of her career and in exchange she got slut-shamed in the biggest music magazine in America.

Mitchell retreated from public life, headed to her rustic homestead in Canada, and returned sounding confident for 1972's *For the Roses*. Up until *Roses* she'd kept things minimal, here she stacked multitracks of impossible vocal harmonies, mimicking a horn section ("Let the Wind Carry Me") or interpolating and dueling with jazzer sideman Tom Scott's riffing woodwinds. Mitchell's vocals, fluttering unpredictably and with stunning control between the bottom of her range and the top of her crystalline contralto, were given a new stop; her heavy smoking had given her a heretofore nonexistent midrange. There's really no singing along with *Roses*, which is a fabulous fuck-you for any pop artist; these songs were hers alone.

Though part of the reason that she'd retired from performing in 1969 was to avoid the default of writing about the myopic rock 'n' roll life, *Roses*' standout track, "Blonde in the Bleachers," shows that she may have understood it better than any of the boys; it is one of the best songs ever written about the rules and (gender) roles of the road. "It seems like you've got to give up / Such a piece of your soul / When you give up the chase," she sings about finding identity and meaning in who you fuck, be you groupie or star. Freedom is an evergreen subject for Mitchell, but "Blonde in the Bleachers" gets beyond the thrill in partaking of what—or, rather, who—is offered up backstage. The quiet story here is seemingly one about the ebbing power of a woman once she's been conquered.

Though Mitchell was criticized for not making blatantly feminist or political (read: sloganeering) albums, her work was often tacitly so. Her songs spotlight the unspoken roles of women ("Barandgrill"), who they were *unrelated* to men; she gave them names, details, desire, motivations; there is hardly a more feminist topic than striving for a freedom that life and love has never allowed you. On "Woman of Heart and Mind," it's hard to tell whether she is mocking herself or the man she is singing to (or both): "Push your papers / Win your medals / Fuck your strangers / Don't it leave you on the empty side / I'm looking for affection and respect." On *Roses*, Mitchell sounds like a woman who's had enough of everyone else's shit, an attitude that certainly put her in line with the libbers.

Her 1974 commercial breakout, *Court and Spark*, found her backed by first-call jazz session band L.A. Express. It was her official severance from folk music. *Court* is her most pop album and gave her three chart hits, going gold five weeks after its release. Mitchell's production features heavy and sudden multitracked swells of

her voice that spike melodies like a choir of accusing angels and mimic strings and horns. Her arrangement on
"Down to You" (aided by Express bandleader Tom Scott)
is stunning in its complexity, yet it never shakes you; it is
still utterly a pop song.

Now six albums deep on the topic of love and loss,
Court has a marked cynicism. It's a grown-up album
about arriving at the intractable issues of adult love.
"Help Me," which was Mitchell's only Top 10 hit, is
cautious about romance; she's "hoping for the future /
And worrying about the past." The refrain is weighted
by the dawnlight realizations of that post–free love era:
"We love our lovin' / But not like we love our freedom."
For the largeness of her band (which included Joe Sample
of the Crusaders, and Larry Carlton, soon to be of every memorable Steely Dan guitar solo), they are nimble
throughout; finally she had a band whose deftness and
dexterity matched her own.

While promoting *Court*, which would become the
commercial and artistic high-water mark of her career, in
the pages of *Rolling Stone*, the album's musical sophisti-
cation was credited to her sideman Tom Scott. Her genius
was somehow still not her own. At this same time, many
of her peers were headed further toward the mainstream,
toward syncopation, toward rock, toward retro revival-
ism. As a woman in her early thirties, Mitchell saw there
was not much of a place for her among the new talents
and the Peter Pan–ing crew she came up with; she saw
jazz as a genre that would allow her to age gracefully and

expand as an artist, and so there she went. She was trying to find or develop a place to belong.

Through all of this, she arrived at *The Hissing of Summer Lawns*. The 1975 album marks Mitchell's official departure from the mainstream, her embarking upon her jazzbo journey. It's the album of an artist absolutely assured of herself, and it's addressed to anyone who might not consider her a *serious* musician, who believed all she could do was confess her heartache. Though it doesn't have the rhapsodic rep of *Blue*, it's unquestionably one of Mitchell's finest albums, and it is certainly her most timeless. Yet *The Hissing of Summer Lawns* was viewed as not merely a stylistic departure but a *betrayal* of her own image as well as a betrayal of her fans.

It opens easy enough with "In France They Kiss on Main Street," a soft, linear move from *Court*. What follows is jarring if you were expecting more of the same: "The Jungle Line" runs over a distorting sample of the Royal Drummers of Burundi tribal pounding and chanting, Mitchell going from husky to enunciation so precise about "the mathematic circuits of the modern nights," the long, low whirring of a Moog running the melody line under Mitchell's acoustic strumming. The rest of the record is dark, tense, and lilts unapologetically toward something softer and more ornate than jazz fusion with Mitchell singing observationally, about the place of women in the world, about the trade-offs they make for power and freedom.

Women of Mitchell's generation had been brought up with the idea that marriage to a man who took care of them would fulfill them entirely; it sealed their fate. Ambitions beyond homemaking were considered frivolous. The album is a reckoning reflective of culture at the time; *Hissing* is an album of women trying to find their real selves in a world that had groomed them for quiet obeisance to men. On "Harry's House," Mitchell sings of a curdling domestic scene, of wives who "paper the walls to keep their gut reactions hid." The song dovetails into the jazz standard "Centerpiece," which she sings in a voice not her own, playacting with an ultra-feminine one, creating a critical distance when she sings the lines: "I'm building all my dreams around you / Our happiness will never cease / 'Cause nothing's any good without you / Baby, you're my centerpiece." And on the devastating "Sweet Bird," she sings of women wielding power through beauty and youth, and what is lost and gained in that bargaining: "Power ideals and beauty / Fading in everyone's hand" and "Calendars of our lives / Circled with compromise."

Mitchell had never made a record that wasn't bigger than the one before and was shocked that her fans and many critics saw her new sound as an abandonment of them and a misguided move, respectively. Reviewers chastised her again and again for her "ego." While the album went gold and brought her a Grammy nod, as her 1974 live album, *Miles of Aisles*, attests, there were still plenty of people shouting for "Big Yellow Taxi." But that Joni didn't live here anymore; *Hissing* was proof. The era of Mitchell doing no wrong was over, and if her audience couldn't hang, she wasn't interested in trying to reel them back in. In the wake of the release, Mitchell went to go see Dylan's comeback-of-sorts, the Rolling Thunder Revue, and wound up joining the tour. At the time, she was a peer of Dylan, commercially and as a songwriter. She had a song in the *Billboard* Top 10, had established herself as a cultural icon, and, still, *she was opening*. When Mitchell recounts this in later interviews, she talks about how being on the tour was a matter of constantly having to subvert her ego to those of the men around her.

The two albums that followed are where Mitchell went off the grid. *Hejira*, from 1976, was written while road-tripping alone from Maine to L.A. and is a meditation on the value and melancholy of being alone, her guitar imitating the rhythms and expanse of the road. In spots it's as emotionally bare as *Blue*. It's a real *grown woman* album and may not make tremendous sense to anyone under thirty. Musically, Mitchell says she was trying to see how far she could get from traditional rhythm; the songs are long and lovely, burbling and unspooling. Whether or not you feel this era of Mitchell is unfairly maligned depends on how you feel about Jaco Pastorious and his fretless bass and its many, many notes fardling way up high in the mix. His playing lends a darkly cinematic feeling to the album, but in the decades since his trademark sound and style have been taken to such unpleasant extremes by jam and light-jazz bands, it's understandable to experience a visceral revulsion.

Inspired by the rhythms of Brazilian music, Mitchell issued the experimental double album *Don Juan's Reckless Daughter* in '77. Her experiments went further than just musical; she appears in blackface and an afro wig as a man on the cover. Less commented on is Mitchell in Native American costume on the back, palm raised, a bubble above her head reading "How!" (Her cringe-inducing arguments about it later on included self-justifying statements about how she has a "black man's soul.") The album is *solidly* jazz-fusion, indulgent in epic run time, with still plenty of Jaco-dominance. But! There is reward in the album's centerpiece: the sixteen-minute "Paprika Plains" is a freak-out of a song suite, inspired in part by a conversation with prickly ol' Bob Dylan. Even if you cannot abide the album, one must be grateful for it, as it is Björk's number one favorite album and source of inspiration. The last piece in the box, *Mingus*, her 1979 collaboration with Charles Mingus before his death, makes her seem like the jazz dilettante that people accused her of being. The ultimate result doesn't serve either of their legacies particularly well.

Though Mitchell's weird escapade through pop doesn't end where the box set does, she never recaptured the thread of popular imagination. Her '80s albums, like many of her hippie-era peers', were overbearing and scolding and featured awkward embraces of technology. She retired from music for long stretches to focus on her painting. Her last great record was 2000's *Both Sides Now*, where, her range ravaged by decades of smoking, she sings the definitive version of the titular song that launched her career and finally sounds like she's seen enough to know.

SLEATER-KINNEY

A Certain Rebellion

PITCHFORK, JANUARY 2015

There was supposed to be someone else, some other band that blazed the path Sleater-Kinney made, some fiery young upstarts who took up that banner and made us true believers, set the awful world right, stamping and railing under those stage lights, loosing that feminist fury, and earning the right to rule upon us in hot waves of punk pummel. Instead, we were left with a Sleater-Kinney-shaped hole in our musical cosmos for nearly a decade. Like Fugazi, Nirvana, or Bad Brains before them—each a singular force, so powerfully perfect—there was no replicating what or who they were. They ghosted as America's last truly great punk band, the last bridge out of Something Pure, an indomitable, baleful force, born out of pre-internet riot grrrl polemics and Olympia DIY, and just as equally a refusal to be hemmed in by the dogmatic rules of those schools. They peacocked their ambition with solos and stage moves. Their existence was political as much as their band was fun. Sleater-Kinney served as a revivifying re-enforcement of resistance, pissed dissenters in an era pocked by war, corporate creep, and high irony. They cared. Their early discography was stripped of blandishment and filled with songs that had the cause of duty. Their music was their way to argue, to assert one's right to exist outside the margins, to coalesce an insurgency, to give the girls and the queer kids and the weirdos the language and anthems they needed. Their shows were ecstatic, sure, but they were serious, purposed—when this band came unhinged in a song or onstage, it was torrential, an act of abandon, explosion as an expression of power. So now that they're back, the question becomes: Are they *still* that band?

Listen to their first new album in a decade, and the difference between Sleater-Kinney then and Sleater-Kinney 2.0 is fairly obvious. While *No Cities to Love* is suffused with that familiar intensity born of the trio's dynamic, the record breathes with pleasure; there is a tenacious sheen covering these renegade blues, more melodic indelibility, and more engagement of the same pop forms the band previously subverted. Singer/guitarists Carrie Brownstein and Corin Tucker, and drummer Janet Weiss, have coaxed the best of their abilities into refined songs that may be less wild, but are no less intense. They know the rules now, which means they can break them that much better. After a staggering run of albums that fought to prove this trio's truth and demanded the world give their spectacular motion its rightful berth, *No Cities* is a return imbued with canonical confidence. Sleater-Kinney's truth now has more beauty.

To get the revolutionary weight of that beauty, there must be some discussion of the painful reasons of Why

Sleater-Kinney Matter So Much. The band began as a way of recording obscured lives, with the riot grrrl movement serving as a catalyst. They were women speaking to other women with their songs. Their success was emblematic, their critical validation totemic; Sleater-Kinney became a front line. Waging a war for a right to be, they pulled their fans out from the margins as they moved into the light. The hysteria in Tucker's voice, the caustic edges in a Brownstein phrase—each word was an act of refusal: to be quiet, to be the good girl, to play a game built for women to lose. Their sound illuminated what it was to be alive, be queer, be feminist, be disgusted by America, to fight for a dignity denied, to want to dance and revel in love and resist death. Sleater-Kinney didn't mean something; they meant *everything*.

Their return is not a victory lap. It is a re-declaration of all they were, all they built. It is a claim of glory after all that toil. We still need Sleater-Kinney. And so do they.

"It was sad. It was real. I was crying pretty hard." Corin Tucker turns solemn sitting in a Portland bar late last year as she explains the moments that followed the band's final encore in 2006. "Did you stay sad?" I ask.

"I did."

On *No Cities*'s closer, "Fade," Tucker sings of the tidal pull of the stage and weighs the last gasp of Sleater-Kinney's inaugural run, which still rings in her ears. It may seem like a strange place to lament the band's end, to leave it like a postscript to this glorious comeback album, one that revels in all they have staked claim to since those Olympia basement days. Yet it has to be aired.

What happened in the intervening years informs the new record as much as their six albums of shared history. During the months leading up to that farewell show, the band had discussed the need for a hiatus. Tucker was anxious to have a second child; mothering her young son amid the widely successful tour for 2005 breakthrough *The Woods* was taxing to her family. Brownstein was similarly exhausted and hoping to pursue her comedy project—which would eventually become *Portlandia*, her hit sketch television show with Fred Armisen—or get a job at the Humane Society.

"It was bittersweet," explains Brownstein, smiling. "It was the end of a chapter, but there was a sense of accomplishment to have not skidded to a halt—we beat [Gwyneth] Paltrow on 'conscious uncoupling' by about ten years." She doesn't seem to have Tucker's melancholy on the subject. Yet, after spending the intervening years fulfilling her ambitions as a writer, performer, and musician, Sleater-Kinney's return is clearly the cherry on top of it all for Brownstein. "The band was such an intense commitment, so we knew if we stopped it would be a full stop," adds Tucker. Though, in her mind, she envisioned the hiatus lasting only two years. The door was not shut all the way.

Tucker began pursuing a career (that she still enjoys) in website development and made solo records; sometimes, she would start to write a song and then stop, realizing it was more like a Sleater-Kinney song. Weiss, meanwhile, was occupied by touring and recording with Stephen Malkmus and the Jicks, Bright Eyes, and Wild

Flag; the drummer also got a job as the permitting manager on *Portlandia*. "We're all friends, so we respected that we had other things going on in our lives," Tucker says. "We really waited until it was like, 'Is the opportunity going to pass us by if we don't do it again?'"

There is some disagreement about the moment when the idea of getting the band back together was first floated. Sitting across the table from each other at a friend's bar near downtown, Brownstein and Tucker recall their new origin story. "We were watching the debates," says Tucker. "And I said something about Sleater-Kinney and then asked, 'Are we ever going to do that again?'"

Brownstein corrects: "We were sitting around on the couch, showing you new episodes of *Portlandia*, and Lance [Bangs, Tucker's husband] and Fred [Armisen] were like, 'Yeah, you should do it.'"

Weiss says the choice was simple: "We had no reason not to." The band nixed the idea of a quick go-round—a few shows, rolling out the hits. ("That would have been hard given that we had no hits," laughs Brownstein.) They were in for a proper album or nothing at all. Easy nostalgia wasn't an option. They wouldn't do it unless they were sure they could build something worthy of their own legacy. They wanted to get it right.

"We didn't want to put out something where people were like, 'Wow, they really fucked this up!'" says Brownstein. "On your third record, there is a next time. But there would not be a next time if we fucked this record up. We did a ton of work on the songs—we would throw away a song we had been practicing for two weeks.

The three of us can get in a room and start making songs that sound like Sleater-Kinney pretty fast, but that's not necessarily good enough. We had to find a new approach to the band."

Starting in May 2012, Sleater-Kinney began tuning back up, bit by bit, in Tucker's basement, cadging together hours between everyone's hectic schedules. While the songs "No Cities to Love" and "Hey Darling" came right away, the rest of the album was as much a process of winnowing and editing as it was creating. They recorded hundreds of ideas; anything that endured on the merit of being catchy and succinct was subject to multiple rewrites. After years of being on what Brownstein calls "the hamster wheel of touring and putting out albums," this was the first time the trio had so much time and space to deliberate and woodshed, with the only pressure to get it right coming from within the band. "We had to push ourselves," says Brownstein. "It was painful."

Somehow, through two years of writing and practicing and recording, news of their reunion never leaked. They laugh about it now. "I was shocked the word didn't get out, I was blabbing about it left and right to friends," says Tucker.

"At the White House Correspondents' Dinner, [*The New Yorker* editor] David Remnick was like, 'What are you doing?' and I told him!" admits Brownstein, though she quickly qualifies, laughing, "That's not a name-drop, just an idea of how loose I was about it."

This aside is one of the small-but-constant reminders that while Brownstein is still as committed to Sleater-Kinney as she's ever been, she has another orbit these days. She is the one who gets lingering glances of recognition at the bar where we do our initial interview. She is the one who gets us courtside, under-the-basket seats for a Portland Trail Blazers game later that night, from her friend (and team owner) Paul Allen. (I ask her how close she is to the billionaire Microsoft cofounder. "We email." Do they text? "No. We're not text-level friends.") At halftime, Allen (*avec* body man) ventures over to talk to her about how things are going with the Sleater-Kinney reunion; he high-fives us roundly when the Blazers win.

It's not just that Brownstein is breathing the rarefied air of magnates and PR-ballers (she occasionally goes record shopping with Blazers center Robin Lopez); she's actually famous now. It's new enough that she alternately seems giddy and unfazed. As she guides us through the labyrinth of the basketball arena's VIP concourse, she's greeted with gasps, and gamely poses for selfies with fans. She gets an expectant, "Hey, Carrie!" from a particularly thirsty local singer, who, after singing the national anthem, circles us like a shark, trying to get a moment or shoehorn in on the cypher with Allen.

Brownstein is, historically speaking, one of punk's biggest pop-culture exports. When you google her, red-carpet pics come up before images of her onstage with a guitar. While she has transformed some, it's hard to imagine her posing sans makeup, T-shirt sleeves pushed up, giving the camera her tough-Patti sneer, as she did in an earlier Sleater-Kinney publicity photo. The nonmusical work she puts into the world now is a natural extension. Nothing is lost in translation. It all calls to mind the famous *Life* magazine cover featuring *The Female Eunuch* author Germaine Greer and the words "Saucy Feminist That Even Men Like." For Brownstein, going to comedy and acting was a relief. "On a personal level, I wanted to be judged by what I am doing now, not everything from my twenties," she says. "That's an intense reality."

Sleater-Kinney's story has often been, for better or worse, lensed by their gender. Their myriad successes were never fully realized until mainstream indie (and male) audiences set aside the gee-whiz of low expectations and recognized them as a canonical act. Which makes the recent box set collecting their first seven albums, *Start Together*, especially important: its feminist significance cannot be understated when so few other women's punk bands (five by my count, and that's including Lydia Lunch's spoken-word set) have gotten such treatment. Even now, we are still at the nascence of marginalized participants in underground music having their contributions and perspectives properly documented; it's fitting that Sleater-Kinney help claim that ground. As Weiss explains it, the making of the box set deeply informed the new album: "Being connected to the past and going through the catalog together—that was a big part of being a band again."

At the center of *No Cities* is the theme of power: economic, political, personal, musical. It begins with "Price Tag," which examines the lure of American capitalism and its toll on working families, and ends with "Fade," Tucker's lament about the price of being an artist driven by the need to perform. "Gimme Love" and "Fangless" are sung from perspectives of people refusing to feel small and actualizing their anguish; "Bury Our Friends" goes with a literal "We won't give in!" It's all post-recession *Spartacus* vibes and feminist resistance.

Brownstein jokes that she'd suggested calling the album *Power*—"It'd be the hardcore thing to do," she laughs. All three admit that their understanding of power and the true shape of it has changed dramatically since the band began, and Tucker says that the recession threw this into high relief. "I understand the weight of power, as an older person, especially economic power," she says. "The reality of making a living and keeping a family together carries a much greater weight for me than it did at twenty."

For Brownstein, Sleater-Kinney's rebellion has evolved: "When the band first started, it was so much about carving out some space for myself and our audience and our songs. I felt like power meant that you had to be engaged in a certain kind of struggle, by force of movement and battle—and that's very exhausting. Now power is more about certainty and stillness, and realizing that the infrastructures that we gather around and worship are the least powerful things."

"It's different when you are a young band," says

Weiss. "We are much more aware. Being adults with lives and families and careers forces us into the moment. We have a lot to say in a short amount of time, and that plays to our intensity. We're not building—we want it to be big, *now*."

THE INVISIBLE WOMAN

A Conversation with Björk

PITCHFORK, JANUARY 2015

With each album, Björk immerses us in a fantastical universe of her own design. Now, on *Vulnicura*, she's letting us into *her* world. The album outlines the dissolution of Björk's relationship with her longtime partner, the artist Matthew Barney. She confesses the devastation with candor. By the third song, "History of Touches," she's lying awake in bed, indexing the past with startling intimacy: "Every single fuck we had together is in a wondrous time-lapse with us here at this moment," she laments over glistening synths. She details her struggle to keep her family intact, limning distance, rejection, and the death of their covenant. The blunt force of her words is striking. And damning. The cast of *Vulnicura* is limited to a "you" that is only Barney, Björk, and their child; the "we" of it is fleeting. There is a joyous, striving *before*, which only makes the familial fragmenting that plays across these long, dramatic songs even more wrenching. She tries to staunch the ruin with love, but it's no use. The album ends with Björk's reclamation of herself, her voice, and her music, turning *Vulnicura* into a document of salvation, albeit a fraught one. "When I'm broken I am whole," she sings on closer "Quicksand," "and when I'm whole I'm broken."

Sitting in a hotel room in London's East End on Halloween, Björk, casually clad in a flamingo-pink kimono, red tights, and platform high-tops, is as eager to talk about *Vulnicura* as she is reticent to talk about what inspired it. The love, struggle, and dissolution are all plain in the lyrics, which are uncharacteristically diaristic; singing about a desire for "emotional respect" is more what you'd expect from Mary J. Blige than an artist whose previous album considered the world atomically. The few metaphors that do arise involve natural, immovable objects like stones, a lake, quicksand—dark forces, being consumed, certain destruction. The album's centerpiece, the ten-minute "Black Lake," is the relational postmortem, a litany of incompatibilities over rising strings, before Björk spits the rhetorical "Did I love you too much?" as if the question curdled in her mouth as she conjured the words. As much as this record is about *him*, it is also about Björk returning to herself. In motherhood, one quite literally becomes a vessel—a role that often continues postpartum. The young family takes precedence, and ambition takes a back seat; a mother can become the net around her loved ones, their needs veiling her own. It is the natural exile of domestic life. And it is a strange and powerful thing to imagine that one of the most singular vocalists in modern music could lose the tether, just like any of us. But here, Björk opens up about coming back to music from such a scene, filling her house and her days with loud songs. Over the few hours that we talked, she became emotional whenever we broached the album's core themes.

The pall would lift immediately, though, whenever she touched on the music that had pulled her back into the light: befriending and exchanging ideas with the album's Venezuelan coproducer, Arca; waking up to mixes by anarchic DJ Total Freedom; her lifelong love of Chaka Khan, Joni Mitchell, and Kate Bush; her desire to stand up for other women artists. *Vulnicura* may be the most tenderhearted work Björk has ever issued, but it also finds her most sure of her power as a woman, a producer, and an artist, all of her invisible work made clear.

PITCHFORK: How does it feel to be putting out a record this personal?

BJÖRK: I'm a little nervous. Definitely. Especially coming from an album like *Biophilia*, which was about the universe. This is more of a traditional singer/songwriter thing. When I started writing, I fought against it. I thought it was way too boring and predictable. But most of the time, it just happens; there's nothing you can do. You have to let it be what it is.

PITCHFORK: Did you know this was the record that was going to come out of you?

BJÖRK: No, no. With most of my albums, I don't really know what I'm doing for the first year or so. It's afterward, when it's almost ready and I start mixing and doing the photographs, that I can see it for what it is.

With this album, it was a big surprise. When I listen to the songs, it is almost like a diary.

PITCHFORK: It sounds like an album about partnership, motherhood, and family—things that bond us—and your worst fears about them ...

BJÖRK: [*Chokes up.*] I'm sorry.

PITCHFORK: The minute your children are born, underneath every thought is: How do I protect them? How do I keep this family surrounded in love? Then you quickly figure out that you can't always protect them. All of that is on this album, very nakedly.

BJÖRK: That's why I was nervous. I've never done an album like this. With *Biophilia*, I was being like Kofi Annan—I had to be the pacifist to try to unite the impossible. Maybe that was a strange, personal job between me and myself, to show how overreaching I was being as a woman. The only way I could express that was by comparing it to the universe. If you can make nature and technology friends, then you can make everyone friends; you can make everyone intact. That's what women do a lot—they're the glue between a lot of things. Not only artists, but whatever job they do: in the office, or homemakers. *Biophilia* was like my own personal slapstick joke, showing I had to reach so long—between solar systems—to connect everything. It's like the end scene in *Mary Poppins*, when she's made everyone friends, and the father realizes that kids are more important than money—and [then] she has to leave. [*Chokes up.*] It's a strange moment. Women are the glue. It's invisible, what women do. It's not rewarded as much. When I did this album—it all just collapsed. I didn't have *anything*. It was the most painful thing I ever experienced in my life. The only way I could deal with that was to start writing for strings; I decided to become a violin nerd and arrange everything for fifteen strings and take a step further than what I've done before. I had like twenty technological threads of things I could have done, but the album couldn't be futuristic. It had to be singer/songwriter. Old-school. It had to be blunt. I was sort of going into the Bergman movies with Liv Ullmann when it gets really self-pitying and psychological, where you're kind of performing surgery on yourself, like, *What went wrong?* Then I got really lucky. I'm not religious but I must have earned some good karma at some point, because as one thing got taken away from me, Alejandra [Ghersi, aka Arca] came. [*Smiles, tears up.*] I don't want to brag, but I get a lot of requests to work with musicians, and a lot of the time, I say, "I'm very flattered, but it's not right." But she approached me almost two years ago, and it was just the most perfect timing ever. I'd just written like a scrillion songs and done these string arrangements, and the subject matter was so difficult that I wanted to move away from it. Then she came on a visit to Iceland, and we just had the best time ever. She's the most generous, funny person I've ever met. It was such a contrast, the most fun music-making I've ever had, with the most tragic subject matter. Somehow, she could just take it on. Usually I do half of the beats and then I will get someone like Matthew Herbert to help me with the chorus of the song, or another guy to help me do other bits. But this time around, maybe because it's a relationship album about the duality between you and that person, doing a whole album with just one person made perfect sense. Toward the end, we needed someone to mix it, so the only other person who came into it was a guy called Haxan Cloak. Literally, just the three of us. Really simple. That's been really fun.

Alejandra knew all of my albums from her childhood—apparently, I'm big in Venezuela. [*Laughs.*] She knew my songs better than me. I would say, "Oh, can you make that third beat like . . ." And she'd say, "Oh, you mean like the third break of song five of album two?" She was like a library of my music. At first, I was really defensive; I'm not good with people who are fans. But it just wasn't that energy *at all*. It was a really healthy energy, like a student. Suddenly, I got to be a strange kind of teacher. I would literally sit next to her and, for the first few songs, the heartbreak songs, I would be the back-seat driver. I would describe all the beats, and then she would do them and add stuff. We did it together. I've never done that before. So I just sat next to her for weeks, and we did the whole album. It's the quickest I've ever worked. She's so incredibly talented and so eager to learn. It's one of those crazy things in life where people from opposite ends meet, and you've got so much to teach each other. It's really equal, what you've got to give to each other. It's been a strange album—the most painful one I've done, but also the most magic one.

PITCHFORK: In the first two songs on the record, you're singing about wanting to find clarity. Does writing a song about something that has happened bring you clarity on the other end?

BJÖRK: Yeah, I think so. When it works. I go for a lot of walks and I sing. That's when you find an angle on things, where it makes sense for that particular moment. It's more *that feeling*. In a way, I also rediscovered music, because [*chokes up*]—I'm sorry—it's so miraculous what it can do to you; when you are in a really fucked situation, it's the only thing that can save you. *Nothing else will*. And it does, it really does. I'm hoping the album will document the journey through. It is liberation in the end. It comes out as a healing process, because that's how I experienced it myself.

PITCHFORK: It very much does. Toward the end of the record, there is a Buddhist sentiment about the obstacle being the path. You sing, "Don't remove my pain, it's my chance to heal." That's how we figure things out, isn't it? That the only way out is through, that having things be easier is not helpful in the long run.

BJÖRK: When I say that, it might come across that I'm incredibly wise. But it's the other way around. I'm fucked and I'm trying to talk myself into it, like, "Go, girl! You can do it!" It's me advising myself. It's not me knowing it all—not at all. It's just a certain route you just have to go; I went through it. It's really hard for me to talk about it. It really is in the lyrics. I've never really done lyrics like this, because they're so teenage, so simple. I wrote them really quickly. But I also spent a long time on them to get them just right. It's so hard to talk about the subject matter; it's impossible— I'm sorry. [*Tears up.*] There's so many songs about [heartbreak] that exist in the world, because music is somehow the perfect medium to express something like this. When I did the interviews about *Biophilia*, I could talk for four hours about tech and education and science and instruments and pendulums—all the things we did. This one, I couldn't put any of that stuff on top of it, because it has to be *what it is*. And I can't talk about it. It's not that I don't want to, I'm not trying to be difficult. It really is all in there.

PITCHFORK: The song "Black Lake" illuminates these parts of partnership, or marriage, that you don't even want to give voice to, the stuff that you never want to think or say, because it feels too worst-case-scenario, too charged, too deep—because it's so unmooring to consider.

BJÖRK: I was really embarrassed about that song. I can still hardly listen to it.

PITCHFORK: How will you perform these songs, then?

BJÖRK: I have no idea. But it's like you were saying, there's no easy exit through. I wish. I would have taken it if I could. [*Long pause.*] It'll be emotional. I'm just going to have to cry and be a mess and do it. Right now, my life is not getting any discount, as we say in Iceland. There's no easy access. I have to go through that to

get to the next bit. I'm blessed that Alejandra is going to do the gigs with me. That's gonna be fun. It's
going to be concert halls, because I'm going to have
a fifteen-piece orchestra: five violins, five violas, and
five cellos, so the sound is really dark. It's very muddy.
Earthy. We're going to start in Carnegie Hall; I've
never played there, but it's perfect for this. It doesn't
really have an orchestra pit, so the string players have
to be on the stage. Carnegie Hall is also good for beats.
It's no coincidence that Duke Ellington played there.

PITCHFORK: Who are confessional singer/songwriters that
you like?

BJÖRK: Funnily enough, with my favorite music like that,
I don't understand the words. I really like fado singers
like Amália Rodrigues, but I don't speak Portuguese.
[*Laughs.*] I really like Abida Parveen from Pakistan,
but I don't understand a word she sings, either. As
for American singers, you know who I've loved almost since my childhood? Chaka Khan. *I love Chaka
Khan.* I've totally fallen in love with a remix album of
hers from the '80s. I don't know if it's a guilty pleasure. It's just pleasure. Obviously, I really love Joni
Mitchell. I think it was that accidental thing in Iceland, where the wrong albums arrive to shore, because
I was obsessed with *Don Juan's Reckless Daughter*
and *Hejira* as a teenager. I hear much more of *her* in
those albums. She almost made her own type of music
style with those, it's more a woman's world.

PITCHFORK: *Hejira* is one of the most feminist albums ever.

BJÖRK: Right? The lyrics! And *The Hissing of Summer*

Lawns as well. I love "The Jungle Line," it sounds like something somebody would make now, it's crazy. Maybe it's because it's not my generation, but when I hear the folk stuff that she did before that, I hear it as a lot of people and not just her. It's a zeitgeist.

PITCHFORK: When it was originally misreported that *Vulnicura* was produced by Arca, instead of coproduced by you and Arca, it reminded me of the Joni Mitchell quote from the height of her fame about how whichever man was in the room with her got credit for her genius.

BJÖRK: Yeah, I didn't want to talk about that kind of thing for ten years, but then I thought, "You're a coward if you don't stand up. Not for you, but for women. Say something." So around 2006, I put something on my website where I cleared something up, because it'd been online so many times that it was becoming a fact. It wasn't just one journalist getting it wrong, *everybody* was getting it wrong. I've done music for, what, *thirty years*? I've been in the studio since I was eleven; Alejandra had never done an album when I worked with her. She wanted to put something on her own Twitter, just to say it's coproduced. I said, "No, we're never going to win this battle. Let's just leave it." But she insisted. I've sometimes thought about releasing a map of all my albums and just making it clear who did what. But it always comes across as so defensive that, like, it's pathetic. I could obviously talk about this for a long time.

PITCHFORK: The world has a difficult time with a woman auteur.

BJÖRK: I have nothing against Kanye West. Help me with this—I'm not dissing him—this is about how people talk about him. With the last album he did, he got all the best beatmakers on the planet at the time to make beats for him. A lot of the time, he wasn't even there. Yet no one would question his authorship *for a second*. If whatever I'm saying to you now helps women, I'm up for saying it. For example, I did eighty percent of the beats on *Vespertine* and it took me *three years* to work on that album, because it was all microbeats—it was like doing a huge embroidery piece. Matmos came in the last two weeks and added percussion on top of the songs, but they didn't do any of the main parts, and they are credited *everywhere* as having done the whole album. [Matmos's] Drew [Daniel] is a close friend of mine, and in every single interview he did, he corrected it. And they don't even listen to him. It really is strange.

PITCHFORK: How does it make you feel when this happens now?

BJÖRK: I have to say—I got a feeling I am going to win in the long run, but I want to be part of the zeitgeist, too. I want to support young girls who are in their twenties now and tell them: *You're not just imagining things.* It's tough. Everything that a guy says once, you have to say five times. Girls now are also faced with different problems. I've been guilty of one thing: after being the only girl in bands for ten years, I learned—the hard way—that if I was going to get my ideas through, I was going to have to pretend that they—men—had the ideas. I became really good at this and I don't even notice it myself. I don't really have an ego. I'm not that bothered. I just want the whole thing to be good. And I'm not saying one bad thing about the guys who were with me in the bands, because they're all amazing and creative, and they're doing incredible things now. But I come from a generation where *that* was the only way to get things done. So I have to play stupid and just do everything with five times the amount of energy, and then it will come through. When people don't credit me for the stuff I've done, it's for several reasons. I'm going to get very methodical now! [*Laughs.*] One! I learned what a lot of women have to do is make the guys in the room think it was *their* idea, and then you back them up. Two! I spend eighty percent of the writing process of my albums on my own. I write the melodies. I'm by the computer. I edit a lot. That for me is very solitary. I don't want to be photographed when I'm doing that. I don't invite people around. The twenty percent of the album process when I bring in the string orchestras, the extras, that's documented more. That's the side people see. When I met M.I.A., she was moaning about this, and I told her, "Just photograph yourself in front of the mixing desk in the studio, and people will go, 'Oh, okay! A woman with a tool, like a man with a guitar.'" Not that I've done that much myself, but sometimes you're better at giving people advice than doing it yourself. I remember seeing a photo of Missy Elliott at the mixing desk in the studio and being like, *a-ha!* It's a lot of what people *see*. During a show, because there are people onstage doing the other bits, I'm *just a singer*. For example, I asked Matmos to play all the beats for the *Vespertine* tour, so maybe that's kind of understandable that people think they made them. So maybe it's not *all* sexist evil. [*Laughs.*] But it's an ongoing battle. I hope it doesn't come across as too defensive, but it is the truth. I definitely can feel the third or fourth feminist wave in the air, so maybe this is a good time to open that Pandora's box a little bit and air it out.

A WOMAN EVERY HOUR

How Nashville's Women Are Fighting Country's Bro Rule

ELLE, OCTOBER 2018

It's Monday night at the Listening Room Cafe in Nashville's SoBro neighborhood, and the venue is nearly full for the dinner seating. The air is thick with the smell of barbecue; the servers are apologetic—they're out of the pulled pork. The crowd is here to see "Song Suffragettes," Nashville's only weekly showcase for female songwriters. The lights come up, and out strides Kalie Shorr, a regular presence on the Song Suffragettes stage, followed by four young women holding acoustic guitars. Shorr sits on the center stool. Next to her is Candi Carpenter, her best friend and occasional writing partner. The rapport between all five women is collegial and affirming; the group is more racially diverse than mainstream country would lead you to anticipate. They sing along to each other's choruses. Their collective talent is palpable—and on a few songs, chill-inducing. By way of an intro, Shorr explains why this night is necessary: "Women in Nashville deserve to be heard, even if they are not on the radio." The audience, a few hundred deep, whoops and whistles in agreement.

In the past few years, the number of women artists on country radio has been steadily declining. According to trade publication *Country Aircheck*, in 2016, women made up 13 percent of radio play; by 2017, that figure was down to a meager 10.4 percent. The country radio programmer quota-cum-excuse that fuels this inequity is that "one woman an hour" is plenty. In response, labels have grown reluctant to sign women, knowing that radio won't support them. Festival and tour promoters excuse the dearth of female country acts on lineups by pointing fingers at radio and labels, insisting that there are not enough bankable women artists to draw from—just superstar headliners like Miranda Lambert and Carrie Underwood.

All of this, as both artists and activists attest, has created an environment in which women are locked out of opportunities and subject to systemic discrimination and barriers, and one in which a growing pool of talented young women are pitted against one another. Industry insiders say that the mechanisms that help establish an artist's career—radio airplay, recording contracts, support slots on major tours, promotional commitments from labels, festival bookings—now rarely exist for women artists. This has created two classes of women in Nashville: superstars, and those whose careers are stalled on country music's lowest rungs.

The issue has been in plain sight in Nashville for years,

though efforts to address gender inequity are more recent. Change the Conversation, an organization founded by CMT executive Leslie Fram, industry stalwart Tracy Gershon, and journalist Beverly Keel, began holding meetings with industry leaders in 2015 to raise awareness and advocate for change. The organization—and also Shorr's career-launching anthem "Fight Like a Girl"—gained momentum in the wake of "SaladGate," a 2015 incident in which radio consultant Keith Hill told *Country Aircheck* that female artists are the tomatoes, and not the lettuce, of the country music salad, and should be programmed sparingly. His evidence: In 1997, spotting a downward trend of listenership on thirty-five-plus country stations, Hill theorized the issue was too many women artists. He tested the hypothesis with four stations, which he says saw a ratings boost after cutting the number of spins of women stars. His thin argument has subsequently been used to justify the erasure of women from country radio in the two decades since.

Political economist Devarati Ghosh's 2015 study on gender disparity in country airplay reinforces a popular theory that the less often women are played, the more jarring it can be when they do pop up. In her research, she discovered that women artists were given fewer opportunities to develop an audience or to get airplay beyond their first singles. Ghosh noted that while roughly the same number of women artists were being brought to market as in years past, their success rate at country radio showed a significant decline. Women country artists receive much less sustained airplay than men; men routinely see their songs remain in rotation weeks, and even months, longer. These are the sorts of programming commitments necessary to establish a new artist, as well as maintain momentum for a veteran artist.

Hill insists the declining number of women on country radio is a direct result of SaladGate, not because of his comments, but rather the protest in the wake of them, that their outcry has just publicized his reasoning. "The efforts on the part of females to get more females played on country radio have actually caused the numbers to go down," he says. "The metric always existed. All I did was give voice to it." He also suggests that the reason women don't want to hear women is, in fact, biological. "Women have ears that hear the higher range," he says, so that they can be attuned to the cries of babies, and the higher frequency of women's singing voices is "an irritant" to women listeners. This theory has further codified the sexism of country radio; many programmers insist that women listeners of country radio don't like to hear women's voices. And if stations play more than 13 to 15 percent women—at least, according to Hill—ratings dip.

Kacey Musgraves, whose latest album, *Golden Hour*, debuted at number one on the country charts with only modest radio support, isn't buying it. "On a recent road trip, my husband and I decided, out of sheer boredom, to listen to country radio and tally the number of males versus females we heard," she says. "It was, not shockingly, so offensive—two females among thirty-one males in about a couple of hours. We also tallied the number of times—thirty-five—we heard references to a woman's body or skimpy clothing, or the actions the man wanted her to do: cook for him, please him sexually, bring him a beer. And we're being told women want to hear that over hearing other women?"

Carrie Underwood, whose total global sales of 65 million records have made her the biggest artist in the history of country music, agrees with Musgraves's assessment. "I think it's really great that there's fan advocacy and social media support around women in country music, because there are so many incredible female artists who, for some reason, are not being given a chance," she says. "We are told time and time again that the women listeners who make up the majority of country music radio listeners don't want to hear other women on the radio, which I think is not true. Growing up, it was incredibly important to hear strong, amazing, talented women on the radio. It let me know that I could do that, too."

The Nashville-based Women of Music Action Network (WOMAN), a group of artists and industry folks founded in the wake of #MeToo and Time's Up, has moved toward concrete action. "Every industry was having a time of reflection, looking at how women are treated. Country music just didn't seem to be having that same moment," says a representative of the organization (whose members remain anonymous in order to speak freely). "It's concerning from an economic perspective for the female artists, and then, obviously, it's at its most severe in terms of the sexual harassment and abuse that permeate a culture where women aren't really present as leaders, and their voices aren't being heard."

WOMAN's work for a more equitable industry extends beyond airplay. As Marissa R. Moss's recent investigation for *Rolling Stone* uncovered, sexual harassment in the realm of country radio promotion—in which young women are cajoled into sitting on programmers' or DJs' laps and subject to unwanted advances—is widespread. Taylor Swift's lawsuit against the DJ who groped her in 2013 evidences that women artists are surrounded by a culture of men's entitlement, be they upstarts or superstars. Swift's charges hardly seemed to impact the DJ's career; earlier this year he landed a new job cohosting a morning show in Mississippi.

WOMAN Nashville's tactics are a strategic pivot from the way Change the Conversation and others have been operating so far; the group is public-facing in its presentation of solutions. They tweet screenshots of what Hot Country weekly playlists would look like without male artists, often highlighting a lone female artist in rotation—naming and shaming dozens of stations directly. They've had some success with request campaigns and have offered research to Country Radio Seminar and advocated for Time's Up messaging at the Country Music Association Awards. Still, what has gotten the most notice is artists being the change, namely Carrie Underwood's decision to only bring women artists (Maddie & Tae and Runaway June) as support on her Cry Pretty Tour 360, specifically. Underwood says her choice was based on her desire to give young talent a boost, adding, "It's really wonderful to see female artists supporting each other. That is one amazing thing that has come out of the lack of females being supported in country music: we are all rallying together."

KACEY MUSGRAVES, JANELLE MONÁE, AND THE YEAR OF THE WOMAN . . . AGAIN

VILLAGE VOICE PAZZ & JOP CRITICS POLL, FEBRUARY 2019

This year, I spent more time listening to the radio than I have since high school, when the college station was still my primary method of music discovery outside of singles bins. I sensed that the tyranny of streaming services' endless options was deadening my connection, so, here amid the hissing exurban lawns of Chicago, I kept the radio on. I drank deep from the bygone pleasure of *no choice*—my options being either "listen patiently and trust the DJ" or "turn it off." WLUW (Loyola's student/community station) and Vocalo (Chicago Public Radio's urban alternative station) were my primary waves, occasionally supplemented by the low-wattage high school station near me for its mix of Soundcloud ultra-now and a previous generation's Slint carts. Radio remains a relief, a direct signal: there was no mediating digital platform capitalizing on my listening habits; what I liked and didn't was kept to the confines of my nucleus accumbens and the confidences of whoever was riding shotgun in my car. I routinely found myself patiently parked at my destination awaiting a giddy, too-quiet back announcement of a six-song set, in hopes the DJ would sate my curiosity (most recent discoveries being Serengeti's "West of Western," Jean Deaux's "Energy," Pill's "Midtown," and KGB's 1995 gem "Bless Ya Life"). While some of the comfort of this routine was fundamentally due to nostalgia, the sense of moderation it offered—wherein algorithmic personalization was impossible, wherein the contract of the music experience was without exploitation—was as thrillingly novel as it was revivifying.

Many of the records crowded atop this year's Pazz & Jop poll offer a similar feeling; they are albums that built discrete new worlds, or at least felt blessedly different from this one. They transported. They immersed the listener deep in the maker's vision. They offered songs that recognize diffuse sexual, social, racial realities, and vividly imagined what might lie beyond chaos, strife, and dysfunction; these are albums that collectively beckon their listeners forward. They mourn what is lost and survive it. More than a collective "Thank U, Next," the eight women-made albums of the Top 10—*Golden Hour*, *Dirty Computer*, *Invasion of Privacy*, *Be the Cowboy*, *Honey*, *Room 25*, *Historian*, and the Mimi-murmurs within Low's *Double Negative*—imbued potentiality into a year that felt bereft of it; you could trust their vision. These records asserted power that was nutritive, power that was symbiotic and psychically sustentative, amid a year defined by grievous abuses of power.

Perhaps this is part of the reason *Golden Hour* triumphed like it did this year. With the breezy dissolve of "Lonely Weekend" and the sweet, disco-y kiss-off of "High Horse," it was a languorous album that offered a space to arrest your very necessary cynicism. In a different but similarly masterful way to Cardi B's *Invasion of Privacy*, Janelle Monáe's *Dirty Computer*, and especially Robyn's *Honey*, *Golden Hour* was a balm of transcendence and space of possibility. Perhaps, as critic Marissa Moss suggested, *Golden Hour* "presents a different breed of protest song: one where there's protest in kindness, in the appreciation of beauty and a sense of being grateful about the world." While no one is imagining a praxis of *posi vibes* in the face of the whipsaw horrors of America's foreign and domestic policy, *Golden Hour* was forty-six minutes of stoned connection and the earth spinning at a reasonable pace. This year's top three albums, most particularly, felt life-affirming: Monáe's earthbound resistance-funk was brought into high relief for me as I watched young people holler, dance, and wipe away tears in the aisles of a *Dirty Computer* screening in Atlanta. And the pure joy of Cardi B, like Sylvia Plath's imagined Lady Lazarus, rising elegant and powerful from the ash of the earth and eating men like air—may her reign never end.

This year is unprecedented in the history of the Pazz & Jop Critics Poll in the number of women artists that populate the Top 10, the fact that women make up the Top 5, and that they positively dominate the Top 35—and, yet, they are anything but a uniform bloc. It's hard not to take this year's poll as a sure sign that Music Culture Has Changed, or that the patriarchal paradigm has shifted. What unifies these artists is not gender, but that they are making ambitious albums too bold and exciting to be ignored. This *momentous occasion* cannot and should not be seen as these artists being suddenly exceptional, or a rushing of the gates. To suggest women have arrived erases the fact that they have, in fact, always been here. As with any group marginalized within music culture, their being continually situated as breaking through has only reinforced their exteriority to structural power, framing their successes as an illegitimate seizure of that power. Women have been making ambitious music *too bold to be ignored* as long as women have been making music (Hildegard of Bingen dropped *Ordo Virtutum* in 1151!), but that didn't help their work from being ignored and woefully misunderstood anyway. Apologies to LL, but you can't call it a comeback when they've been here for millennia.

As one of the writers who regularly gets called up when some jeremiad or pronouncement about *women in music* is needed (a living [sorta, still] that I am goddamned grateful for), I'm keen to note it is year twenty-four, for me, of pounding my shoe on the table yelling, *The time is now!* As Nina Simone once put it, "Same old game / Same old thing." In his 1993 P & J missive, Robert Christgau notes it's the fifth (or sixth) "Year of the Woman" in the poll's history, and that was a quarter-century ago. The earliest Women in Rock trend pieces and Women Finally Have Arrived pronouncements were published in 1968. That's a long-ass insurgency. Fifty years of perpetual arrival. If this was the Old Testament, we woulda been back in Canaan a decade ago. So, are women here yet?

If this poll's results have any relationship to the still-burgeoning #MeToo movement, perhaps it is that they evidence a wizened deliberative body (lord, hear my prayer). The toll of music's Great Men is *known*, and just who has been obscured by their long shadows and music journalism's role in perpetuating the Great Man myth is no longer going unexamined. All that has been ignored to preserve the reputation of these so-called Great Men, all that has been justified by saying it's the nature of the music industry, that it's sex drugs and rock 'n' roll, that it's a tough business and survival of the fittest (note: that was allegedly Kim Fowley's wretched justifying excuse for sexually abusing young women, to toughen them for the abuse they would encounter as artists)—it's a weight music culture can no longer bear. All this reckoning, overdue and cyclical and triggering and enraging as it is, presents a challenge to anyone who truly gives a shit about music, which presumably includes the nearly four hundred folks (85 percent male-identifying respondents) that voted this year.

The other obvious factor, as critic Laura Snapes, my friend and colleague, suggested, is that "#MeToo has made it suspect to undyingly praise the male *auteurs* who would otherwise have populated the upper reaches of these charts." Plus, in 2018 a bunch of revered dudes released albums that were vestigial at best. You don't even start hitting clumps of cis-het white dudes until the bottom fifty. (In the past few years, the Top 10 has crept toward this trend—notably, in 2015, the Top 5 was women-plus-Kendrick, the best showing since the high-water mark of a few PJ/Hole/Phair/Breeders triumphs in the mid-'90s.)

Despite claiming the top slot twice since 2010, and being tied with Bob Dylan for the most number ones in the poll's history, Kanye only tied for 273rd place this year, with just three measly votes for *Ye* total. Drake's at 82, Jeff Tweedy at 84, Jack White a squeaker, tied for 95th; the poll's historically lauded artists David Byrne (tied at 69), Elvis Costello (at 45), and Paul McCartney (tied for 120) are left behind. The artistic and commercial failure of men's work is often written off, and even celebrated as evidence of a calculated experiment from a risk-taking visionary, so I am sure they all will be just fine despite their collective paucity of resonant ideas in 2018.

All of this is to say that for every Pazz & Jop poll, there is surely a shadow Top 10, comprising othered artists whose work didn't fit the image prescribed, whose albums were the wrong kind of confrontational or flamboyant, albums that were created to speak to or uphold a community which those critics were not part of, not interested in, not attuned to, or—in the case of Black, feminist, or queer work—music that disrupted and threatened the critical agenda. From #MeToo's rupture of music's mythologies, a phantom canon emerges. Let it haunt all of us.

Robert Christgau rather keenly diagnosed the dominance of women in the 1993 poll, writing of Liz Phair's *Exile in Guyville* and its femme cohort, "The big story in 1993 was girls learning to play a boys' game by boys' rules, and play it to win," and suggested that the critical body of voters were a bunch of rockists (true then, less true now, but c'mon, *Parquet Courts*?) who were just waiting, rather prescriptively, for women to "*come on strong.*" Girls learning boys' rules was and is inherent to a career, success, survival, and safety in music, yet it is forever posited as an aspirational achievement, a signal of one's ambition or women's artistic legitimacy. Later in the essay, Christgau shuts down some racist grousing in the critical ranks about certain artists not being "Black enough," which is another grim fucking reminder of the havoc that whiteness and patriarchal mores have wrought on both the canon and individual artists' careers. And what is the white heteropatriarchy if not the biggest algorithm of 'em all?

Yet what is "girls learning to play a boys' game by boys' rules" if not the game itself? Was there ever a time in the music industry and music journalism when those weren't the terms? Music's cruelest lie has always been the assertion that it's a meritocracy. The idea that if you play by their rules, and are exceptional enough, the rules might change in order to allow you in—it's an awful paradox, one that keeps people jumping and performing like trick poodles. And it's a lie I mistakenly believed for, well, too long. When I was all of twenty-two, I wished, in my *Punk Planet* column, for something like an all-girl Crosby, Stills, Nash & Young; perhaps I was fantasizing something akin to Boygenius (at number 26) or Pistol Annies (at number 15), but at the time I was hoping for an equalizer and not an analogue. I believed perhaps if women's work could be exceptional enough, something might change. The path might widen. I was just looking for some magic key that would fit the lock, something to remediate the sad ache I felt as a young woman at shows, or the sinking feeling reading music history books and reviews sections. I wanted something to fix the feeling that the bands, the big ideas, and people and politics that I valued most in music were without consequence to the men in music, the men that had power and shaped everything around me. I bought their lie. I thought that it was a matter of women being inscrutable, that it was on women to puncture and petition the boys' club. It was a faulty reasoning, one that disregarded any hierarchy but *theirs*, one that disregarded the fact that women had been putting out works of virtuosic genius since the dawn of recorded music.

This belief contorted my opinions and writing about music; it warped my experience of music and my understanding of music's history; it shifted my goals and allegiances; it disoriented my sense of where I belonged and what I could do. I spent a decade as a Sherpa for patriarchal bullshit before I realized that in playing a "boys' game by boys' rules," contrary to Christgau's assertion, there is no way to ever actually "win." As Sasha Geffen writes in *Glitter Up the Dark*, "Patriarchy relies on the illusion of its own inevitability to survive."

The first time I voted in this poll I was eighteen years old. I am forty-two now. As scholar Mary Beard writes in *Women & Power*, the cultural mechanisms that silence women are deeply embedded. Even in ourselves. Too often, Pazz & Jop's findings legitimated women's exclusion in music, they gendered and racialized genius, designated music's mythopoetics as white and male. The poll served many purposes and helped legitimize music criticism as a crucial form of cultural dialogue, but it also served to reinscribe patriarchy, prescribe heteronormativity, and center whiteness. Early on, Pazz & Jop celebrated work that reflected the identity of its voters—predominantly white, heterosexual, and male; the deliberative body was basically twenty-five guys and Ellen Willis. Typically, between two and five of the thirty slots went to women artists or bands with front women, with Joni's *Court and Spark* (1974) being the lone album by a woman to claim number one that decade; the total doesn't crack double digits until it hits eleven of forty in 1981, though 1979 is a solid showing with Donna Summer, the Roches, and the Slits. (Also, how the actual fuck did Labelle escape making a single P & J appearance for the whole of the seventies?) The results stay pretty seriously white until 1980, and diversified significantly after 1986 as hip-hop's presence grew. This deliberative body, incomplete as it may be in 2019, is heir to such malignancy.

The forty-fifth (or forty-sixth) Pazz & Jop poll—with its Top 35 that celebrates queer, nonbinary, and trans voices, womanist work, multiple albums steeped in Afrofuturism, one sung entirely in Spanish, an album by a teenage girl as well as two by women over forty, and women delivering third-person character studies—might signal less a paradigm shift than an uncoupling. It's an unmooring from some of music criticism's faultiest frameworks and conventions and its most painful omissions and enshrinements. It is a necessary move in order for music journalism to have any argument that it is (still) crucial to music's community.

There's unquestionably been a progressive shift within music journalism in recent years, owing in part to a host of writers whose work is incandescent and has drawn even more new talent in. Notably, there's Hanif Abdurraqib's *They Can't Kill Us Until They Kill Us*, which has beckoned folks in with open arms, and the exceptional work of Doreen St. Félix, Julianne Escobedo Shepherd, Suzy Esposito, Lindsay Zoladz, Jia Tolentino, Hua Hsu, Sasha Geffen, Carvell Wallace, Jenn Pelly, and Liz Pelly. Others have risen up through *Remezcla*, *She Shreds*, *Bandcamp*, or *Rookie* (RIP), drawn in by what those sites mirrored back to them. Some have arrived via the mentorship of Ann Powers, Greg Tate, Charles Aaron, Jeff Weiss, Jes Skolnik; others through their critic-professors Amanda Petrusich, Karen Tongson, Josh Kun, and more. In this moment, wherein music journalism feels strikingly akin to the final verse of Springsteen's "Atlantic City," it's hard to get a handle on how music journalism sustains itself long enough to hand a generation of bright and enterprising young writers the reins. Music journalism has no bulwarks; unlike poetry, fiction, and investigative reporting, it has no formal institutions; there are no stalwart journals to endow-into-eternity like Ruth Lilly did *Poetry* magazine, no Sunday special sections dedicated to album reviews; unlike book critics, we do not have prestigious awards to honor the artists we revere. There are no dedicated grants or residencies for music journalism, no cash-prize honors. It's glory-free, operates on net-ninety-day terms, and there's hardly a toehold to be had. The upside: at least there's plenty of room to build something.

And what *could* be next? So many music freelancers are subsidizing low-word-rate assignments by doing un-bylined bios and blurbs for Big Algorithm or corpo #content; only a handful of paying, music-focused publications and sections still exist. Will the next Greg Tate get a come-up when there is no *Village Voice*? Does the Eve Babitz of 2019 miss her *East Village Other* stepping-stone and just detour into teaching hot yoga instead? A decade ago, when shit went sideways for print and digital media, some folks that didn't or couldn't break into books or academia got by on in-flight magazine bylines, lifestyle pubs, B2B gigs, the ever-nebulous "editorial consulting." Doing the scammy side hustle you have to in order to keep on doing the meaningful work elsewhere is old hat for many freelancers, but there has to *be* an elsewhere. It all calls to mind Rimbaud's *A Season in Hell*: "To whom shall I hire myself out? What beast must I adore?" What happens when the only career opportunity left is entry-level Beast Adoration?

Journalism is one of many industries gripped in the gnashing maw of surveillance capitalism (call social media's con by its true name), but there has to be a future beyond servitude to merciless info-mining Goliaths, one seemingly sustained only by the heroic enterprise of billionaires, and/or the wild ideas of the dude from *Bustle*. It's confoundingly bleak, to be sure. Yet, still, there are folks in our midst who remember how to build a thing and tend a flame. I am heartened by the publication of *The LAnd*, the passion project of a bunch of former *LA Weekly* staffers. There's also the incredible turnaround of my old country home, the *Chicago Reader*, despite its just barely surviving successive perilous changes in ownership. The now non-profit paper has been righted by a dynamic consortium of four women who are veterans of local independent publishing; they are expanding and diversifying the paper's coverage and reach to better serve the city. A half-dozen newsrooms have successfully unionized in as many months. So maybe it's time to pivot back to fanzine. Pivot to local underground newspaper. Pivot to supermarket circular. Pivot back to listservs and anonymous blogspots. Pivot to a publication for teenage girls that doesn't die because it refused to be an app and a vehicle for selling *things* to an elusive and valuable market. Pivot to a publisher who doesn't nuke the newsroom for unionizing. Pivot to a music journalism where the fate of young Black writers and freelancers of color doesn't depend on one white editor staying employed at a dying publication. Pivot to bartending or shifts at California Pizza Kitchen because weeklies still only pay nine cents a word, but at least they let you go off when a record sucks and you gotta make rent somehow. What the hell can you do but keep on swingin'?

AFTERWORD

When I was fifteen, I was furious at the world; it was boring, depleting, unjust, and assumed teenage girls were stupid. Punk music introduced me to awe I had not known. Helpful obeisance was the peak virtue of girlhood, of womanhood; punk's rejection of silence drew me in. I felt right amid such amateur and calamitous noise. In interviews for the first edition of this book, I told the story of my birth as a music writer: how, at fifteen, I read a piece about the all-woman noise trio Babes in Toyland and knew the critic got it wrong and that I, a fan, could get it right. That my entrance to music criticism was a rebuttal is a significant point, given much of my early career was me yelling *But you're wrong!* over the transom.

It's just as meaningful that the first music I felt empowered by was a woman screaming. Kat Bjelland's screaming, which cut through the din like a scythe, was art. To lift the scream aloft in a song, to form it over again and again—the immensity was almost mythical, taunting, a dare against silence. Her scream was a seed; its intemperance and sheer extremity offered a new, glamorous destiny for my feral self. It forced me to consider what would happen if I screamed, too.

What Angela Davis wrote of early blueswomen held true for punk women decades later: in creating art from her own emotional turmoil, Bjelland was "giving herself aesthetic control over the forces that threaten[ed] to overwhelm her." What I felt and heard in Bjelland's scream was an exorcism of everything the world had tried to put upon her. The power of this scream-as-rebuke rightly unsettled listeners; the idea that a woman screaming was evidence she was unhinged and artless informed much of the writing I read about women in punk. Yet, for me, this woman making her own ecstatic rage the centerpiece of her artistic expression cleaved my whole world open. Her scream was pure possibility. Her scream was contagious and it endowed my work. My life as a writer is built on top of that holy scream.

When the local magazine wouldn't let me write a corrective piece about Babes in Toyland, I went to work making my own Xeroxed magazine, *Hit It or Quit It*. I was fortunate to grow up in Minneapolis at the dawn of the nineties, when active participation in underground culture was an expectation. You couldn't just come in and consume, you had to contribute *ideas* and *work*, not just the five bucks you paid at the door. After the first issue was published, I started writing for other fanzines, some reviews for the local alt-weekly *City Pages*; my prose was breathless and hyperbolic and the gossipy slings plentiful. I immediately encountered hostility and resistance from adult dudes in the scene. I was elbowing my way in and I didn't aspire to their tutelage or their hierarchies of cool. The latter was especially a problem for them. I didn't want what they had. I was in tenth grade and propelled by the burgeoning riot grrrl movement. I wanted to nuke those dudes' whole fucking scene on general principle.

Knowledge that my writing unsettled people was a liberatory gift. It wouldn't endear me into anyone's graces or onto their masthead. I had nothing much to lose, and, in the absence of permission, that'll do just fine.

■ ■ ■

When I was nineteen, I flew to Washington, D.C., to interview Ian MacKaye from Fugazi. It was as much a pilgrimage as it was an interview. It was an unusual expense for my fanzine, which, in 1995, had a circulation of about twelve hundred. I arrived early, and when I walked into the Dischord house Ian was on a little mat doing yoga in what looked like a ceremonial cloth diaper. Most of my questions were covert requests for advice, though I wasn't so much asking for his ideas as I was looking for direction on how to pursue mine. I was seeking instruction from punk's no-bullshit guru on how to reject the world as it was being presented to me, to challenge capitalist ideals, to challenge my own cultural inheritance as a teenage girl. I had life experiences that had served me, and others that had been a bad education. To alight on this path of independence was to be true to myself, to give soft breath to this little flame of altruism, feminism, and punk in my heart.

Somewhere in the wake of my question about why Fugazi rejects the mainstream, Ian explained that Fugazi is for the people who want it. And if you keep your head down, do your good work, stick to your principles, the people who are looking for that work will find you. They will dig until they find it. And those are the people you want as fans, not people who got into you because they see your ad every month in a magazine.

I took what he told me to heart. I wanted to live by a code, an imperative that centered around connection and creation. I wanted to abide by a kind of asceticism that simplified a world that confused and diminished me. It wasn't just my teen punk idealism that wanted something pure and reliable to cling to; believing in something gave me a way of belonging. Writing about music was a way of seeking coherence.

I moved to Chicago, when I was twenty-one, to find fellowship. Everyone here had a fanzine and/or a band and/or a label; there were more all-ages shows, and more trees, than in L.A. I was running a small P.R. firm for indie bands and labels and still making my fanzine. Within a few years, I was tired of backburnering my own dreams. My rent was $250. I lived on cheap tacos, Topo Chico, and cigarettes. I was debtless because I didn't go to college and so the stakes for pursuing music writing full-time were low and relative. I figured if I could find a way to make $850 a month writing about music, I could manage. As Deborah Levy wrote, you either die of the past or you become an artist. And so I did.

I went to shows most every night, came home and worked on my fanzine, skated on the basketball court across the street, wrote some more. I listened to a lot of Mary J., Teddy Pendergrass, and Prince; hardcore was leaving me cold. I started going to church for the first time in my life, mostly for the music. I volunteered, protested, and put together benefit shows. I went on epic walks with my friend JR, where he filled the gaps in my education with Chicago poets, free jazz, and Lester Bangs lore.

I tried to stay fast to what Ian MacKaye had told me, and what his band modeled. Cloistered in the Midwest and writing for a weekly print paper that didn't even have a website simplified things. I was not in the New York music journalism hothouse. I didn't have a college buddy network or even a degree. In lieu of mentors, I had my friends, fellow dirtbags and weird kids, who were trying to build a thing, make something cool and courageous on their own because they had to.

While I wanted a music journalism career, I disdained the system that might deign to give me one. I received a lot of unbidden advice from men, many of whom I barely knew, about my work. They usually offered the same paternalistic scolding: that it was perverse to tangle up music criticism with feminism or my personal experience, moral judgments about music didn't belong in reviews and I should stick to merely aesthetic ones. They'd tell me what kind of woman, fan, or writer I was. They insisted the ways in which my critical perspective deviated from theirs were wrong and needlessly political, and that to revel in—let alone actively expand—that distance was futile. If I took their advice, I might have a chance to become a *real* writer, like them.

I did not share their particular concerns about my writing.

I wrote to argue for a different world, to change the scene—an ambition that is, by turns, naive and wistful, small-stakes and lofty. I wrote to impress my friends. I wrote to impress my editor (I needed to keep those sixty-dollar checks coming). I wrote because it was exhilarating and there was nothing like digging into what a song *meant* until I hit the bedrock of how I felt about it and why, or sitting on the porch of my decrepit apartment at 4:00 a.m., reading my third draft under the yellow motion-activated security light, waving my smoking hand to turn it back on every minute or two, just to make deadline. This was my dream, on whatever terms I could make it. I was twenty-eight, but I was just getting born. In the space of a review, I could be as smart, dumb, profane, prosaic, poetic, pointed, feminist, and furious as I wanted. My writing was an articulation of my absolute self and a way to be in a relationship with music and a city that I loved. I just wanted to do what I was good at. Maybe get great at what I was good at.

What was real to me was speed-walking home alone from the show at 1:00 a.m., darting down the middle of the street for an elusive sense of safety beneath the streetlights. Real was continuing to write despite knowing that being young, feminist, Midwestern, and a woman meant my work was less valuable. While my whiteness conferred significant ease in navigating my music journalism career, the barrier these men posed helped me understand something crucial: They didn't want to help me, they just wanted me to want what they had. They wanted me to align with their values, mirror them, be an acolyte in their church of boy kings. But why would I?! What they did with their power was boring.

A decade later in my career, when these same men would ask me for my cooperation, I knew what they were really asking for was my silence.

I wrote anyway. I wrote till something gave way.

Is there even another way in?

If your voice, your work, is not your own, then whose is it?

■ ■ ■

A decade ago, when I initially proposed a collection of my music writing to different editors, publishers, and agents, I was told there was no precedent. To be without precedence is to be disenfranchised from history, to be denied lineage. I existed, and the feminist tradition within criticism existed, yet none of it was real enough. Ellen Willis's anthologies, and out-of-print editions of *Rock She Wrote*, one editor pointed out, as if this proved the relative worth of feminist criticism, were retailing for a dollar on Amazon. What I was fighting for wasn't just the value of my own writing, but fighting against the erasure of work that endowed my own.

What *The First Collection* became and where it took me were far beyond what I had imagined possible. In the eighteen months following publication in May of 2015, I spoke in seven countries on four continents, and did more than sixty events. It was a gift to hear stories of the strength and struggles of women and young people in music from around the world; it was enraging how awful those struggles had been. Justifications and tolerance for racism, misogyny, and transphobia within the scene and industry had dispirited people, and forced out those who confronted it. The audience Q&As of these events were frequently full of revelations and topics that have now become much more commonplace in the wake of #MeToo. Young women asked me for advice on how to deal with their boss at the college radio station who took credit for their work, or the talent agent who wouldn't book their band unless they went on a date with him. They waited at the very end of the signing line to tell me everything that they had survived. They told me what sustained and empowered their art and writing.

In Melbourne, a woman spoke of her recent return to making music; it took her a decade to pick up her instrument after being raped by her famous mentor. In Germany, a woman spoke of quitting an acclaimed band at its peak because of her abusive boyfriend-bandmate who used the band as a way to control her; her agents and labels told her to tough it out for the sake of the money everyone was making, and ostracized her when she couldn't. I met artists from Austria who described the process of releasing a record in their country, which required petitioning an arts council run by geriatric men who decided what was worthy. (Only 9 percent of the records released in Austria the year before were made by women.) In Chile, I met a DJ/producer who was moving to another country so she could be out as a queer woman and still get bookings. In Austin I talked with an artist whose opportunities disappeared after she confronted her renowned collaborator over his misogynoir and taking credit for her work. I received a letter from one of the half-dozen women working as sound engineers in Australia; she had abandoned her career because bands didn't want to hire a woman, the gigs she got came as a result of offering to work for free.

In Dublin, I met the powerful women who ran the music scene, and who had created spaces and mentorship networks in order to support the young women coming up behind them. In Santiago, Chile, I met two young friends, Barbara and Barbara, who had mail-ordered my book from America. They brandished their copies like talismans, declared they wanted to be music critics now, too. After that event, I marched with my hosts in an International Women's Day parade and protest. Amid the hundreds of thousands of demonstrators, the noise we made—deep, loud, furious—was riotously musical. I was grateful to witness this massive collective strength, this forbearance and tenacity from women around the world, the remarkable lengths people were willing to go in order to be seen and heard, to make music.

Still, by the end of the tour, when asked the inevitable question "What's your advice for young women who are entering music journalism/the music industry?" I often struggled to find a useful or encouraging reply. Gone was my pragmatic advice about peer mentorship, DIY can-do, and self-confidence. By virtue of having stuck around, the assumption was that I had figured out something they hadn't about surviving; I had not. I knew music journalism and the music industry were not particularly safe places. I told them: guard your art and ambition, build something precious elsewhere. During one event, as I read from an essay I had written nearly two decades earlier, "Emo: Where the Girls Aren't," it hit me just how little things had changed. I had an uneasy expertise from hearing twenty years of people's stories of the dehumanization they'd faced in music spaces, people who were just trying to live their love of music. I knew the weight of half a lifetime of being told, "That's the way it is. If you don't like it, leave." What Ellen Willis wrote in 1971 still stands: "Rock culture has not merely assimilated male supremacy but, with its own Orwellian logic, tried to pass it off as liberation."

I decided it was time to stop touring after a talk I gave at South by Southwest in 2016; as soon as I started talking about the music industry's rape culture, the few men in the audience left, save for one, who waited until the Q&A to ask how to get his reviews published on *Pitchfork*.

After the talk, I walked off the sprawling festival campus, fleeing the beered-up hordes, the indifference of the men at my talk, the pain I heard during the Q&A. I followed a single street out of downtown, taking a straight path so I wouldn't get lost. While attending SXSW five years earlier, six months pregnant, I had become stranded late at night at a DIY show in a residential exurb. I'd walked alone for several miles until I saw a city bus coming and got on. When I noticed a group of old kids hanging out in a parking lot where a band was playing, I got off, knowing instinctively I would find someone who would help me get back to where I was staying. As soon as I stepped off the bus, I ran right into my friend Esme Barrera, the coolest girl in Austin. Tearfully gulping down a PBR, she blurted, "Alex Chilton's dead. I cannot believe Alex Chilton is dead." She insisted on walking me back to my hotel; she wanted to make sure I got home safe. We talked about Big Star, about new bands she loved, about what she wanted to do with her life.

I thought of Esme, now, five years later, as I walked along some busy industrial byway heading toward the outskirts of Austin. She had been murdered January 1, 2012, coming home from a show. I prayed to her spirit for guidance; what would the indomitable girl-punk spirit of Esme demand?

In the midday Texas sun, I sobbed behind my sunglasses, angrily paced the edges of a Home Depot parking lot, Cocteau Twins loud in my headphones, trying to drum up some fugitive hope and clarity. I was thankfully too far from anyone I would have to explain my tears to; I didn't have it in me to explain any of this anymore, to try to cajole someone into caring. I thought about how the truth of women's experiences had reoriented and rearranged my work. I thought about what it would be like to feel safe, for all of the women and the folks in the scene and at the shows to feel safe, to be heard, to be seen, to be revered, for their history and contributions to be documented and exalted. Was I asking too much? Was this even the right fucking question anymore?

■ ■ ■

The publication of *The First Collection* bore out Ian MacKaye's maxim. The people who wanted this book found it. Seeing this book meet its *true* audience was validating, but it also gave me a mandate. It gave me a better understanding of the complexity and the joy within people's relationships to music. It allowed me to see how the constancy of my struggle to stay in music journalism had disoriented me, how the fight had estranged me from community and the joy within my relationship with music. I am grateful to have the opportunity to remake *The First Collection* on the other side of all of that, as well as to the friends, readers, and colleagues who continue to bring me to clarity.

The writing collected here is a fraction of my work; most of my living has been made by writing concert previews, short reviews, quick Q&As with local bands and touring pop stars. What is included in this collection is primarily critical writing about women artists, my interpretations and examinations of their work, and my efforts to integrate feminist music criticism into conversations about popular music. When my longtime editor Naomi Huffman and I were remaking this book in 2019 and early 2020, I often thought of the Barbara and Barbara that I met in Chile: *we are making a book for them*. I wondered about the Barbara and Barbara of Des Moines and Sioux City and Mobile, who I have not met yet, whose fanzines and bylines are perhaps still just dreams.

In the introduction to the 2015 edition of this book, I wrote that the title of the book was about planting a flag for those whose dreams languished due to a lack of support and bad faith arguments about "precedent." My hope for this second edition is more that it can be used as a tool, perhaps to prop or pry a door open wider, for young writers and fans to use to interrogate or reject all that came before them. I want this new edition of this book to be a link between the path blazed by the visionary work of Lillian Roxon, Ellen Willis, Ann Powers, and others who came before and alongside me, and the Barbaras working in our wake. I wrote it to endow the feminist lineage within music criticism. Long may it run.

ACKNOWLEDGMENTS

Much of the work in this book, as well as the work of making this book, was possible due to the support work of others. Thank you to Sasha Geffen for astute and diligent research assistance. Thank you to my editor, my co-conspirator, my manuscript midwife, Naomi Huffman. Your vision for this book expanded and ennobled my own understanding of what it could and should be. Thank you to the pride of Evanston, Samantha Irby, for your generosity and enthusiasm. Thank you to my agent, Claudia Ballard at WME, for being vigilant and steadfast. Thank you, Jessie Chasan Taber and Camille Morgan, for your valuable assistance.

Deep gratitude to Megan Stielstra, Hanif Abdurraqib, Carvell Wallace, Darcie Wilder, Dylan Tupper Rupert, Charles Aaron, Casey Kittrell, JR Nelson, Alex Pappademas, Dan Fierman, Jenn Pelly, Nikki Darling, and David Dark for their editorial advice, careful reads, and feedback on pieces that appear in this book. Also to Eloisa Amezcua, Lisa Bralts-Kelly, Michael Catano, Danielle Henderson, Beth Pickens, Ann Powers, and Bob Mehr for their cheerleading and encouragement. Thank you to Robin Harris, Morgan Thoryk, Nora Brank, Molly Raskin, Jane Marie, Yasi Salek, and Heidi for the sustaining sorority and support. And to Francisca Valenzuela and the Ruidosa folks for bringing me to Chile, Angela Dorgan for bringing me to Ireland, and everyone else who helped *The First Collection* get 'round the world the first time. And thank you, David Bazan and Bob Andrews, for help with permissions.

Forever thanks to all the independent booksellers who championed and supported my work, most especially my hometown crew, Women and Children First, The Book Stall, and Volumes.

Bless the Farrar, Straus and Giroux / MCD crew who helped make *Revised and Expanded*: Jackson Howard for your enthusiasm and for being such a great shepherd, and Sean McDonald, Gretchen Achilles, Alex Merto, Na Kim, Stephen Weil, and Claire Tobin.

Thank you to all the original editors of these pieces: Simon Vozick-Levinson, Rob Harvilla, Charles Aaron, Kiki Yablon, Phillip Montoro, Melissa Marerz, Keith Harris, Alison True, David Wilcox, Steve Kandell, Christopher Weingarten, Jon Dolan, Caryn Ganz, Maura Johnston, Robert Christgau, Brian McManus, Dan Sinker, Ezra Caraeff, Steve Haruch, Randall Roberts, Cassie Walker, Phoebe Connelly, Julianne Escobedo Shepherd, Kevin Williams, Neila Orr, Melissa Giannini, and my editors at *The Cut* and *Vanity Fair*.

This book wouldn't exist without the support of my family: Matthew Hale Clark, Lauren Redding, William, Jude, Mom, and Dad. Thank you to Steve and Louise, Jeanine, Sarah-Marie, and Alice for childcare that allowed me to do this work.